# The Scotsman Guide
# to
# Scottish Politics

### Edited by
### MATTHEW SPICER

© The Scotsman Publications Ltd, 2002

The Scotsman Publications Ltd
Barclay House
108 Holyrood Road, Edinburgh

Distributed by
Polygon at Edinburgh
22 George Square, Edinburgh

Typeset in Minion by
Pioneer Associates, Perthshire, and
printed and bound in Great Britain by
Creative Print & Design, Ebbw Vale, Wales

A CIP Record for this book is available from the British Library

ISBN 1 902930 34 7 (paperback)

# Contents

# Foreword

The Rt Hon Sir David Steel KBE MSP

Two years into the first term of the Scottish Parliament and the political landscape in Scotland is unrecognisable. The Parliament has found a personality and I believe it is now a key focal point in Scots life.

Our new and inclusive approach to politics has enabled every Scot in the land to have his or her say in the decision-making process. Important legislation has been passed which is positively impacting on the lives of many Scots. No fewer than thirty Bills have been introduced in the Scottish Parliament to date. Important areas of social concern have been addressed: most notably in the areas of education – both school and further education – land tenure, transport and the introduction in Scotland after many decades of debate of a system of national parks. These are achievements that we can all be proud of.

This is an important book which brings together respected politicians and commentators impressions of devolution and a post-devolution Scotland. I commend this thoughtful and meaningful publication which has been skilfully brought together. I am sure it will be enjoyed by all who read it.

David Steel
*Presiding Officer of the Scottish Parliament*

# Notes on Contributors

**John Curtice** is Professor of Politics and Director of the Social Statistics Laboratory at Strathclyde University; and Deputy Director of the Centre for Research into Elections and Social Trends (CREST).

**Graham Leicester** is Director of the Scottish Council Foundation.

**Donald MacCormick** is a journalist and broadcaster who was a university contemporary and lifelong friend of Donald Dewar.

**Joyce McMillan** is a journalist, critic and political activist who held the Chair of the Constitutional Commission, a key committee of the Constitutional Convention.

**Allan Massie** is a novelist, essayist and commentator who opposed devolution in the referendum.

**George Reid MSP** is a former journalist and broadcaster who is now Deputy Presiding Officer of the Scottish Parliament.

**Iain Martin** is Editor of *The Scotsman*.

**George Kerevan, Kirsty Milne** and **Robert McNeil** are staff writers with The Scotsman Publications Ltd.

**Matthew Spicer** is a journalist, producer and former Editor, Television Current Affairs, at BBC Scotland.

# Introduction

Andrew Neil

'That incendiary newspaper' was how one furious laird and fully paid-up member of the Scottish establishment described the then fledgling *Scotsman*. Almost two hundred years on, many members of the Scottish Parliament and MPs at Westminster must know how he felt.

Since its launch on 25 January 1817, *The Scotsman* has made it its business to take on the political establishment when necessary. It has earned respect by combining a spirit of serious-minded enquiry with trenchant analysis and pomposity-pricking coverage of Scotland's politicians down the ages.

Those qualities have never been required more than they are now. *The Scotsman*, one of the most consistent supporters of the need for a devolved Scottish legislature, reflected the national sense of achievement when the Parliament met again for the first time in almost three hundred years in Edinburgh in 1999. However, passion for the principle has not stopped *The Scotsman* from exposing its failings and suggesting positive improvements to our young Parliament and the policies pursued by the parties within it.

*The Scotsman* sees no conflict in being a supporter of devolution and a firm friend of the Union with England; we are convinced that it is a mutually beneficial and rewarding relationship. It is now down to a devolved administration to display drive and determination in proving that the new constitutional arrangements of the reformed Union can help make Scotland an enterprising and more prosperous country.

The Scottish Parliament has command over significant swathes of policy. It is, though, far from being the only institution which makes an impact on the lives of Scots. Westminster continues to be hugely important. *The Scotsman*, as befits a truly national daily newspaper, is committed to reflecting that reality with its unparalleled coverage of politics in Edinburgh and London.

In this, the first comprehensive guide of its kind, we hope to make an invaluable contribution to the understanding of a transformed political landscape. It offers expert analysis of the situation at Westminster as well as Edinburgh. A full guide to the personalities in both parliaments is included.

*The Scotsman* continues to be 'that incendiary newspaper'. It has long been an influential player in the shaping of Scottish affairs. It will not shirk its responsibility in the years ahead. The publication of this guide is a guarantee of our continued commitment to promoting a healthy Scottish body politic.

Andrew Neil
Publisher, *The Scotsman*

# CHAPTER 1

# Towards 2003: Lessons from the Westminster General Election 2001, the fall of a First Minister and the Battle to Come

Iain Martin

When he fell, fatally wounded by the row over his office expenses, he was a broken man. Henry Baird McLeish's entire parliamentary career had been driven by his desire to take power in his own right. In opposition he was an expert operator with the media, as a minister a naked populist whose initiatives never seemed to quite live up to their headline-seeking billing. But as a First Minister? Perhaps McLeish had expended so much energy struggling to get to the top of Scottish politics that when he achieved his wish he had little idea about what, exactly, he should do with this new power.

His administration lasted for little more than a year. It was not a glorious twelve months. Desperate to find the big idea that would distinguish him from his predecessor, he rushed into unwise commitments such as agreeing to the implementation of the Sutherland Report on free care for the elderly. Hampered by his oratorical limitations and mocked for his pioneering way with the English language, McLeish – a loner in politics by nature – found himself with few friends prepared to save him when his moment of crisis came. He had alienated the Labour leadership in London. Central to his strategy had been a determination to prove that he was no plaything of the Chancellor or the Prime Minister. He believed strongly that appropriating some nationalist language would enable him to out-flank the SNP. Instead, it confused his Labour colleagues and was added to the charge list being drawn up by those who regarded 'Team McLeish' as unstable and intellectually incoherent.

With a resignation statement to the Scottish Parliament, he was gone. Jack McConnell – a politician with no Westminster upbringing – represents a break with the past. He is also relatively young and more nimble than McLeish on his feet. But McConnell's elevation sets Labour up for a fascinating test: how much has it been damaged by the Officegate scandals that consumed McLeish and dogged other Labour figures in the autumn of 2001? Charges of cronyism, and sleaze, which have threatened to dog Scottish Labour in the past, are starting to stick. Can McConnell clear his party's name by running an effective administration?

The authority of the Scottish Parliament is also on the line. Disappointment is certainly more widespread, earlier, than even most devo-sceptics had suggested would be the case. But 2001 as a whole illustrates that Scottish politics is not, as the nationalists would have it, solely about the parliament in Edinburgh. All the par-ties are struggling to adapt to new realities. One of the main lessons of the years since the 1997 devolution referendum is that Westminster should continue to matter to the majority of Scots.

**The Westminster General Election 2001**
The Westminster 2001 contest was profoundly confusing for all those involved in Scotland. The first post-devolution campaign was always going to be a disorientating affair. The drive of Scottish politics and the interests of so much of the political class since the Thatcher years had been primarily geared towards the constitution, or at least using the constitutional argument as a basis for constructing a social policy agenda different from that favoured south of the border. But by the beginning of 2001 an Edinburgh parliament had been operational for eighteen months and the constitutional argument was dead, or asleep. We had swapped the administrative devolution of the old Scottish Office for democratic control over health, educa-tion, law and order, some of transport, other policy areas and the block grant from the Treasury. It was not that pre-devolution UK elections had been of a unitary character – all of the parties offered distinctive domestic policies (the Conservatives favouring the

Scottish Office, devolutionists arguing they needed a new democratic institution to implement truly distinctive measures). Even Labour strategists recognised the peculiarity of this contest, though. The constitutional settlement which followed Labour's 1997 landslide altered forever the nature of the Caledonian end of Westminster elections. How would the public react to a contest in which so much of the UK campaign – conducted principally through the media – centred on issues which had been devolved to Edinburgh? Would it illustrate that, far from devolution having created a wholly separatist mindset, enough of the electorate was aware of the continuing importance of the UK Parliament to the lives of Scots – on the economy, welfare, defence and foreign affairs?

As the preparations for the 2001 election intensified, each of the parties had to grapple with these questions. The choices they made and the positions they adopted tell us much about how they envisage handling the new duality of Scottish politics – Westminster for reserved matters and Holyrood, or rather the Mound until construction work is completed on the site opposite Her Majesty's Scottish residence, for that which was devolved in Donald Dewar's Scotland Act. This was a new type of contest, confusing to commentators as well as participants. The SNP's leader, for example, was not a candidate. Labour's manifesto contained little if anything new in the way of Scottish policy. The Conservatives had trouble deciding which elements of UK policy would play with a Scottish electorate and then just got swamped again. The Scottish Liberal Democrats sat around a cabinet table with Labour ministers in Bute House, the First Minister's official residence in Edinburgh, while fighting a campaign against Labour in the country. Each party plotted a different course through the maze that is post-devolution politics. Only one exited the maze happy, and even then its success owed more to the campaign fought from its UK headquarters in London than it did to the ramshackle efforts of Scottish Labour.

## 2001: Policy, Positioning and the Result

It is true that Scottish Labour, under the guidance of Secretary of State Helen Liddell, decided – or was told by Scots then at the heart of Millbank such as Douglas Alexander MP or his mentor Gordon Brown – that as little disruption as possible of the lines of communication between the London UK machine and the Scottish electorate was required. The British-wide message that the Conservatives could not be trusted with government and that low turnout and apathy risked a Tory revival, no matter how small, was the principal Labour message here. On policy the party decided to avoid making too many specific Scottish policy statements in its manifesto.

It ran into one row on taxation which did illustrate that Labour was struggling with this new form of Westminster election. On May 16, as David Scott reported in *The Scotsman* of the following day, Liddell's team was forced to admit that it could not guarantee that voters would not pay income tax rises under a Labour government (a principal plank of the UK manifesto). The decision on whether to advocate the use of the Tartan Tax after the 2003 devolution elections lies with the Scottish Labour Party and the senior figures who serve in the Executive. It remains unlikely that Labour will campaign in 2003 for the use of the Tartan Tax. Instead, the row was proof that Labour figures at Westminster have to recognise the technical distinctions and that they cannot bind the hands of politicians in their own party who will have to fight elections for a different parliament, the Holyrood one. Labour also had to contest with an SNP operation that was far less chaotic than in 1999. Out went the rather shambolic approach to party events and press conferences, and in came a slicker, more modern-looking Nationalist machine. Liddell has a reputation running back to the 1970s for fierce opposition to the Nationalists; her rhetoric is regarded even by members of the Labour high command as unhelpful in being so exaggerated. She chose to focus much of her fire on apathetic voters – with limited results, as low turnouts on polling day proved. Liddell did also attempt to revive the strongly anti-Nationalist rhetoric of the Gordon Brown-led 1999 devolution campaign, but as a study of the pages of *The Scotsman* and other Scottish newspapers during the campaign illustrates, such attacks received far less coverage than they had in 1999 and can, arguably, be said to have made less of an impact on voters than in the past. Senior Nationalists close to the leadership believe that is the result of the Scottish public seeing the SNP in operation as a large parliamentary group on the Mound. It may be more that the party is not seen as such a significant threat to the Union as it was in the run-up to the 1999 contest.

If Labour's strategy was aimed at providing the minimum of distractions from the UK campaign – adding only the occasional purely

Scottish flourishes – then the SNP had to do the opposite and make itself heard in a UK election after the creation of a Scottish parliament. The campaign launch might have been slicker than in the past, this time an almost New Labour-style event at the Dynamic Earth building in Edinburgh, but a successful campaign is made of more than such occasions, critical though they can be. John Swinney and his closest advisers, such as Fiona Hyslop MSP, attempted to counter charges that this was an election in which a vote for the SNP would be wasted (why vote SNP for Westminster, a parliament the SNP want Scots to reject and in which they can never hope for influence on UK reserved matters?). The SNP defence never really took off. It is difficult for a nationalist party to complain that Scotland's interests are not protected when a devolved parliament has been created and many of those running the reserved areas of policy in Westminster and Whitehall are Scottish. The loss of Alex Salmond as leader did not help in that area. The most easily identified Nationalist figure played a prominent part, but Swinney – largely unknown to many voters – was the leader.

The Conservatives found themselves in the most difficult position of all. At the time of the autumn 2000 fuel protests, the party's campaign managers had envisaged the party recapturing as many as eight seats in the subsequent elections. By the time the campaign proper started, they had privately scaled down their expectations to one to two seats. They eventually made virtually no attempt to differentiate themselves from the London-based party on policy, arguing that they accepted the reality that their Westminster candidates could not trespass on areas on which the Scottish Parliament has responsibility and that they were at one with the UK party on reserved matters. But that meant that opposition to British entry to the European Single Currency and proposals to limit the numbers of those seeking asylum became the principal messages north of the border.

The Scottish Liberal Democrats might have expected to suffer a backlash as a result of their involvement in a coalition with Labour. A number of their better-known MPs with solid local reputations were standing down with new candidates taking their place. The party also made a U-turn, mid-campaign, which illustrated the difficulty of fighting a Westminster election. The initial manifesto launch was criticised in the media for failing to contain anything specifically Scottish; a subsequent extra document emphasising the relevance of

UK party policy to Scots voters and the Lib Dems' work in the
Scottish Executive had to be produced.

Thus, each of the four main parties struggled to acclimatise to a
varying extent. But the Labour campaign in Scotland – in terms of
share of the vote and number of seats – was clearly a success. The
party's strategy, implemented ineptly on occasion as the row over the
Tartan Tax illustrated, was astute. It meant few distinctively Scottish
Labour events or initiatives confused the message emanating from
London that Tony Blair and his team were the only ones fit to run the
country in a straight fight between Blair and William Hague. The
SNP failed to find a message of its own to counter the Labour logic
that this was an election in which the UK parties were doing battle.
However, the lower national turnout in Scotland than in the rest of
Britain is evidence that some voters believed the contest to be irrelevant and opted not to vote. The poor showing for the Tories implies
that the party's chances on the Mound will not improve until a
national recovery – if it is possible at all – takes place. The Liberal
Democrats benefited from the continuing weakness of the Conservatives and the failure of the SNP to penetrate. Charles Kennedy
fought a more spirited campaign than envisaged. But perhaps the
results also indicate that any presumption that devolution would
somehow alter voting behaviour radically for Westminster was
incorrect. Almost 80 per cent of those who voted did so for British
parties who want the Union to survive, and the campaign was
dominated by UK matters. It was the first concrete evidence that
voters may understand the distinction between the two types of
elections more clearly than the politicians had imagined.

## 2003 and Beyond

McLeish is gone and for Labour 2003 will be McConnell's show. He
started the drive towards polling day in the oddest of fashions. Billed,
by himself, as a moderniser, he appointed a very left-wing cabinet. At
the time of writing, he has yet to define his administration with
much clarity of vision. He sent his cabinet enemies to the backbenches in a brutal reshuffle. He has also been slow to move to
counter the reputation for cronyism and sleaze that his party is
gaining.

The SNP had based its plan for 2003 around Henry McLeish and they did not want him replaced with a stronger Labour leader. McConnell may have begun slowly, but he is much more likely to be able to adapt to the new constitutional arrangements. Expect him to be presented as a young leader, his own man and a First Minister with good links with Westminster on the issues that matter most to voters. Swinney is also about to be tested. He will be marketed by his party as 'honest John', the antidote to Labour practices. The Scottish Conservatives need a UK revival to build their credibility. It appears unlikely, and even the increase in stature of their Scottish leader, David McLetchie, who played a leading role in bringing down McLeish, does not appear to be helping them much with the voters. In areas such as health policy, in which the Scottish Executive appears to be restrained by its own ideological obsessions, there is room for the party to rebuild its base. The Liberal Democrats have proved their critics wrong in one respect at least: that it is possible to share an administration with Labour in Scotland and hold on to Scottish seats.

But most of all, 2003 will be a very different kind of contest to that fought in 1999. We know the limitations of the Scottish Parliament now. Most of the voting electorate want the continuation of the United Kingdom. The feeling in the first devolution elections that the Union might break seems quite distant now. The parties in 2003 will be competing to run a devolved Scotland; it will not be a referendum on the constitution. There is room for the opposition to damage, perhaps even defeat, Labour on public services, corruption and good governance. McConnell will fight to prove that he merits a decent run as First Minister. However, the 2001 campaign stands as a reminder that substantial numbers of Scottish voters continue to view politics through a British lens as well as a Scottish one. They were playing a part in electing a UK Prime Minister and government. Despite some reservations connected to low turnout, the new constitutional set-up finds enough of the electorate able to see beyond devolved affairs. The 2003 election will be vitally important, but British elections still matter to Scotland.

CHAPTER 2

# Adding up the Figures:
# Conclusions from 2001

Professor John Curtice

In Scotland the 2001 Westminster election was, of course, the first to be held since the creation of the Scottish Parliament. As a result it was another significant stage in the nation's devolution journey. For it meant we would begin to discover what impact, if any, devolution might have on Scots voters' attitudes towards and attachment to the UK Parliament at Westminster.

Why might the presence of a Scottish parliament have implications for the way that Westminster elections are won and lost? The first possibility is that it might affect how many people vote. For now that Scots have their own parliament there would appear to be a danger that some of them at least would decide that it was no longer worthwhile voting in UK parliament elections because they no longer felt that Westminster had much impact on their lives north of the border. After all, the various local, devolved and European elections held throughout Britain between 1998 and 2000 had already suggested that it was proving more difficult to persuade voters to go to the polls. So there would seem every chance that if Scots no longer felt that Westminster mattered that they would stay at home in droves. But even if Scots did go to the polls, the Scottish Parliament might make its presence felt in a different way. For what would Scots be voting in the election about? The delivery of key services in

Scotland, such as health and education, was now the responsibility of the Scottish Executive, rather than the UK government at Westminster. So in theory such devolved issues were now an irrelevance north of the border, and voters should be focusing their attention on matters that were still reserved to Westminster, such as tax and Europe, leaving subjects like health and education to one side.

But, of course, there was no guarantee that voters would ignore devolved matters, not least perhaps because many of them would be unaware of which subjects were Westminster's responsibilities and which not. And even if they were aware of the distinction, some might decide to use the election as an opportunity to send a message to Holyrood about how well they thought the Scottish Executive was performing – much as they often use local and European elections to express their view about the current performance of the UK government. In short, voters might use the election as an opportunity to comment on the performance of the Executive in Edinburgh rather than the government in London.

If any of this speculation were to prove correct then there would be a clear consequence – the election in Scotland would be rather different from that in England. The turnout would be lower because fewer people thought it mattered. And those Scots who did vote could well behave differently from both their counterparts in England and indeed also from how Scots themselves voted at Westminster elections in the past – either because they were voting about different issues or casting a judgement on different bodies. And even if none of these possibilities were to come true, it would certainly be the case that the parties themselves would no longer just be focusing on how well they could do at this election, as they might have done in the past, but rather would also be considering how they might use the opportunity created by the Westminster election to advance their prospects in the next Scottish Parliament election in 2003.

This chapter examines what impact devolution did in fact have on the 2001 Westminster election. Did voters stay away because they thought Westminster no longer mattered? Did the existence of Holyrood affect what the election was about? And what are the implications of the answers to these questions for the parties' prospects in 2003?

Apathy is one enemy all politicians share in common. If voters do not bother to participate in elections then politicians cannot claim to be speaking on behalf of the people. So the one message that came from all the political parties, including the SNP, was that this Westminster election did indeed matter. In particular they all accepted that while Holyrood might decide how services were delivered in Scotland, it was still Westminster that decided the total amount of money that Holyrood had at its disposal in order to discharge its responsibilities.

In fact the politicians were largely talking to the converted. Even before the election one opinion poll conducted by ICM for *Scotland on Sunday* in February found that two-thirds of Scots believed that recent trends in the health service were either mainly the result of the UK government's policies or else the result of the work of the UK government and the Scottish Executive equally. Only 6 per cent thought that the Scottish Executive was principally responsible. This picture was confirmed when in a poll conducted by ICM for *The Scotsman* at the beginning of the election campaign, 65 per cent said they thought that Westminster either had most or at least equal influence over the quality of the NHS and schools in Scotland, whereas only 27 per cent thought that the Scottish Executive had most influence.

So in reality there was little reason to anticipate that Scots would be particularly reluctant to go to the polls. In the event, 58.2 per cent cast a ballot, just 0.9 per cent fewer than did so in England. This figure of course represented a substantial drop of no less than 13.1 percentage points on the 1997 figure, but this largely reflects the reluctance of voters to go to the polls throughout Britain. At 12.1 percentage points the drop in England was almost as high.

The advent of the Scottish Parliament appears then to have had little or no impact on the salience of the 2001 Westminster election in the eyes of the Scots. They took as much – or more accurately as little – interest in the election as did their counterparts south of the border. On this measure at least devolution did not have quite the impact that its critics might have feared.

But what did those who went to the polls vote about? It looks as though we might be able to discount one possible answer to that question, that is that those who voted did so solely about devolved issues. If Scots believe that Westminster still has a significant influence on the quality of health and education in Scotland, then there seems little reason to believe that in deciding how to vote they would confine their attention to reserved matters. Moreover one might anticipate that the continued perceived importance of Westminster in voters' eyes would also mean that they would be unlikely to vote on the basis of the performance of the parties at Holyrood rather than at Westminster.

In practice the parties happily mixed devolved and reserved matters in their election campaigns. Thus, for example, three of the five pledges on the Scottish version of Labour's pledge card referred to devolved rather than reserved issues. And here also, the parties' messages were in conformity to what voters were expecting to hear. Thus when asked what were the most important issues in the election, Scots voters gave the same answers as their English counterparts – health and education. For example, 67 per cent of Scots told ICM that the NHS was a crucial issue for them in deciding how to vote in the election, while 59 per cent said the same of education. The only other issue to approach this figure was law and order (56 per cent) – also of course a devolved issue. In contrast, the most important reserved matter, taxes, was regarded as crucial by just 36 per cent.

So there seems little reason to believe that voters in Scotland were voting on different issues to their counterparts in England. And equally there is little evidence that they were basing their judgement of those issues according to how well Holyrood rather than Westminster was performing. Thus the polls conducted by ICM for *The Scotsman* during the election campaign continued to find much as they did during the Scottish Parliament election in 1999, that many voters were saying that they were voting differently in the Westminster election from how they would vote in a Holyrood election.

ICM found that SNP support for the Westminster election was running at no less than eleven points below what it would have been on the first vote of a Holyrood one. Meanwhile Labour's share was running at no less than seven points above what it would be in a Holyrood contest. This pattern of higher SNP support in a Holyrood election and lower support in a Westminster one – with Labour exhibiting the reverse – is similar to that found in polls conducted before the 1999 Scottish Parliament election. It would appear that far from voting in the Westminster election on the basis of the performance of the parties at Holyrood, a significant proportion of Scots voters was still drawing a distinction between the two bodies much as they did even before the new parliament was actually a reality. The result itself is also consistent with this interpretation. At 43.9 per cent, Labour's share of the vote was much closer to the 45.6 per cent it won in 1997 than the 38.8 per cent it secured in the constituency vote for the Scottish Parliament two years previously. The same is true of the SNP's 20.1 per cent, down just two points on its 1997 tally, but no less than 8.6 points lower than its score in 1999.

Moreover many of the trends in party support in Scotland were a mirror image of what happened south of the border. Thus the fall of 1.6 points in Labour's share of the vote was similar to the 2.2 points drop the party experienced in England. Moreover, as in the rest of the UK, Labour's share of the vote fell most heavily (as indeed did the turnout) in those seats where the party was strongest in 1997, a pattern that is suggestive of some dissatisfaction among more traditional Labour voters with their party's more centrist tone under Tony Blair.

True, not everything was the same in England. The Liberal Democrats advanced rather more strongly in Scotland (up 3.4 points), than they did in England (up 1.5 points). But if this performance was occasioned by the party's presence in the coalition government north of the border it indicates that, contrary to the claims of many commentators, being the junior coalition at Holyrood is enhancing rather than undermining the party's credibility. Certainly, only 29 per cent of Scots told ICM that they agreed with the claim that 'the Liberal Democrats these days are no different from Labour'.

Meanwhile, the Conservative performance was even more lamentable than it was south of the border. The party's share of the vote actually fell by 1.9 percentage points in contrast to the one and half point increase support the party achieved south of the border. However, if it were the case that the presence of Holyrood was making much of a difference to the way that Scots were voting then one would have anticipated that the Conservatives would have done better in Scotland than in England rather than worse. After all, the party has now come to accept the existence of the Scottish Parliament and has a significant presence inside it. Yet perhaps in a tell-tale sign that, despite this, the party still has to rehabilitate itself in the eyes of many Scots, no less than 45 per cent told ICM during the campaign that the Scottish Conservatives were still mainly an English party.

So the presence of the Scottish Parliament appears to have relatively little impact on what the 2001 election was about in the eyes of the voters or on how well the parties performed. That is not necessarily to the detriment of the new body. After all it would have done the new Parliament little good to be blamed for inducing a low turnout or distracting voters from what a Westminster election should be about. But it does suggest that we should exercise some caution in examining the implications of the results for 2003. Unless, for example, Labour can close the hitherto persistent gap between the proportion of voters who are willing to vote for it in a Westminster contest and the proportion who are willing to do so in a Holyrood one, the party will find the contest in 2003 a much tougher challenge than 2001 was, even if it were not the case that it benefits far less from the Holyrood electoral system than it does the Westminster one.

Equally, although the SNP must undoubtedly be disappointed by the unexpected drop in their support in the 2001 election, 2003 still looks like a much happier hunting ground for the party than 2001 was. What it did achieve in 2001 was to retain second place in votes – for the first time the party has come second in votes in two Westminster contests in a row. It has thus maintained its relatively recently acquired status as Scotland's principal alternative to Labour. Still, one indication of the substantial challenge that the party still faces in getting its message across about the alleged disadvantages of the current constitutional settlement comes from ICM's finding at the end of the campaign that less than one in five Scots accept that the current formula for funding public expenditure in Scotland will result in a reduction in Scotland's share of the UK government expenditure. This reading was obtained despite the fact that significant attention was given to the issue of the future funding of public expenditure in Scotland during the election campaign.

But there is perhaps one signal from the 2001 election that should not be ignored – and that is the record low turnout. If only 58 per cent of Scots consider it worthwhile voting for a body that they evidently still consider to be more influential than the Holyrood Parliament, to what level might the turnout in 2003 potentially fall? ICM found in their final poll in 2001 that 10 per cent fewer people said they were certain to vote in a Holyrood election than said they were certain to do so in this year's Westminster election. If the

# CHAPTER 3

# Westminster and Edinburgh: Conflict or Co-operation?

Kirsty Milne

The threads connecting Westminster to the Scottish Parliament are already under strain, but the general election frayed them a little further. A group of politicians cut their links with the Commons and proclaimed their preference for a future at Holyrood. The 'dual mandate', which allowed MPs who wanted a devolutionary career to serve out their term at Westminster, had come to an end. Yet scarcely anyone noticed as the likes of Jim Wallace, John McAllion, Malcolm Chisholm and Margaret Ewing – familiar figures in the House of Commons – slid quietly north of the border once and for all. Dennis Canavan made a fuss by going early and forcing a by-election in Falkirk West. Alex Salmond caused a stir by changing his mind and sticking with Westminster. But the rest evaporated without fanfare or regret.

Devolution in Labour's first term was a drama. In the second term it will be a slow drift, as the Scottish Parliament becomes more self-contained and autonomous. Analysts alert for political or legislative challenges to Westminster miss the bigger cultural effect of two parliaments coexisting in mutual ignorance. The media plays a part in this. Journalists who have made the Scottish Parliament their career choice pay little attention to what is happening at Westminster, while most lobby correspondents are dismissive of devolution and know little about it.

This leads to some curious anomalies. Outside the general election campaign, Scots politicians operating at UK level get little coverage in their own country. Alistair Darling, the Social Security Secretary, is on a mission to reform the welfare state. Gus Macdonald is the Prime Minister's personal 'progress chaser' at the Cabinet Office. Yet neither can hope for the profile that devolutionary ministers such as Wendy Alexander or Andy Kerr will enjoy north of the border over the next few years. The interesting thing is that voters know where real power lives. The first *Scottish Social Attitudes* survey showed that two-thirds of those questioned thought that Westminster had more influence over the way Scotland is run – even though three-quarters felt that Holyrood ought to have the more important role. The finding is gratifying for Helen Liddell, who likes to point out that the spending she controls as Secretary of State for Scotland exceeds the budget for the whole of the Scottish Executive.

When Westminster politicians do intrude into the world of Holyrood, it is usually in the role of pantomime villains obstructing the Parliament or failing to communicate with it. Nick Brown, when agriculture minister, played the latter role in rows over foot and mouth and genetically modified crop trials. Gordon Brown has often been invoked as a louring presence in discussions over free long-term care for the elderly, usually without any evidence of his actual intervention. The effect of this staged antagonism and mutual ignorance is to let the UK Labour Party off the hook. Ideological divisions inside the party tend to be recast as differences with Westminster – by political opponents and by the press.

Thus, Henry McLeish's decision to follow the recommendations of the Royal Commission on long-term care, chaired by Sir Stewart Sutherland, was portrayed purely as an act of devolutionary defiance, prompted by pressure from Mr McLeish's coalition partners, the Liberal Democrats. It is true that the Health Secretary, Alan Milburn, who refused to fund free personal care for the elderly south of the border, was less than enchanted by the move. But just as significant were tensions between the former First Minister and members of his own cabinet, such as Susan Deacon, who believed that help should be targeted at the poorest pensioners. The difference of opinion over universal versus means-tested benefits is a fault-line that runs through the UK Labour Party. It showed up prominently in the row over the state pension during the 2000 party conference. But it has been obscured in the Holyrood debate over long-term care.

The decision to implement the Sutherland Report can be attributed to the demands of coalition government. But the general election saw a more radical, if less widely noticed, swerve away from Westminster. Mr McLeish obtained an exemption from the major battleground of Tony Blair's second term. The pledge to involve private-sector companies in health and education was missing from the Scottish version of Labour's manifesto.

It was not the Liberal Democrats who insisted on a different approach. It was Labour ministers, principally Jack McConnell and Susan Deacon. They objected to the timing rather than the principle of involving the private sector. To march in step with the Prime Minister, they argued, would upset trade unions and councils, who had already been asked to accept health service reform and the McCrone deal on teachers' pay and conditions. It could also leave Labour's left flank vulnerable to the Scottish National Party. The result was that the UK party tailored its message to suit a federal electorate, and Labour in Scotland postponed the public–private debate to another day.

Scottish Labour MPs will be used to voting on measures from which their constituents are constitutionally exempt. Now, in an intensified version of the West Lothian Question, they are voting on measures from which their constituents are ideologically exempt as well. This approach is made possible by the scant Westminster interest in devolved areas of the United Kingdom. Labour MPs do get irritated when they hear that tuition fees, which many found painful to support, have been replaced by a graduate repayment. But divergent policies north of the border will only start to register when elderly constituents move north to take advantage of free long-term care, or when local teachers cast envious eyes on the better pay and conditions brought to Scotland by the McCrone deal.

But if MPs are vague on the details of what is happening in Scotland, they have a strong sense that other regions of the UK – usually their own – are losing out in the distribution wars. The campaign for regional assemblies, boosted by Gordon Brown's sudden interest in regional economic policy and bolstered by the surprise conversion of Peter Mandelson, has gathered strength and pace. The push for a review of spending across the UK (which goes wider than the Barnett Formula) is backed by an unlikely coalition ranging from MPs in the north-east of England to Ken Livingstone, the mayor of London, the Scottish National Party and Plaid Cymru in Wales. Alex Salmond is happy to stir the debate over Barnett because it suits the SNP's short-term aim: fiscal autonomy for the Scottish Parliament. His decision to stay at Westminster and lead the small, inexperienced SNP group shows that his party has realised it needs to take the House of Commons seriously, even after devolution, maximising opportunities to embarrass the Executive by keeping lines open to the south.

Scottish Labour MPs are likely to find themselves fighting on several fronts. Besides Barnett, there will be the struggle for survival as the Boundary Commission prepares to cut the number of Scottish MPs. There will be bare-knuckle fights within parties as well as between them, with rivals battling over a reduced number of seats.

The Liberal Democrats, with a Scottish leader, are in an interesting position. In Scotland and Wales, they sit round the cabinet table with Labour, with voting reform for local government high on their list of demands. Yet at Westminster, Charles Kennedy has retreated from co-operation to a more critical stance, and the prospects for a referendum on Lord Jenkins's proposals seem bleak.

With a lone representative in the Commons, the Scottish Conservatives will barely feature at Westminster in Tony Blair's second term. During his unsuccessful general election campaign, Malcolm Rifkind, the former Foreign Secretary, emphasised that without Conservative MPs, Scots who oppose the European Single Currency would not be represented in the UK debate over the Euro. No doubt Peter Duncan, the surprise victor for Galloway and Upper Nithsdale, will do his best. But if Tony Blair were to call a referendum before the next election, Eurosceptics north of the border will have no official voice at Westminster.

Could the Scottish Parliament act as a focus for debate on the Euro? MSPs, while gaining confidence on their own turf, remain nervous about commenting on reserved matters such as media regulation or anti-terrorism laws. But the climate is slowly changing. The campaign to preserve MSP numbers – boundary changes required by the Scotland Act imply a cut in numbers – has bred cross-party esprit de corps. The notion of fiscal autonomy, giving the Parliament responsibility for raising the money that it spends, is no longer seen as a Nationalist eccentricity but as a legitimate subject for discussion.

The biggest and most symbolic break with Westminster was the election, in November 2001, of a home-grown First Minister. Unlike Donald Dewar and Henry McLeish, Jack McConnell has never been an MP. His only experience of elected office has been at Holyrood. What a contrast with the early days of the Scottish Parliament, when there was speculation that Robin Cook or Alistair Darling could be parachuted into Edinburgh to take over as First Minister on Donald Dewar's retirement. That would be unthinkable now. The umbilical cord has been cut – and not just with Westminster. Mr McConnell has ruptured the special relationship between Scotland and Gordon Brown.

Mr Brown has been described by David Clark, a former aide to Robin Cook, as 'kingmaker' in Scotland, with 'absolute authority' from Tony Blair. The Chancellor lobbied for Henry McLeish in the leadership contest that took place after Mr Dewar's sudden death, a contest in which Jack McConnell was the only challenger. On gaining power a year later, Mr McConnell cleared the Brownites from his cabinet, leaving Wendy Alexander a lone but important link to the Treasury and the departments of Social Security and Trade and Industry, where her brother Douglas is a minister.

But while the First Minister's loyalties lie in Scotland, his views put him on the same wavelength as Labour in London. Mr McConnell is not hostile to involving the private sector in public services, though more sensitive to council and trade union opinion than Tony Blair would be. He has set his face against changing the Barnett Formula or pushing for fiscal autonomy, insisting that Scotland enjoys 'record levels of resources' and that modernisation is not just about money.

Gordon Brown ought to be delighted with the script, if not with the speaker. Mr McConnell may be making a break with Westminster, but he is staying close to Millbank.

CHAPTER 4

# After 300 Years:
# The Road to Home Rule

Joyce McMillan

Political systems change, but some things endure. 'Once upon a time,' writes Liz Lochhead at the beginning of her 1987 play *Mary Queen of Scots Got Her Head Chopped Off*, 'there were twa queens on the wan green island, and the wan green island was split inty twa kingdoms. But no' equal kingdoms, naebody in their richt mind would insist on that. For the northern kingdom was cold and sma'. And the people were low-statured and ignorant and feart o' their lords and poor! They were starvin'. . . . The other kingdom in the island was large, and prosperous, with wheat and barley and fat kye in the fields o' her yeomen fermers, and wool in her looms, and beer in her barrels and, at the mouth of her greatest river, a great port, a glistening city that sucked all wealth to its centre.'

Lochhead writes in a spirit of sparkling irony, of course, conjuring up stereotypes of both Scotland and England that exist as much in imagination as they ever did in reality. But still, most of us here in the northern kingdom recognise the psychological truth of the image without hesitation. The fact is that ever since the two kingdoms began to emerge in recognisable shape, around the turn of the last millennium, Scotland has been a smaller and less populous nation sharing an island off the north-west coast of Europe with a larger and more powerful neighbour, and our political history has inevitably been dominated by the quality of that relationship, its terms, conditions and relative harmony. Throughout the middle ages, the relationship was one of actual or threatened war, during which Scotland survived as an independent kingdom by a combination of guile, guts, stubbornness and sheer battlefield luck. After 1603, it was a question of sullen union under a single monarch, overshadowed by fierce religious differences and civil war in England; after 1707, it was a full incorporating Union with the Westminster political system, in which the Scots swallowed their pride, suspended their parliament, and relieved England for good of any threat of invasion from the north, in return for full junior-partner status in the growing enterprise of British Empire.

But always, insofar as public opinion can be measured, Scots seem to have seen the Union primarily as a practical alliance of two closely linked peoples, a treaty aimed at promoting peace, prosperity and economic development; whereas for everyone else, it was simply a matter of Scotland finally throwing in the towel, and effectively becoming part of England. Whatever their views on the Union, in other words, Scots of all persuasions remained much more strongly aware than their Union partners of their continuing existence as a nation, and of the character of the United Kingdom as a Union state rather than a unitary one; so it was hardly surprising that in the nineteenth century, as the electoral franchise began to extend beyond the landed and wealthy elites who had been most effectively bound into the Union establishment, organised movements for various degrees of home rule immediately began to appear on Scotland's political map.

The organisation widely recognised as the first modern home-rule campaign was the Scottish Home Rule Association of 1886, an alliance of Gladstonian Liberals and early socialist trade unionists which featured the young Ramsay MacDonald among its leading members, and was much influenced by Gladstone's idea of 'home rule all round' as a solution to the Irish Question; and over the next century, plethora of home rule alliances and initiatives came and went, both inside the unionist Labour and Liberal parties, and beyond them. The National Party of Scotland – the parent of today's SNP – was formed in 1928, at a rally at Bannockburn, from an alliance of small nationalist groupings. But the Scottish Home Rule Association stood aloof because of its traditional links with Labour; and so the broad home rule movement began its exhausting seventy-year struggle to achieve a degree of unity in the fight for a Scottish Parliament, despite the deep and persistent split between those who were mainly concerned with democratic reform within the British state, and those whose passion was to assert Scotland's full national sovereignty, and complete freedom from London rule.

Throughout the twentieth century – apart from a brief Labour hiatus during the post-war high tide of Unionism between 1950 and 1970 – home rule for Scotland was the official policy of both the Labour and Liberal parties, and even the Conservatives would embrace the idea from time to time. In the years between 1880 and 1992, no fewer than nineteen Bills for Scottish home rule were introduced at Westminster, only to be voted down, talked out, or – like the famous Home Rule Bill of 1914, which seemed set to become law just before the outbreak of the First World War – overtaken by events; as Andrew Marr puts it in his vivid 1992 history *The Battle for Scotland*, Conservative governments in power tended to change their tune about home rule, while Labour governments were unable to deliver.

But despite these repeated disappointments, the presence of the SNP and its forerunners always kept the issue alive, and there were periods when the cause of Scottish home rule attracted such a broad alliance of Scottish opinion that the coming of a parliament within a year or two seemed almost inevitable. It happened in the years following the First World War, when Scotland sent the blazing social-ist–nationalist Red Clydesiders to Westminster. It happened in the idealistic post-war atmosphere of the late 1940s, when almost two million Scots signed the great National Covenant; and it happened again around 1974, when the discovery of North Sea oil produced a historic reversal in Scotland's sense of itself as small and poor, and a significant surge in support for the SNP. Each time support for home rule surged and failed, some campaigners would fall victim to one of the great psychological bear-traps of life in a stateless nation, the hectic mood-swings between exaggerated self-assertion and moody self-contempt that Scots nowadays call the 'Argentina syndrome', after the roller-coaster of exaggerated hope and sickening humiliation that accompanied the appearance of Scotland's football team in the World Cup finals of 1978.

And when the last of the nineteen failed home rule Bills collapsed in ignominy in the Commons in March 1979 – following a referendum in which fewer than a third of Scots voters turned out to support the measure – it seemed to many that Scotland, and Scotland's divided and disorganised movement for self-government, had finally shot itself in the foot so comprehensively that it would never walk the home rule road again.

But as it turned out, the impression of abject failure was even more false than the dream of inevitable victory that preceded it, for beneath the surface of British and European politics, tectonic plates had begun to move, removing many of the major obstacles to Scottish home rule. In practical terms, it's easy enough to outline what was done, after 1979, to keep the cause of Scottish home rule alive.

Soon after the general election of that year, a group of activists led by Isobel Lindsay of the SNP, the former Scottish Office civil servant Jim Ross, and Labour home rulers Dennis Canavan and George Foulkes among others, met in Glasgow, and set up a cross-party group called the Campaign for a Scottish Assembly (CSA), with the sole objective of keeping the issue alive in difficult times. Five or six lean years followed, but by 1987, when the Conservatives lost eleven of their twenty-one Scottish seats in the general election, the CSA was ready to capitalise on growing unease among Scottish MPs and politicians about the widening political gap between Thatcherite southern England and anti-Thatcherite Scotland, and about the powerlessness of Labour's 'feeble fifty' Westminster MPs to influence policy in Scotland.

In 1987–8, they convened a committee of Scottish grandees who produced a Claim of Right for Scotland, outlining Scotland's ancient claim to self-rule, and in March 1989, after long and fraught negotiations among the non-Tory political parties (the SNP decided at the last minute not to take part), along with other social partners in the churches, trade unions and voluntary sector, the CSA presided over the launch of the Scottish Constitutional Convention at the Church of Scotland Assembly Hall on the Mound. This was an astonishing event in British constitutional terms, at which 58 of Scotland's 72 MPs, along with 7 of its 8 MEPs, 59 of its 65 local authorities, 7 political parties, and a huge range of civil society organisations and activists, signed up to the Claim of Right, and undertook to campaign for Scottish self-government. It was an initiative that owed much to the history of broad-based Scottish campaigning for home rule; the scene at the signing strongly recalled the launch of the National Covenant, thirty-eight years earlier in the same hall. But it was also an example of the new wave of 'civil politics' that was beginning to spread across Europe as the old Cold War system crumbled; citizens from beyond the party-political system were beginning to intervene and demand their say, and were often asking for a new age of cross-party co-operation to achieve common ends.

And despite repeated predictions of its demise, after 1989 the Convention worked away in reasonable harmony, producing increasingly detailed and innovative draft schemes for a Scottish Parliament in 1990 and 1995. There were two more fierce crises of confidence, the first following John Major's unexpected general election victory in April 1992, and the second in the summer of 1996, when Tony Blair's Shadow Cabinet suddenly decided that the decision to go ahead with Scottish home rule would have to be confirmed by a referendum.

But after Tony Blair's massive election victory of May 1997, and Donald Dewar's appointment as Secretary of State, the Convention scheme was swiftly developed into a White Paper. In September 1997 the 68 per cent of Scots who went to the polls voted by a margin of three to one for the setting up of the Parliament, and by two to one for the Parliament's small tax-varying power. In 1998 the Scotland Act – with its ringing opening phrase 'There shall be a Scottish Parliament' – became law. In May 1999 the 129-strong Parliament was duly elected by an additional member system of proportional representation, and on 1 July 1999, on a bright, blustery summer day in Edinburgh, the Queen formally opened the Parliament at its temporary home in the Assembly Hall, and delivered to its presiding officer – the lifelong Liberal Democrat, home-rule campaigner and Constitutional Convention Co-Chair Sir David Steel – a Scottish silver mace emblazoned with the words 'Justice, Wisdom, Integrity, Compassion'.

Many of us, at home or in the Assembly Hall, could only watch with tears running down our cheeks, of relief as much as of joy. This was the day generations of Scots had imagined, and had thought they would not live to see; now it was here, and looking not only magnificent, but absolutely ordinary and right.

But why, in this final rush of years after 1987, did what had for so long seemed next to impossible suddenly become almost easy? In the first place, because the Britain of the late 1990s was no longer the place it had been for most of the years since 1707. It was more populist, less aristocratic, more driven by cash and less concerned with custom and history. Most crucially, despite the last-ditch stridency of the Thatcher years, it was slowly losing the near-mystical faith in its own institutions that had sustained it through the mighty years of Empire and war, and the postwar creation of the welfare state, and it had all but ceased to produce a leadership elite who knew or cared how to defend the Union in its traditional form.

Margaret Thatcher was a formidable leader in many ways, and took herself for a great sentimental Unionist. But in reality – unlike the older Tory aristocrats who had led the party in its pre-democratic era – she had very little feeling for any of the checks and balances which traditionally moderated the immense power of the Prime Minister in the British system.

Between 1979 and 1997, the number of Tory MPs elected in Scotland fell from twenty-two to zero, but the once-shrewd grandees of the Tory Party seemed past caring, or even asking why. By 1988, anger at Margaret Thatcher's cavalier way with the old British constitution had reached such a pitch, across the country, that a large UK-wide movement was launched under the name Charter 88, a campaign for constitutional reform which embraced the case for devolution alongside demands for proportional representation, reform of the House of Lords, and a radical freedom of information Act. Charter 88 consciously modelled itself on the great Czech civic movement of the previous decade, Charter 77, and the fact that Scottish home rule activists could now see their constitutional unease explicitly reflected in a UK-wide movement added a whole new dimension of psychological robustness to the Scottish home-rule argument, which was no longer only about Scotland and its private griefs, but also about general and widely-recognised principles of good governance for the twenty-first century.

And the Labour Party, too, had undergone a deep cultural change since the 1960s, as the old tradition of patriotic Labour Unionism was swept away, particularly in England, by a generation of radical new left activists, creating years of strife in the party, and leaving it shorn of half a generation of credible English leaders. By 1997, easily the most impressive group of politicians in the Commons was Tony Blair's inner Shadow Cabinet; but this time around, an unusually high proportion of these new Labour grandees – including Gordon

Brown, Robin Cook, Alistair Darling, George Robertson, Donald Dewar, John Reid – were post-war Scots, signatories to the Claim of Right, and committed home rulers.

But if the resistance to Scottish home rule at the heart of the British system had begun to melt away, Scotland, too, was no longer the place it had been through most of the years since 1707. During all that time, Scotland had had to live with the sense that its path to modernity, prosperity and the future inevitably led to and through London. Generations of Scots grew up with the idea that to be 'too Scottish' was to be somehow backward, old-fashioned, unambitious, and as late as the 1960s – with *The White Heather Club* playing on television alongside images of Swinging London – Scots teenagers were growing up with the idea that Scottish national identity was a couthy, nostalgic thing, while the future lay elsewhere.

But after 1970, the age of centralising modernism began to give way to the more complex patchwork culture of post-modernism, and a higher premium began to be placed on 'roots', belonging, local identities. Britain joined the European Union, with its complex structures of federal and regional government, and the London-centred establishment, struggling to come to terms with this new world, continued its slow decline in cultural prestige and dominance. A brilliant new wave of Scottish writers and artists burst onto the scene, through the novels of Alasdair Gray, the plays and paintings of John Byrne, the theatre shows of John McGrath, the poems and plays of Liz Lochhead, the music of James Macmillan, the great 1980s wave of Scottish rock and pop, and all the work associated with Glasgow's flagship role, around 1990, as a post-industrial city using culture to come to terms with its past.

And it began to seem as though Scotland and small nations like it, with their long habit of sustaining dual identities, their sophistication in recognising and negotiating different cultures, and their natural inclination to seek federal solutions to the problem of combining unity and diversity, might actually be better placed to cope with the new age of European Union and rapid globalisation than Britain's old metropolitan establishment.

Even more importantly, the concept of Scottishness gently exploded, between 1970 and 1990, to the point where it could accommodate every aspect of modern Scottish experience and every strand of influence on modern Scottish culture – the Irish, the American, the

Asian, the Italian, the Jewish, the English – and yet still remain confident of its distinctive Scottish voice. And once the idea of Scottishness was no longer trapped in the past, and paralysed by fear of dilution and loss, it began to storm towards the future, attracting waves of young people as it went, drawing inspiration from 'Celtic tiger' Ireland to the west, and moving rapidly beyond the point where it could easily be frightened by old concepts of Scotland as second rate or provincial. At a crucial moment in the 1990s, that flood-tide of cultural confidence and exuberance gave Scots a powerful new image of their nation, complex, dynamic, forward looking, diverse, thoroughly modern at last; and without that vision, and the artists who helped make it, the massive 'yes' vote of September 1997 might never have been possible.

None of which, of course, guarantees a happy and harmonious future for the Scottish Parliament itself. Born into an age of crushing cynicism about the value of democracy and the usefulness of political institutions, the Parliament runs a heavy risk of rapidly becoming just another despised institution among many, unless it seizes its chance to become a powerful advocate and laboratory for some of the new ideas about participatory and consultative democracy that emerged through the home-rule process of the 1990s, and through the wider UK and European movements for constitutional reform of the same decade.

But in the end there is a profound satisfaction, for all those who worked and campaigned for home rule, in the thought that no future crisis, in the British state or beyond it, will ever find the Scottish people as bereft of a true and representative national voice as they were between 1707 and 1999. Now, the main instrument of democracy is in our hands, to use as we see fit. And although post-devolution Scotland remains a long way from paradise, it's a place where an old and painful breach in the life of the nation seems healed at last, and where, on a bright day in Edinburgh, we can once again stand in the Lawnmarket and watch our own representatives walk up the street, to take their seats in the Parliament of Scotland.

# CHAPTER 5

# The Scottish Parliament:
# (a) How it Works

George Reid MSP

## From Principles to Practice

> 'I ken when we had a King,' wrote Sir Walter Scott, 'and a Chancellor and a Parliament – men o'our ain – we could aye peeble them wi' stanes when they werena gude bairns. But naebody's nails can reach the length o' Lunnon . . .'

Old habits die hard. Outside the back door of the Assembly Hall, an elderly man is regularly stationed with a poster calling for repentance by all who enter therein. In the Royal Mile, there are Border farmers, disabled children in wheelchairs, men and women made redundant – all perfectly clear about their basic right to require MSPs to stop and listen to their views. Inside, there lurk the parliamentary press corps – always ready to rake their nails across those who stray from the path of righteousness.

Westminster it isn't. Like it or not, the people have already taken ownership of the Parliament – voicing their criticisms while viewing it with a sort of grudging affection, liking its lack of affectation and the fact that it does is business in a very Scots, democratic way.

## Doing Business the Scottish Way

For those of us who have served in the House of Commons,

Holyrood is a joy. No more trailing around the lobbies, in division after division, at an hour when decent citizens are in their beds. Decision time at Holyrood, with electronic voting at five o'clock, takes no more than ten minutes – after which three-quarters of members can go home to their families and constituents.

No more squeezing up the green benches, or sitting on the steps, roaring abuse at the opposite side across two swords' lengths of green carpet. Instead, each MSP has a desk in the European-style hemicycle. The fact that almost 40 per cent of the members are women (the highest of any Commonwealth legislature) also makes it a Chamber with a much lower testosterone count. No more bowing and scraping before dropping a petition in a poke at the back of the Speaker's Chair, after which to all intents and purposes it disappears. In the Scottish Parliament, all petitioners must be told, within a defined timescale, what action has been taken.

No more pomp and circumstance. Buddhists, Baptists, Muslims and Mormons all share the Wednesday *Time for Reflection* slot with the Kirk and the Roman Catholics. Deaf-signers have appeared on the floor. And nursing mothers have discreetly breastfed their babies in the gallery during debate. It is a comfortable, family-friendly way of conducting our affairs. But it is only the cultural framework within which the Chamber and the committees do their business.

### Dealing with the Democratic Deficit

Two years on from the opening of parliament on 1 July 1999, thirty-one Bills have been introduced covering such issues as education, transport, land tenure and national parks–with twenty-two of them having made it to the Statute Book, and another two awaiting Royal Assent.

It would have taken between two and three Parliaments at Westminster to achieve the same results. Indeed such measures as the Leasehold Casualties (Scotland) Act and the Abolition of Feudal Tenure (Scotland) Bill have been waiting in the wings for years for a slot in the Commons. And the Protection from Abuse (Scotland) Bill has many provisions that closely mirror the Domestic Violence (Scotland) Bill that I tried to introduce at Westminster in the late 1970s.

The volume of work by the Parliament's seventeen committees which, unlike Westminster, have the dual role of scrutinising legislation and conducting their own enquiries – and which can initiate their own Bills – has been equally impressive. When the SQA scandal broke in 2000, affecting the exam results of Scotland's school-leavers, the Education and Enterprise Committees both conducted immediate inquiries – subjecting ministers and civil servants to detailed questioning, and producing fifty-six recommendations for change. In the old Westminster days – apart from questions and letters to ministers – there could never have been such a rapid reaction.

In their chambers in Edinburgh – and up and down the country in town halls, prisons, factories, universities and even gypsy caravans – other committees have held hearings on such varied subjects as domestic abuse, housing, regional development funds, fishing policy, special educational needs, local government finance, community care, genetically modified organisms, foot and mouth disease, commercial lobbyists and roadside drug-testing. Scotland, after years of being managed, is now open to an unprecedented degree of public scrutiny. While those who ran the old patronage state may not like it, decades of democratic deficit are now being addressed.

**The Fundamental Principles**
Following the overwhelming mandate for a parliament in the 1997 referendum, the new Labour government established the Consultative Steering Group under the chairmanship of Henry McLeish MP to devise an operational structure for the new legislature. Building on the work already done by the Scottish Constitutional Convention, and after examining best practice from around the world, the group published its final report, *Shaping Scotland's Parliament*, in December 1998. There was, of course, no Erskine May to pull off the shelf, listing centuries of precedent and practice. In the Scots tradition, the group therefore sought to identify a number of principles which would inform the Parliament's work and provide evaluators against which its performance might be judged. These were:

- Sharing the power: the Parliament should embody and reflect the sharing of power between the people of Scotland, the legislators and the Scottish Executive.
- Accountability: the Scottish Executive should be accountable to the Scottish Parliament, and the Parliament and Executive should be accountable to the people of Scotland.

- Access and participation: the Scottish Parliament should be accessible, open, responsive and develop procedures which make possible a participative approach to the development, consideration and scrutiny of policy and legislation.
- Equal opportunities: the Scottish Parliament in its operation and appointments should recognise the need to promote equal opportunities.

These principles were adopted by members in plenary session in June 1999 and are also explicitly agreed by the Executive in its Scottish Ministerial Code. They establish a means of evaluating the Parliament's daily work in making laws on devolved matters; in holding the Scottish Executive to account through scrutiny by committees and by oral and written questions; in debating important topical matters; and in conducting inquiries and publishing reports. They also provide a way of judging the extent to which the Parliament has met Henry McLeish's promise that it would 'offer the opportunity to put in place a new sort of democracy in Scotland, closer to the Scottish people and more in tune with Scottish needs'.

### The Power of the Parliament

Westminster, of course, does not share power with anyone. The Crown in Parliament, which in reality means the government of the day, is sovereign. The Scottish Executive is, however, hedged in by the various vires tests laid down in the Scotland Act and is subject to a number of constraints.

First, it has to discuss its forward business programme collectively in the Parliamentary Bureau, chaired by the Presiding Officer, where each of the Business Managers of the main parties holds votes equivalent to their number of MSPs. The Bureau meets behind closed doors, and publishes only a brief summary note of its decisions.

Second, it has to get its proposals through the committees, which have a far more central role in the legislative procedure than at Westminster. Since there is no revising chamber in Scotland, it is important to get it right the first time round. When the Executive brings forward a Bill, it has to provide a policy memorandum outlining who it has consulted with, what alternatives were considered and the likely effects on equal opportunities, human rights, island communities and sustainable development. In addition, there is a separate Financial Memorandum. Unlike Westminster, the Bill is then examined in Committee before going to the Chamber for a Stage I vote on its general principles. Thereafter it goes back for line by line Stage II examination by the lead, and possibly other, committees.

Third, the Executive has to get its proposals through plenary. This can be a delicate moment in a coalition government, as in the case of the Education (Graduate Endowment and Student Support) Bill. It can also be a moment when backbenchers dig their heels in, leading to outright defeat of the Executive, as happened with Tommy Sheridan's Abolition of Poindings and Warrant Sales Bill.

Fourth, the Executive has to deal with the Presiding Officer, elected to represent Parliament as a whole, who has a great deal of discretion but no book of precedent to guide him, and for whom Standing Orders are sometimes only too silent. This has led to a number of spats – on how his casting vote should be used, and on his ban on ministerial statements that have already appeared widely in the press.

In general, however, the Executive can argue that, midway through the first Parliament, it has been successful in securing its programme on a whole raft of issues covering housing, the end of up-front student loans, teachers' pay and conditions, rape law and the abolition of Section 28 on the promotion of homosexuality in schools.

### The Power of Committees

There are seventeen parliamentary committees. Eight are mandatory – Audit, Equal Opportunities, Europe, Finance, Public Petitions, Procedures, Standards and Subordinate Legislation. And nine are subject committees – Education, Culture and Sport; Enterprise and Lifelong Learning; Health and Community Care; Justice 1; Justice 2; Local Government; Rural Development; Social Justice; and Transport and the Environment.

Given their joint scrutiny and inquiry role, committees are the engine room of the Parliament. On the Housing (Scotland) Bill alone, it took the Social Justice Committee over 24 hours to work its way through amendments. And vast amounts of work have gone into major committee investigations into such subjects as the SQA (broadcast on line, with an IT chat room for teachers and parents), the Common Fisheries Policy, and local enterprise. Committees also have fiscal responsibilities, reviewing the budget and sometimes securing extra money – for victim support or payments to the mentally ill, for example – in the process. The Audit Committee, in particular, has carried out major investigations on the cost of the new Holyrood building and on the NHS deficit in Tayside.

For the first two years, committee conveners had no collegial status. They met informally as a group to share experience, apportion research moneys and agree travel outside Edinburgh. But increasingly they have begun to discuss any matter of common interest and to relay views to the Bureau and, on finance and personnel matters, to the Corporate Body. Now the group is to be officially recognised in Standing Orders. This will give conveners a stronger voice in expressing concerns about expertise being lost by too much shuffling of MSPs between committees by the Business Managers. There will also be attempts to tailor parliamentary business much closer to their work programme – dovetailing their half-day debates, when they decide the subject, to their own work programme and trying to ensure that they are not reviewing the budget simultaneously with carrying out an inquiry or scrutinising a Bill.

**The Power of the People**

In many ways it was civic Scotland – the voluntary organisations, the trade unions and the churches – that kept the light burning for a Scottish Parliament during the long years when the country had a government imposed on it for which it did not vote. Regardless of left–right and constitutional issues, civic Scotland wanted a more modern, participatory parliament in which its voice would be heard. The level of expectation was so high that, inevitably, some have voiced disappointment – particularly that it is not possible to co-opt experts as non-voting members of committees.

Nonetheless, compared to Westminster, the level of participation is extremely high. Committees regularly take evidence in witness sessions from the voluntary and civic sector. The Assembly Hall of the Parliament is also made available (which the Commons never would be) for events in which non-MSPs give voice on public issues. 'Business in the Chamber', featuring 130 industrialists, led to substantial changes in the Enterprise Committee report on local enterprise services. The Social Justice Committee brought together a similar number of people to debate Exclusion, in a project which will inform its work programme to the end of the Parliament. The Education service filled the Committee Rooms and Chamber with young people, who over a day took through their own dummy Bill on health care.

The Equal Opportunities Committee has also reached out to the disadvantaged, appointing Reporters with special responsibility for Race, Religion and Gender. It has made special efforts to communicate with its audiences, be it through Braille, audiotapes, or large type. Finally, Gaelic is present throughout the Parliament since all the signage is bilingual. With the appointment of a Gaelic officer, there are also regular outputs in the language via the website, media releases and the occasional speech from the floor. In 2001 a dictionary of parliamentary usage, *Fàclair na Parlamaid*, was produced.

**An Accessible Parliament**

Perhaps the main test of a legislature's appeal to its people is whether they come and watch. In Edinburgh, even during the most technical of debates, there is always someone in the galleries and for First Minister's Questions on a Thursday, the queue regularly stretches out into the Royal Mile. When the Public Petitions Committee met in Galashiels to consider the reinstitution of the Borders' railway, the hall was jampacked. And when the Audit Committee met to consider the NHS deficit in Tayside in the City Chambers of Dundee, the largest space available, so many people turned up that video cameras had to relay the meeting to other locations.

Members' business debates, given 45 minutes after the five o'clock vote, also attract specific interest on subjects as diverse as Endiometriosis, Women's Pay, Credit Unions, Debt Awareness, and Autistic Spectrum Disorder. The parliamentary website receives around 600,000 hits a month, and has registered viewers for its live coverage of committees and Plenary across the globe. Partner libraries – one in each constituency – are also on line and able to provide documentation to visitors. There is a free phone line for callers seeking background information. And the schools service, now serving as a model for other legislatures, has, after two years, processed 10,000 students in a planned work programme – with almost as many again simply coming to watch from the gallery.

In all this work, members of all parties are very conscious of what Tony Blair called the 'corrosive cynicism' of many citizens towards parliamentary democracy. While it is easier to maintain links in a small country like Scotland, the Parliament is determined to do all it can to maintain the link between electors and elected in an ongoing programme of outreach and accessibility.

## A Process, not an Event

We Scots are a pragmatic people. We don't like fully to endorse principles until they have been proved in practice. Judging by the large survey carried out by in the 2000 Social Attitudes Survey, however, most Scots seem to like the principle of the Parliament. Two-thirds want it to have more powers, and three-quarters want it to have more influence than Westminster over their daily lives. They're just not sure about the practice to date.

Jack McConnell and his team will argue that they are providing Scottish answers to Scottish issues. They will cite the work already done on free personal care for the elderly, nursery education, school and hospital buildings, the better salaries and conditions for teachers, land reform and concessionary fares. For the Opposition, John Swinney will argue that much more could be done with greater fiscal autonomy – 'completing the powers of the parliament' – and stronger Scottish links to the European Union. What is clear is that the Parliament has already made a difference. Scotland, a quintessentially social democratic country, has taken on that profile inside the British state.

What was promised, after the long years of taking largely second place at Westminster, is already being delivered. The label on the box was correct. The parliament *has* been open, accessible, accountable and has shared power with the people. But the Parliament was never an end in itself. It is simply a means of delivering a more open, democratic, just and caring Scotland. Virtually everyone agrees that devolution was not an event, a once-and-for-all transfer of powers from London. Rather it was part of a process which would be driven forward by the principles. The best thing at this stage of the process is that we Scots stopped girning about Westminster and blaming the Mother of Parliaments for all our ills. If we make mistakes in future, they'll be largely our mistakes. And, for sure, we will hear about them. It would not, after all, be a proper Scottish Parliament unless the people, from time to time, could feel free to peeble their politicians wi' stanes.

CHAPTER 6

# The Scottish Parliament:
# (b) Does it Work?

Graham Leicester

Devolution in Scotland brought into being two new institutions in Scotland: the Scottish Parliament and the Scottish Executive. It is necessary to begin with this simple point, because it is not self-evident. The fact that we tend to interpret 'devolution' as meaning the setting up of a Scottish Parliament illustrates that it is all too easy to forget that the Executive is a new institution, too.

In the early months people tended to see Parliament and Executive as the same thing – an error too often compounded in the press. Many still do. In any event, even those who saw the Executive as a separate organisation did not see it as 'new'. After all, it looked just like the old Scottish Office – the same group of officials serving many of the same ministers augmented by a number of new recruits from the Scottish elections.

Hence most political energy in the run up to devolution was devoted to how the new Parliament might work. My own organisation, the Scottish Council Foundation, is an exception to that rule. In a series of publications – from *Holistic Government* through *Promise and Practice* to *As Good as it Gets?* – we have analysed in detail the opportunities inherent in setting up a new Executive, how they might be realised, and the performance of the new institution in practice. That material is available on the web at HYPERLINK 'http://www.scottishpolicynet.org.uk'.

This article will touch on the Executive, therefore, but concentrates on the Parliament: in particular on new research conducted in partnership with Manchester Metropolitan University. For three years now we have conducted a series of interviews with a panel of Members of the Scottish Parliament (MSPs), with the first interviews taking place in the summer of 1999. Our aim has been to record the early aspirations of the first members of the Parliament and to track their changing views over time as the new institution has developed. We were promised a 'high-tech and family friendly' Parliament by the Consultative Steering Group, a Parliament fit for the modern world. Yet the results of our study show a significant level of disillusion with a Parliament that has fallen short of its promises to be inclusive, family friendly, different from Westminster and based on a new collaborative politics.

As one MSP told us: 'What started out as a vocation has turned into a job, and a very hard one at that.' The 2000 *Scottish Social Attitudes Survey*, just completed, shows that only 10 per cent of people think the Scottish Parliament has greater influence than Westminster, only 45 per cent think it has given them more say in how they are governed, and nearly 70 per cent think devolution has had a negligible impact on their lives. It would not be surprising in these circumstances if, come the 2003 elections, more MSPs follow the lead of Labour backbencher Ian Welsh, who resigned from the Parliament after only six months because he was not prepared to endure the damage to his lifestyle for so little reward.

Some argue that the Parliament can only be truly effective with more powers. This article instead looks at other reasons why the settlement has failed to live up to expectations. These reasons are independent of the precise nature of the balance of power between Scotland and London. They lie for the most part deep in the British political culture. Take the Parliament's promise to be 'family friendly'. The Parliament sits only during the school term, from Monday afternoon to Friday lunchtime, with a full day running from 09.30 to 17.30. Yet still MSPs are working 60–70-hour weeks. Why? The simple answer is that politics has an endemic long hours culture. Many of us argued in advance of devolution for a part-time legislature, as is the norm in many US states. That would have encouraged longer term policy making and might have broadened the range of people tempted to go into politics. But there were feelings that Scotland needed a 'real' Parliament, and that means one that makes constant demands on its members.

The press surrounding the early days of the new Parliament did not help. The first decision of the Parliament concerned the allowances for MSPs. Labour led with a transparent attempt to cement their territorial advantage. They forced through a package giving fewer allowances to MSPs elected on the regional list under the Additional Member System (AMS) of PR than to those elected from a constituency (Labour had only three list MSPs out of fifty-six). Naturally there was a row, suggesting to the public that their new politicians were interested only in feathering their nests. It also ensured that list MSPs – the most distinctive break from Westminster and potentially a valuable resource – were treated officially from the start as second-class members. Much of the hard work put in since by diligent MSPs can be seen as trying to make up for a poorly handled start.

The politics of AMS has also added to the workload. Every Scot is now represented by one MP, one constituency MSP, seven MSPs for the region (list MSPs) and a local councillor. An embarrassment of riches for the constituent with a grievance or a problem, who can now pick and choose both the level of government to approach, and – because of the list system – the party to represent her. Much of the MSP's caseload, as for Westminster, is about local government matters. And constituents are not making a distinction between devolved and reserved issues: if an MSP proves effective on one issue she will be approached on others, even when they are the responsibility of the UK government. The other consequence of AMS is that even in a safe constituency the other parties are also represented. As one MSP put it, 'Under the Westminster system the opposition effectively disappears for four years. But now there are MSPs everywhere!' That, too, adds to the workload – the campaign never stops.

The Parliament in turn makes demands on the Executive. The statistics for the first full year show that the Executive had nearly 8,500 oral and written questions to answer, over forty ministerial statements and dozens of ministerial or official evidence sessions before committees. As early as November 1999 Donald Dewar chose to make one of the themes of his John P. Mackintosh memorial lecture the strains that devolution had imposed on the system of administration. He noted that more parliamentary questions were put down in the first four months of the Parliament's existence (including during the recess) than in a whole year at Westminster and that there had been a 35 per cent increase in ministerial correspondence.

There were added demands too generated by the expansion in the size of the Executive: a trebling of the number of ministers, and the added challenges of assuring coherence within a coalition government. Added to that, the commitment to a new form of more participative politics had been translated into an Executive that by mid-May 2000 had issued more consultation papers than there had been working days in its life. The strains of all these additional pressures were too much. The machinery of government slowly clogged up: Parliament and Executive locked into a way of working that neither could sustain, yet seemed impossible to reverse.

As for the effectiveness of the Parliament itself, the committees were to have been strong independent voices, challenging and scrutinising the Executive, performing the role of a revising second chamber for legislation, undertaking their own research and even initiating legislation. The shadow of the local government influence – another strong influence on the Scottish Parliament's culture – is evident.

Yet the committees, too, have struggled to define their role and were quickly swamped with Executive legislation. Most MSPs sit on two or three committees each, but as they have become increasingly disillusioned by the grind of committee work, the Parliament has been forced to review arrangements, reducing the number of people on each committee and introducing an additional justice committee to share the workload. Meanwhile there are now thirty-eight formally registered cross-party groups. None is resourced from public funds, but the continued growth of this kind of activity suggests that there is a parallel structure already developing in the Parliament in which MSPs congregate around their interests rather than around the structure or the agenda of the Executive. That looks like an interesting tension in the years ahead.

The same tension has been evident in the way the Parliament has defined itself as in opposition to the Executive. This is more a function of party politics than the mechanics of the institution itself – but it goes to show that it takes more than a horseshoe seating plan to break the mould of Westminster. In the recent parliamentary debate on the Sutherland commission's proposals on the funding of long-term care, for example, neither the Parliament nor the Executive excelled itself. The Executive tabled an emergency motion accepting the opposition's position minutes before the end of the debate in order to avoid a defeat in the Chamber. That reversed their statement of policy made to the Parliament just days before. The Parliament, on the other hand, seemed to get carried away with its power to bring the Executive to heel. What we all needed in that debate was a representative chamber that could seriously deliberate the issues involved, examine the opportunity costs of staking such a large slice of resources in one basket and reach a decision based on evidence and values rather than point-scoring politics. Too much to hope, it transpired, either of the Parliament itself or of the Health and Community Care Committee that considered the issue.

Which brings us finally to the promise of a high-tech Parliament. It is true that there is electronic voting in the Chamber, and a live webcast of proceedings – both plenary and higher profile committee sessions. There is a video-conference facility that has occasionally been used to take evidence remotely. And the Parliament's website is excellent. Yet the members themselves are still resistant to accepting the logic of a high-tech environment. Many parliamentary questions, for example, still ask for information freely available on the Executive's website.

And when it was suggested early on that the official report should be circulated to MSPs only by e-mail – to their standard issue laptops – the decision was rejected. Why? Because what MSPs want to do is to photocopy their own speech and fax it to the local press and too many had assumed that they would have to download and print the entire report in order to do that.

All of which goes to show that it takes more than a new building, a consignment of technology, a library of fine words and a new electoral system to overturn the habits of several lifetimes. The Parliament for the modern age is still very much work in progress.

# CHAPTER 7

# Second Thoughts: Reflections of an Anti-devolutionist

Allan Massie

When the Queen formally opened the Scottish Parliament in the summer of 1999, even some of us who had argued against devolution and voted 'no, no' in the referendum were touched by the sense of history being made, and even shared to some extent in the exhilaration. Now exhilaration and optimism have been replaced by embarrassment and disappointment. The McLeish administration was never impressive and its end was wretched. The confidence many had placed in the Parliament was severely damaged. And yet the Parliament is here to stay. It is inconceivable that the Scotland Act will be repealed. Like it or not, the Scottish Parliament is part of our lives.

In the long run it may even be that the circumstances of the McLeish resignation will be seen to have strengthened the Parliament. Though his misdemeanours were originally exposed in the press, it was the pertinacity with which the Opposition parties pursued the question that ultimately made his position untenable. Some now protest that sections of the media went too far in their attacks on McLeish and in their questioning of his successor Jack McConnell's private life. Yet no-one can or should expect the press to behave like fans with typewriters. No politician should look for press support as a right. Robust, even impertinent, criticism demonstrates confidence in the Parliament – it is not a tender plant that needs to be protected.

In contrast, those of us who didn't want the thing, and never expected much of it, can look on its failings with equanimity. We always thought much that was promised of the Parliament unrealistic, even absurd. A new style of politics? Up to a point perhaps. A new breed of politicians, drawn from a spectrum much wider than the class of professional politicians? Not on your life. One had only to look at the lists of selected candidates, especially Labour's, to see from what a narrow range of background they were drawn.

So while it would be a touch unfair to suggest that the 129 elected MSPs were all party hacks, there was scarcely one who wasn't a good reliable party man or woman. An excessive number had been councillors, council employees, trade union officials, political researchers.

All the List MSPs were there because they had as individuals found favour with their party chiefs rather than with the public. So we discovered that it was possible to be elected an MSP even if you had got fewer than 2,000 votes from a constituency electorate of just under 60,000, as did Keith Harding, who stood as a Tory in Fife Central, but whose position on his Party List got him into the Parliament. More remarkably still, you could be elected on the List even if you had never presented yourself individually to the electorate at all. There will surely be pressure or some change in the way List MSPs are chosen, if not at the 2003 election, certainly by 2007.

So the composition of the Parliament disappointed some enthusiasts, but was not however very different from what we, the opponents of devolution, expected.

What of its performance, and the performance of the Executive?

Well, even the severest critics should admit that it is still early days. Two years is a very short time, the mere blink of an eyelid, in the history of a nation or an institution. Take for instance the Union itself. Two years after the Treaty of 1707, it remained deeply unpopular in Scotland. Even some of its advocates had concluded it was a mistake and were calling for the annulment of the Treaty. The Earl of Mar, a Unionist in 1707, led the Jacobite Rising of 1715 – and the Jacobites promised then, as in 1745, to dissolve the incorporating Union and revert to the seventeenth-century system of one King, Two Parliaments. Yet the Union settled down. After the defeat of the '45 Rising, its merits were scarcely questioned. It had brought peace and prosperity to Scotland.

Some opposed devolution because they thought, as Professor Hamish Keir (formerly Vice-Principal of Aberdeen University) has put it, 'that a Scottish Parliament would be an unnecessary and messy waste of time, effort and taxpayers' money'. He at least still holds to this opinion, saying that 'all could have been achieved through the Scottish Grand Committee in Westminster'. He might well be right, though Liberal Democrats will protest that their presence in the coalition has forced Labour to make certain policy changes – for example, on student fees. But even those who sympathise with Professor Keir's view must admit that the Scottish Grand Committee could function effectively as a substitute Parliament only while the party governing the UK had a majority there, too.

Others opposed devolution because we believed that creating a Scottish Parliament would lead to the dissolution of the Union. (Some of these who advocated it were themselves staunch Unionists, Donald Dewar among them, who were persuaded that only devolution could save the Union). It is too soon to say which view will be proved correct. On the one hand it is clear that the Scottish Parliament is going to press for more power to be devolved to it. The argument about 'full fiscal freedom', or, if you prefer, 'some fiscal responsibility' is only just beginning. The fact that the Scottish Tories, last defenders of the unreconstructed Union, are now flirting with the idea of granting the Parliament much greater revenue-raising powers than the Scotland Act allotted to it, suggests that, even if we are not proceeding fast down that motorway to independence, the Scotland Act is not going to prove that settlement of the constitutional question that Dewar declared it to be. It is more probable that Tam Dalyell's argument that politicians will always seek to extend the powers of the institution of which they are members will be justified. We are unlikely to move to independence in a rapid or dramatic way, but rather incrementally, as the Parliament pushes to extend its powers.

Already we are less than full members of the United Kingdom. Constitutionally, of course, we remain just that. But the Scottish Parliament now receives much more attention from the Scottish media than Westminster does. People are accustoming themselves to thinking of the Executive as the Scottish government. This made the recent general election an odd affair. If people's principal concerns are health and education, devolved subjects, then a Westminster election must matter much more to the English than it does to the

Scots. Some people are happy with the progress of the Parliament to date. Magnus Linklater for instance makes the point that simply by being there it has allowed matters Scottish to be debated as they could never have been in Westminster. This is a fair comment. It is also true that the Parliament is enabling the ministers of the Executive to strike out a distinctively Scottish line on certain questions.

That will please and satisfy many. But it is important that the Executive does not seek to take 'a distinctively Scottish line' merely for the sake of doing things differently. At present it looks as if education and schools in Scotland will not be subjected to the radical treatment that Mr Blair and his education ministers are applying in England. Admittedly the signals are confusing. On the one hand, McConnell has spoken of his impatience with the bureaucratic control of schools by local authorities. On the other hand, he appointed Cathy Jamieson, seen as a left-winger in hard Old Labour mode, as Education Minister – but then it was announced that responsibility for schools would rest with her junior minister, the Liberal Democrat Nicol Stephen. This leaves it unclear at the moment of writing whether there is to be a distinctively Scottish line on schools (no reform of the system?) or whether the McConnell administration will imitate some of the remedies now being promised for failing schools in England. A similar question arises where the NHS is concerned. One begins even to wonder whether, for Labour, the purpose of devolution was to keep things the same – whether 'a distinctively Scottish line' means, simply, 'no change'.

Scottish solutions not driven by England? Fine. But what if the English ones are better? By the same token, who can be confident that if a Scottish Parliament had been set up in 1979, it would have agreed to sell council houses to tenants who wished to buy?

As I say, early days. No doubt the politicians may learn from their mistakes. Perhaps the second Parliament to be elected in 2003 will look rather different, will be more eager to encourage and promote enterprise than to follow the precepts of the politically correct.

The thing is here to stay. But if it is here for our benefit, rather than merely to massage our self-esteem, we must hope MSPs' learning curve proves steep. At present it does too often look like a magnified county council rather than a Parliament. It hasn't yet done much good. But at least it hasn't done a great deal of harm. No better than I expected but no worse than I feared; some consolation, if small.

CHAPTER 8

# Taxing Problems:
# Block Grant or Fiscal Autonomy?

George Kerevan

The Scottish general election debate of 2001 took everyone by surprise. Early predictions suggested it would be dull because Westminster was responsible for so little north of the border. Then, in a most unlikely turn of events, a dozen bespectacled economics professors lobbed a hand grenade into the election debate via a letter to *The Scotsman* on 21 May, the second Monday of the campaign. Led by Professor Andrew Hughes Hallett of Strathclyde University, they argued that the Scottish Parliament should be granted fiscal autonomy. That is, it should be given responsibility for raising its own taxes north of the border, rather than the current system, called the Barnett Formula, whereby Holyrood is given a block grant from London every year. Some in the group were known to be sympathetic to the cause of Scottish independence, but also others were not. They included Professor Rod Cross of Strathclyde University, Professor Mike Danson of Paisley University, Professor Hervey Gibson, a consultant business economist, Professor Hasan Mosala of Dundee University and Professor Anton Muscatelli of Glasgow University.

In retrospect, perhaps the ignition of the fiscal autonomy debate was not so surprising. The election was fundamentally about funding public services, so it was inevitable that, in the devolved Scottish context, the ability of Holyrood to deliver these services would soon come to the fore. The immediate and unexpected political support for the economists' letter took everyone by surprise. Leading Labour Holyrood backbencher John McAllion said the Finance Committee of the Scottish Parliament should be asked to investigate what revenue-raising powers could be transferred from Westminster to Edinburgh. Murdo Fraser, Tory Westminster candidate in North Tayside, said the only way to strengthen the Union was to give Scotland fiscal autonomy.

Official Labour was not convinced. The Scottish Executive finance minister, Angus MacKay, published an article in *The Scotsman* claiming that, even with all the taxes coming to Holyrood, there would still be a £2.5 billion shortfall in public spending to come from somewhere. Scottish Secretary Helen Liddell described the contribution by the twelve leading economists as 'fundamentally flawed' and claimed they had failed to address Scotland's budget deficit, though she doubled MacKay's figure to £5 billion. But the issue finally became too big to ignore when the then First Minister himself, Henry McLeish, declined to dismiss the call for greater fiscal powers eventually. He said that allowing the Scottish Parliament to spend all taxes raised north of the border was 'more plausible' than independence. His coded words were seen as further proof that he was willing to distance his administration from London.

By the last Friday of the election, even the Chancellor of the Exchequer had felt moved to enter the fiscal autonomy debate. He sharply denounced the notion of making Scotland's public services financially dependent on the vagaries of the price of oil. Then just before polling day on 7 June, the debate was rekindled when fiscal autonomy was backed by the Scottish Parliament's Presiding Officer, Sir David Steel. Speaking in Oxford, he said: 'I actually believe the Scottish Parliament should try to acquire a little more fiscal responsibility for raising the money that is spent.'

The clumsy phrase 'fiscal autonomy' covers several distinct issues. One is the principle, near universal from America to Germany, that regional tiers of government should be responsible for raising a significant proportion of the money they themselves spend. This 'fiscal responsibility' argument implies that the elected government of a regional parliament like a US state or a German *Land* should be held accountable by having to convince its own voters to pay for local spending. Thus in the USA, 82 per cent of taxes are levied at the state level and below. In Australia it is 61 per cent, Germany 56 per cent,

Italy 52 per cent, Spain 61 per cent and Switzerland 73 per cent. But in Britain it is only 13 per cent. Why?

It is a residue of two things. First, the Treasury's longtime political desire to control the national purse strings, a centralising tendency reinforced by Chancellor Brown. Second, the peculiar mechanics of the Barnett Formula whereby the Treasury block grant to Scotland, before and now after devolution, is fixed. The Barnett Formula does not determine the overall size of Scottish expenditure, which is a given historic datum. The formula is applied only when there are changes to expenditure headings in England. English increases are automatically applied to comparable expenditure in the three non-English territories (roughly) according to population share. For example, a £100 per head of population increase in spending on schools by the English Department for Education will be matched by a £100 per head of population increase to the Scottish Executive. However, once allocated, Scottish ministers are not obliged to spend this new money in the same spending area as in England. This was also true prior to devolution but clearly the scope for elected ministers under more public pressure to vary programmes has now increased.

The Barnett Formula has civil service antecedents. In 1888, the then Chancellor of the Exchequer, G. J. Goschen, established a system (know as the Goschen Formula) which allocated funding to England, Scotland and Ireland on a population ratio of 80, 11 and 9. This population-derived system survived in one form or another until 1957. But as public expenditures mushroomed during the 1960s and 1970s, the Scottish allocation was largely determined by bargaining among Whitehall departments. Faced with the need to rein in public spending, the Labour government of the late 1970s devised a new approach, based on a formula that would henceforth automatically apply increases in English expenditure to the territorial departments. It became known as the 'Barnett Formula' after the then Chief Secretary to the Treasury, Joel Barnett. When devolution came along, no-one could agree on an alternative to Barnett. Until the fiscal autonomy debate erupted.

Barnett and fiscal autonomy intersect in two ways. First, devolution has made the higher per capita spends in Scotland (and Northern Ireland and Wales) transparent to English voters who are becoming disgruntled with the situation. Barnett should have meant that over the decades the Scottish per capita spend was brought into line with the English – if everyone gets the same annual cash increase per head of population, eventually the original disparity in starting income is eroded. But this did not happen in practice because the real population of Scotland fell while the notional (and now inaccurate) population ratio between Scotland and England enshrined in the original Barnett Formula was adhered to because no-one wanted to start a political fight that would benefit the SNP.

Second, as the devolved administrations feel more politically confident, so they are bound to want control over their own resources rather than be constrained by what the Treasury gives them as an accidental consequence of English spending decisions. How would such fiscal autonomy work? Spain is well used not only to devolution but to giving regional parliaments different degrees of tax freedom and at marginal rates which suit the needs of each specific area. At one extreme, the Basque provinces and Navarre collect all direct taxes themselves and now have different income and corporate tax rates from the rest of the country. That is full fiscal freedom. They pay into the central coffers in Madrid for shared national services like defence and EU membership. Other regions, like Catalonia, levy some of their own taxes but still receive block funding from Madrid.

Growing fiscal autonomy in the main Spanish regions has been used to provide special incentives to make the local economies more competitive. In particular, Catalonia has used its tax-varying powers to boost the quality of education, entice inward investment and provide special tax breaks to the small manufacturing companies who traditionally form the backbone of the Catalan economy. Catalonia, as Spain's main industrial region, had little option but to go it alone tax-wise as it faced brutal competition from France, Germany and northern Italy. But the Spanish regions in the south, which are not so advanced economically, decided to leave more economic and educational responsibilities with Madrid in order to gain extra financial muscle in getting their economies up to a European level.

However, fiscal autonomy in the different Spanish regions has complications. There is always the possibility that one region might try and use taxes to discriminate against another or to attempt to give its companies an unfair advantage. To deal with this potential problem, there is a central Spanish competition tribunal (the TDC) which can adjudicate on unfair regional tax regimes. For instance, the TDC has openly opposed a new tax on hypermarkets that the government of Catalonia introduced last November. The controversial tax aims to discriminate in favour of small Catalan retailers against large Spanish and foreign supermarket chains.

Another model for fiscal autonomy comes from Canada. Again the different Canadian provinces, with their widely disparate economies, have been given their own tax powers separate from the federal government or the local authorities. At the extreme end is Quebec. Unlike other Canadian provinces, Quebec, with a population of 7.3 million, administers and collects its own taxes on the income of individuals and corporations. Other kinds of taxes are collected by the federal government. And, while individual taxes have been high over the past decade, companies that set up in Quebec have traditionally enjoyed one of North America's lowest taxation rates on profits. This is very much the fiscal mix favoured by the SNP.

However, frightened by the prospect of a recession on the back of the US slowdown, the nationalist Quebec government was recently forced into a major change in tax policy in its March 2001 budget. Income tax has been slashed in an attempt to revive economic fortunes and a budget surplus has been programmed to maintain investor confidence. Quebec is now in danger of seeing its economic miracle ended by tax competition from the other Canadian provinces as well as from the USA. Fiscal autonomy is a useful tool but does not isolate you from the economic real world.

The case for some fiscal autonomy is thus hardly revolutionary. Indeed, the Scottish Parliament already has the (unused) power to vary local income tax by up to plus or minus three pence on the standard rate. But nestling inside the British autonomy debate is a complicating factor. The SNP believes not in a degree of fiscal autonomy but in full fiscal freedom, or F3. That is: every penny of tax raised in Scotland, including North Sea oil revenues, should be levied by the Scottish Executive. In most countries, different kinds of taxes are split between the regional and national tier of government. For instance, most US states have a local sales tax but there is still a federal income tax.

However, the SNP sees F3 as the stepping stone to a final divorce with Britain. And it is this Trojan horse that Labour fears. For its part, the SNP eschews anything less than F3 because it thinks partial fiscal autonomy will be used by the Treasury to scrap the Barnett

Formula and cut the relatively high per capita public funding Scotland currently receives. F3 raises another problem. Could Scotland raise enough taxes to support its present public spending or was Angus McKay right in saying Scotland would still need extra cash from England? This is where the economists' letter to *The Scotsman* touched a raw nerve. They claimed that if we include oil revenues then Scotland normally has a comfortable financial surplus over its needs which is used to subsidise the rest of Britain.

This contention was hotly contested by public finance expert Professor Arthur Midwinter, of the politics department of Strathclyde University. He entered the fray arguing that the current Barnett Formula should be retained because it produced 'stable growth'. The SNP would counter-argue that the large fiscal surpluses enjoyed by Norway are part and parcel of its prudent use of oil revenues, these being invested in a special fund to off-set swings in the international price of petroleum. Such a mechanism works inside a devolved structure: witness the Alberta Oil Fund in Canada. However, all countries which grant high degrees of fiscal autonomy to their regional governments ensure there is some system to redistribute tax income from rich to poor areas. In Germany, the state *Länder* governments do this by consensus with minimum interference from the federal government in Berlin.

Parallel with the Scottish debate, the idea of fiscal autonomy is being much discussed in the other devolved regions, for example Northern Ireland. Fearful that the much lower 12.5 per cent corporation tax in the Irish Republic is sucking away foreign investment from the north, the Enterprise Committee of the Northern Ireland Assembly has recently called for increased fiscal autonomy for the Northern Ireland Executive. This could involve letting the Executive set a local corporation tax lower than that of the UK – and that may not be acceptable to Westminster. Alternatively, the business community in the north has suggested letting the Northern Ireland Executive offer 200 per cent capital allowance against tax, which would be a de facto separate corporate tax regime.

Northern Ireland has other tax problems involving fiscal autonomy. One estimate suggests that about 40 per cent of the petrol being used in Northern Ireland is bought south of the border due to the lower tax on petrol. Letting Northern Ireland fix and collect its own fuel duty at a lower level than the UK would actually net more money if it limited this cross-border drain.

The fiscal autonomy debate has also spread to London. Shortly after the general election, Ken Livingstone, the mayor of London, launched a campaign calling for London to be given a better deal, claiming it was missing out on £2 billion a year, despite being the economic engine house for the UK. This English debate is likely to grow if the government proceeds with its proposal to hold referenda in the English regions to test popular support for devolved regional parliaments. The Treasury has a counter-argument to such moves across the UK regions: to introduce internal regional differences would be unacceptable simply because it would distort activity and competition within the UK.

But the Northern Ireland debate shows that without this regional tax flexibility there is a potential constitutional crisis at the UK level. For the alternative to local fiscal autonomy as a solution to the tax competition with the Republic is across-the-board EU tax harmonisation. This would imply Brussels setting common fuel duties, VAT and business taxes. Not just Eurosceptics but Gordon Brown's Treasury will resist that move. Fiscal autonomy within the UK could prove the necessary counter to the siren call for a European level playing field in taxation.

Since the general election of 2001, Labour and the SNP have conspired to keep the fiscal autonomy debate on the narrow issue of total fiscal freedom for Holyrood. However, the issue now has wider ramifications covering European tax law, funding the emerging English regional assemblies and the debate over a prospective British federal constitution. It is clear that a letter from a dozen mild-mannered academics has opened a constitutional can of worms that will still be wriggling during the next Holyrood elections and the next Westminster contest.

# CHAPTER 9

# Donald Dewar: A Reappraisal

Donald MacCormick

Not long before the opening of the Scottish Parliament in 1999, Donald Dewar talked to BBC Radio Scotland about his role in delivering home rule. He insisted he'd just been part of a wider 'team achievement', and said he'd been 'very, very lucky' when Tony Blair asked him to implement devolution. 'I was in the right place at the right time for once in my career.' It was Dewar in typical interview mode – downbeat, unshowy, self-deprecating. But his remarks did less than justice to his contribution. Of course a host of others played their part in winning home rule, but none was more devoted to the cause than he. Yes, his career had some terrible setbacks, but he worked to overcome them and helped to make the good luck that came to him so late. Dewar and the devolutionists were also more lucky than they realised at the time in having Mrs Thatcher as their main enemy on the UK stage. Her long years in power helped feed the appetite for a Scottish Parliament.

Looking back to the beginnings of Dewar's career, no-one should be taken in by the image of him portrayed by some at the time of his death – that of a well-meaning bloke who wandered into public life almost by accident and kept himself a bit above the political fray. As a student debater in Glasgow University Union he honed the famous staccato style of oratory which he used to send up, and squash, opponents. But he was also intensely ambitious for student office. He fought a ruthless campaign to win the presidency of the Union. He was dead set on being a leading figure and running things. He was ambitious to serve. There was no doubt, either, about his gradualist, Gaitskellite views, and his determination to work for them in the real world beyond university. When his friend John Smith, still a student, fought a by-election in East Fife in 1961, Dewar was chief whip and assistant minibus driver for us GU Labour Club members drafted to the campaign front.

His politics obviously owed something to his parents, a well-off middle-class couple of liberal opinions. (As their only child, Dewar inherited from them the basis of his own untapped prosperity, which was to raise a few old Labour eyebrows and a few vindictive headlines, after his estate was published in June 2001.) Dr and Mrs Dewar's influence had a strong Scottish bias. The elegant Dewar home, in a terrace overlooking Glasgow's Kelvingrove Park, was full of Scottish books and Scottish paintings, notably those of the Colourists. Occasionally Dewar's father would take him to a shinty match to broaden his knowledge of Scotland. The cultural atmosphere was nationalist with a small 'n'.

That's why I think Tam Dalyell, the father of the House of Commons, got it completely wrong when his obituary article in *The Independent* speculated that Dewar embraced devolution only after his wife Alison left him in 1972, taking their children south to live with Derry Irvine, now Lord Chancellor. According to Dalyell, this cruel blow caused Dewar, who'd seen himself until then primarily as a UK politician, to 'harbour a deep resentment against London'. First, there was no resentment and, moreover, the Scottish dimension was always part of Dewar's hinterland. What brought it to the fore in the 1970s was not the end of his marriage but the seismic political shock of the Scottish Nationalist victory in the 1967 Hamilton by-election, followed by the earthquake of 1974, from which the SNP emerged with eleven MPs.

In any case, more than two years before his wife left him, Dewar contributed to *The Scottish Debate: Essays on Scottish Nationalism* edited by N. MacCormick (London, Oxford University Press, 1970). His essay made clear his belief in the virtue of devolution and his hope that Labour would develop a constructive devolution policy.

No-one would dispute, though, that the collapse of his marriage was a traumatic event. He had also lost his seat at Aberdeen South in the general election two years earlier, and had undergone major surgery for a painful back problem. Dewar went to ground for a while, then somehow started to come through the ordeal. To his immense credit, he seemed, eventually, to have been mellowed by it. He was never going to be one of life's natural rays of sunshine but friends noticed less acid, more charm than before. Perhaps that period gave him a deeper human understanding as Reporter to the Children's Panel for Lanarkshire, the job he took during exile from the Commons.

His troubles had a clear effect on his political life. He became, as it were, married to the Labour Party. From then on, loyalty was the virtue he prized above all. There was an almost emotional need to have loyal allies around him in Labour's big internal battles of the 1970s and 1980s – over devolution and the challenge of the Bennite left; and in the ongoing external effort to curb the SNP.

The devolution battle was largely won by the mid-1970s. In the October election of 1974 Labour campaigned in favour of devolution and, once elected, put forward plans for a Scottish Assembly. Although he'd become a leading member of Labour's Scottish Executive, Dewar sat out both elections that year and didn't get another chance of a Commons seat until a by-election came up at Glasgow Garscadden in 1978. It was a hazardous re-entry. The country was only a year away from a referendum on the Assembly plans and the Nationalists were tipped to increase their number of MPs to twelve. In the event Dewar won an unexpectedly comfortable majority; the SNP tide had been turned. Congratulating Dewar, John Smith predicted with characteristic ebullience that the referendum to come would be 'a scoosh'. It didn't turn out like that. In March 1979 the cross-party 'yes' campaign got a narrow majority but failed to surmount the 40 per cent hurdle set by Parliament, thus hastening the fall of the government and the election of Mrs Thatcher.

So began the long haul of opposition. Dewar joined the front bench as a Scottish affairs spokesperson under Michael Foot's leadership. Neil Kinnock made him Shadow Scottish Secretary in 1983. The loyalty he set such store by in others he fully paid back, never entertaining a switch to the Social Democrats, despite the apparent suitability of his views, and his past closeness to defecting Labour MPs like Bill Rodgers and Bob Maclennan. He fought on with other moderates against the hard left.

During the 1980s Dewar also made several speeches at UK Labour conferences, preparing the party for another shot at devolution when and if they got back to power. Even after the referendum debacle of 1979 and Labour's successive election drubbings by the Conservatives, the home rule cause was alive and kicking in Scotland. This was partly a result of the seemingly endless run of Tory government. Sir Malcolm Rifkind memorably observed that the Scots wanted to run their own affairs not because they were oppressed by the English, but because they were irritated by the English. And who was the irritant-in-chief during that period? Step forward the victor of the Falklands, the nay-sayer to such a thing as society, Margaret Thatcher herself.

For all her achievements – some of which New Labour has been keen to preserve – Maggie set Scottish teeth on edge. She dismissed home rule as a concern merely of the chattering classes. She patronised the Kirk about the doctrines of Adam Smith. But when she left power there were only half the number of Scottish Tory MPs who had been elected in 1979. She was the best Conservative Prime Minister devolutionists could have wished for.

As Shadow Scottish Secretary Dewar pitched into the government with vigour. Then in 1988 the devolution campaign moved into a new phase and he backed the setting up of the Scottish Constitutional Convention, a cross-party grouping which thrashed out a home rule scheme similar to the one he would later deliver. Dewar supported the Convention's adoption of a PR voting system for the new Parliament, which meant Labour would be unlikely to form a government in Edinburgh on its own. On this occasion party loyalty took second place to his conviction that the nation in all its variety would not embrace a devolution package which entrenched Labour, and thus west-of-Scotland, dominance.

But all this was still just talk. More tough times were to come before Dewar got the job that would enable him to put plans into practice, the job he'd always wanted – Secretary of State for Scotland. ('I'd do it so well', I once heard him say, more wistfully than boastfully.) First came the 1992 election defeat, all the worse for being unexpected. Then followed four uncomfortable years as Shadow Social Security Secretary. Dewar did not welcome the move – he said it was like being back at university doing another degree – but John Smith, now leader of the opposition, asked him to do it and that was that. In 1994 there came the tragic blow of his friend John's sudden death. Like countless others, Dewar was distraught. The friendship did not always run smoothly. Smith was a genuine convert to devolution rather than a prime mover; he had more reservations about PR than Dewar. Dewar was wittier, more caustic, but Smith had the more abrasive personality. Still, they'd been shoulder to shoulder through so much over so many years. Again, that was that. Dewar saw out another two years in charge of social security until Tony Blair made him Chief Whip in early 1996. Shifting one of Labour's best debaters backstage seemed an odd appointment, but Dewar's career never looked back. He kept up the pressure on the ailing Major government with good humour. He also transformed the nature of his new job. Instead of being a traditional, semi-trappist Chief Whip, he became de facto 'Minister for the *Today* programme', defending Labour policy across the board on radio and television.

There was one crisis left. In June 1996, only a year before the general election and with Labour commanding the opinion polls, a Scottish Parliament was clearly in sight. Unlike 1979, there was no referendum to cloud the picture. As John Smith had intended, the 'settled will of the Scottish people', expressed again in the election result, would be enough. Then suddenly, prompted by Tony Blair himself, the Shadow Cabinet switched course. There would be a referendum after all. A referendum, moreover, with two separate questions: one on setting up a parliament, the other on its power to raise taxes.

There was speculation the Prime Minister wanted to torpedo devolution altogether. Labour and Liberal supporters, together with most of the media, were up in arms. Dewar, still Chief Whip, went along to a news conference to support the Shadow Scottish Secretary, George Robertson. The questions were fierce and hostile. Dewar later admitted that the referendum decision had caused 'agony'.

But 1979 did not repeat itself. Labour won its landslide in May 1997 and Dewar became Scottish Secretary. Again reaching out beyond his own party's ranks, he got the SNP on board the 'yes' side in the referendum held that September. Three-quarters of those who voted backed a parliament; two-thirds endorsed the power to alter income tax. Now Dewar had to turn this triumph into legislation. In framing the Scotland Bill he generously acknowledged the help he got from the Lord Chancellor, Derry Irvine, who'd figured in his personal troubles more than quarter of a century earlier and who chaired many of the Cabinet committees involved. When English voices protested about too much being ceded to the Scots, Irvine backed Dewar in arguing that these were the consequences of devolution. Dewar then piloted the Bill through the Commons with comparative ease, and the first election for the Scottish Parliament was held in May 1999. Labour won 56 of the 129 seats. Dewar took office as First Minister in a coalition Executive alongside the Liberal Democrats, with the Scottish Nationalists forming the main opposition.

The first Parliament in Scotland for 300 years was opened by the Queen on 1 July 1999. It was a moving ceremony, simple but impressive.

Soon, however, the long journey to home rule began to look the easy part. Over their first year in office, the First Minister and his Executive were embroiled in a series of crises. The costs of the new Parliament building at Holyrood kept spiralling up, exceeding original estimates by five or six times. Two special advisers in Dewar's office were sacked in controversial circumstances. There was a bitter struggle to repeal Section ii. a (Clause 28 in England), banning the promotion of homosexuality in schools; the Executive were pushed onto the back foot when the Stagecoach tycoon Brian Souter bankrolled a campaign against repeal, which was amplified in the pages of the *Daily Record*. In the summer of 2000, the Scottish Qualifications Authority sent delayed, inaccurate or incomplete exam results to thousands of school pupils waiting to go to university.

This catalogue of woes attracted what Dewar admitted was 'a fusillade of flak' in the press, much of it directed at him personally. Such criticism was not always fair. Certainly he should have questioned his civil servants more closely about estimated costs for the new building, though it was finally Parliament's Corporate Body that had the duty of overseeing the project. Over Section IIa, the Executive had to acknowledge that it might have misread the public mood and sought to reassure parents by inserting a form of words stressing the value of stable family life. The exam-results fiasco was the most damaging crisis, and – with characteristic if unwise loyalty – Dewar stuck by the education minister, his old friend Sam Galbraith. The blame lay mostly with an arm's-length agency, but the press and the public wanted a commensurate sacrifice.

It has been said that Dewar was too often thrown off course by events rather than controlling them; although he'd been the right man to achieve devolution, perhaps he wasn't the right one to run Scotland. Such mutterings were not, seemingly, confined to the media. Even during 1999, ambitious Cabinet colleagues were reported as planning for the succession.

It is probably true that Dewar did not take a tough enough line with wayward or scheming colleagues, whether in the Executive or his own private office. Despite his irreverent, sardonic outlook, he was not a man for head-on confrontation. As one of his close aides put it, 'He loved an argument, but hated a row.' So he preferred to move forward by consensus rather then throw his weight around; he was also constrained by not having an overall majority behind him. But there was never any real alternative to Dewar as the first, First Minister. The only MSP to have served in a British cabinet, he was head and shoulders above all others in experience, ability and vision.

Donald Dewar was someone who believed strongly, all his political life, in the ability of government to alter people's lives for the better. He regarded the Housing Bill, which seeks among other things to reinforce choice and empower tenants in public-sector housing, as the flagship measure of the Executive's first term. The Bill was passed in June 2001, drawing much less media attention than any of the earlier dramas. Perhaps legislation like that will prove the best memorial to the man who declared at the opening of the Parliament: 'We will make mistakes . . . but we will never lose sight of what brought us here: the striving to do right by the people of Scotland; to respect their priorities; to better their lot; and to contribute to the common weal.'

# CHAPTER 10

# A Quizzical View from the Gallery

Robert McNeil

Oh hooray. It's Thursday. It's 2.30 p.m. For 15 minutes, members of the public have been taking their seats and an excited hubbub has been gathering in strength. Broadcasting technicians are checking plugs. Security men in happy-camper blazers take their positions. World-weary journalists start to arrive, casting a cynical eye over the Chamber, and exchanging wry or ribald remarks. Then the stars arrive in their ones and twos until, lo, there are 129, sat in a horse-shoe of curving benches on the main stage or Chamber. The crowd twitters psychically towards silence and Dame Artichoke Steel, the presiding orifice, raps his gavel. Oh, the joy of it. Parliament is under way.

They've been getting under way for two years now but it only seems like yesterday since that gloriously sunny day when crowds lined the streets and jets looped the loop overhead and children on the shoulders of their parents waved little plastic Saltires. Here was hope for future. A Parliament was born and, ever since uttering its first words ('Point of order, Mummy'), it has kept the nation in stitches.

There is a serious side as well, of course. And, while nothing substantial springs to mind immediately in support of that assertion, I do recall that, on the very first day the goons who were to lead us got together, I was lobbed out on my ear by over-enthusiastic security guards. I was only trying to get encouraging comments about the Parliament from the nice folk going into the visitors' gallery, but the nervous tyros at the entrance had been badly afflicted by keepootery, to coin a phrase. The story appeared under the headline, 'How I became the first person chucked out [in 300 years]'. An unhappy boast.

Another unhappy boast might involve the calibre of some representatives. Those who had long argued in favour of a parliament claimed a vast array of talent lay out there. Unfortunately, few of them turned up on the day. OK, cheap joke, and unfair to the majority, but a large rump – and that feels like the right word – seemed to have emerged from an obscurity that had been right for them. Painstakingly, they stumbled through their inspiration-free speeches like abashed children reading essays to the sniggering class. With ill-grace born of poor confidence, they refused to take interventions. Many were overweight. And they were not all from the last hole of the Central Belt either.

The Labour Party was unequivocally to blame for this. Its selection procedures had churned out a batch of yes-men and -women rather than individuals with imagination and phlegm. The Nats have some deadwood too, indicative again of too much party poltroonery, but the Tories are a joy. Irrelevant politically, nevertheless every one of their representatives is a character personally. None has trouble with public speaking. They come across as the parliamentary branch of the Rotary Club. The Lib Dems are a mixed bunch. Around half have Tory-style personality, while the other half are Labour-style hacks.

Together, they have had two years to mature. So, like cheese, do they smell? Or, like wine, do they have bouquet? Putting aside the ill-begotten thought that cheese-and-whine seems a good working definition of politics, they must be given the benefit of the doubt. Sniff them though you may for defects, swill them round your palate for hints of well-blown raspberry, you will admit that this parliament is a cheeky little number.

Taken in order of importance, the security men are now afflicted by a happier cumminery, to coin another phrase. Smiling, friendly and helpful, they have grown into an asset as they escort the elderly to their seats and bid rascally journos good day. The politicians, too, have come on. Only a few still suffer from nerves. Many debates are outstanding, in the sense that a learning process takes place and disputation becomes an engine for progress instead of a grenade-lobbing exercise from entrenched positions. Even the childlike speakers are persevering, and one must admire their pluck. Personality is starting to shine through. Donald Dewar was the largest of these, and perhaps Alex Salmond the nearest to him. Both have departed the place, Donald to that great over-budget Parliament in the sky, where the agenda drips with honey and you can eat as many sausage rolls as you like; Alex to the House of Commons, where the cream of United Kingdom politics sit upon the sherry-soaked sponge of hallowed tradition.

Their respective places, as First Minister and leader of the opposition, were taken by Henry McLeish and John Swinney. Henry came in for much criticism, mainly on the grounds that he was a dork. It seemed a terrible calumny. He mangled the English language. Like a Zen Buddhist in a fever, he uttered gnomic nonsense. He cracked jokes that were inevitably greeted with groans. But he was doing his best and seemed to be getting by – until his Westminster past caught up with him. The Leader of All Scotland was revealed as the Sub-letter of Glenrothes, and Henry went off greeting to the eventide home that is the backbenches.

John Swinney, too, has been pilloried, mainly on the grounds that he is a dweeb. This is an outrageous slur. True, he comes across as the Monty Python accountant who really wants to be a lion-tamer. There is something of the buttoned-up clerk in his appearance. He doesn't do anger well. And, perhaps most fatally to his chances of power, he is bald. But he is doing his best and seems to be getting by. Now he faces Henry's successor, Jack McConnell, survivor of Lobbygate and Trousergate and a smart cookie to boot.

Every Thursday, these two giants clash in the titanic struggle known to the nation as Hamster Wars. Performed perhaps with less wit and verve than in the Donald Days, these have taken on a curious pattern. In the Henry Era, John asked Henry some questions, and Henry answered by complaining that John had to keep spoiling everything by bringing politics into it. Jack is more cocksure, as it were, and less afraid of politics – an attitude that can come in handy in a parliament.

However, it's not all about Jack and John. When one talks personality, one thinks of Margo MacDonald (SNP), matriarch of the nation, Jamie Stone, clubbable Lib Dem with oodles of chutzpah (or is it chutney?), David McLetchie, the Tory leader and – which is the same thing – mordant joker, Frank McAveety (Lab), a funky guy with Glasgow written through him like Blackpool through rock, Phil Gallie (Con), right-wing rough diamond with a heart of gold, Allan Wilson, lowbrow Labour minister for culture but mainly fitba', Bill Aitken (Con) and his performing adenoids, Robert Brown (Lib Dem), king of the complex comb-over, Malcolm 'Jessie' Chisholm (Lab) and his sympathetic period pains, Lord James Douglas-Hamilton (Con), gentleman bumbler, Dotty Grace-Elder (SNP) and her hilarious hyperbole, Ross Finnie (Lib Dem) who *is* Captain Mainwaring, thuggish Kenny Gibson (SNP), scary Karen Gillon (Lab), oh-so-capable Annabel Goldie (Con), mad-as-hell Kenny MacAskill (SNP), Jamie McGrigor (Con), shellfish enthusiast and author of the arguably derivative *Captain Corelli's Prawn*, Duncan McNeil (Lab), the most working-class person in the world, Des McNulty (Lab), never knowingly interesting, John Farquhar Munro (Lib Dem), the sleeping Gael, Elaine Murray (Lab), and the voice that shattered a thousand windows, Lloyd Quinan (SNP), and his ace heckling; and – last but not least, though the point is arguable – Murray Tosh (Con), histrionically bawling and strutting like Mussolini on a balcony, his gestures growing ever more extravagant in inverse proportion to the importance of the subject. And let us not forget the three one-man bands: Robin Harper (Green), Tommy Sheridan (Scottish Socialist), Dennis Canavan (Canavan Popular Alliance).

What a cast of characters. It's a shame they've had such a hard time. No-one can fault them for effort. They work hard and they are trying to improve their country. Yet all they attract is scorn from the hard-nosed hacks, and caricature from the occasional skittish sketch-writer. They never fail to supply him with lines. Take, for instance, the joyous enthusiasm of Donald Gorrie (Lib Dem): 'When I walk up here in the morning from the bus stop my heart lifts.' Or Kay Ullrich – Aggie Schwarzenegger (SNP) – on being urged to criticise the Executive rather than the Tories: 'Keep the faith, baby. I'll get to them.' Or John Young (Con) observing during a debate on the age of consent that, in all his years on Glasgow Council, sex had only been mentioned once. Or Tricia Marwick (SNP) sadly confessing: 'I have never been invited to a club.' Or Donald Dewar recounting the time he was kissed by Tom Conti's wife: 'I may say that is not the sort of thing that happens to me every day.' Or Lyndsay McIntosh (Con) during a debate on corporal punishment: 'I am sure there have been occasions when you have witnessed behaviour here and wished you could administer a smack.' Or Andrew Wilson (SNP) intervening during a speech by Murray Tosh: 'I suspect a call for a medic might be appropriate.' Or Nick Johnston (Con; now retired to normal life) to tourism minister Alasdair Morrison: 'If you've got your head in the sand, the only other place you can talk out is the other end of your anatomy.' Or Dotty-Grace telling the assembled mob we were entering 'a new age of darkness, of witchcraft'. How we laughed.

So, while they may rightly complain about their treatment at the hands and pens of their curmudgeonly critics in the gallery, they should know that, underneath it all, something nobler lurks. For, as I always say sometimes, to lampoon them is to love them.

CHAPTER 11

# Results from the Scottish Parliament Election 1999

## (i) Election by first past the post

| | Con | Lab | LDem | SNP | Other | Majority |
|---|---|---|---|---|---|---|
| *CENTRAL SCOTLAND* | | | | | | |
| Airdrie & Shotts<br>*Karen Whitefield (Lab)** | 3,177 | 18,338* | 2,345 | 9,353 | | 8,985 |
| Coatbridge & Chryston<br>*Elaine Smith (Lab)** | 2,867 | 17,884* | 1,889 | 7,519 | | 10,365 |
| Cumbernauld & Kilsyth<br>*Cathie Craigie (Lab)** | 1,362 | 15,118* | 2,029 | 10,923 | 1,116 | 4,195 |
| East Kilbride<br>*Andy Kerr (Lab)** | 4,665 | 19,987* | 3,373 | 13,488 | | 6,499 |
| Falkirk East<br>*Cathy Peattie (Lab)** | 3,399 | 15,721* | 2,509 | 11,582 | 2,001 | 4,139 |
| Falkirk West<br>*Dennis Canavan (Ind)** | 1,897 | 6,319 | 954 | 5,986 | 18,511* | 12,192 |
| Hamilton North &<br>Bellshill<br>*Michael McMahon (Lab)** | 3,199 | 15,227* | 2,105 | 9,621 | 1,064 | 5,606 |

CENTRAL SCOTLAND

|  | Con | Lab | LDem | SNP | Other | Majority |
|---|---|---|---|---|---|---|
| Hamilton South<br>*Tom McCabe (Lab) | 2,998 | 14,098* | 1,982 | 6,922 |  | 7,176 |
| Kilmarnock & Loudoun<br>*Margaret Jamieson (Lab) | 4,589 | 17,345* | 2,830 | 14,585 |  | 2,760 |
| Motherwell & Wishaw<br>*Jack McConnell (Lab) | 3,694 | 13,925* | 1,895 | 8,879 | 1,941 | 5,046 |

GLASGOW

|  | Con | Lab | LDem | SNP | Other | Majority |
|---|---|---|---|---|---|---|
| Glasgow Anniesland<br>*Bill Butler (Lab) | 3,032 | 16,749* | 1,804 | 5,756 | 1,139 | 10,993 |
| Glasgow Baillieston<br>*Margaret Curran (Lab) | 1,526 | 11,289* | 813 | 8,217 | 1,864 | 3,072 |
| Glasgow Cathcart<br>*Mike Watson (Lab) | 3,311 | 12,966* | 2,187 | 7,592 | 920 | 5,374 |
| Glasgow Govan<br>*Gordon Jackson (Lab) | 2,343 | 11,421* | 1,479 | 9,665 | 1,465 | 1,756 |
| Glasgow Kelvin<br>*Pauline McNeill (Lab) | 2,253 | 12,711* | 3,720 | 8,303 | 1,375 | 4,408 |
| Glasgow Maryhill<br>*Patricia Ferguson (Lab) | 1,194 | 11,455* | 1,793 | 7,129 | 1,439 | 4,326 |
| Glasgow Pollok<br>*Johann Lamont (Lab) | 1,370 | 11,405* | 931 | 6,763 | 5,611 | 4,642 |
| Glasgow Rutherglen<br>*Janis Hughes (Lab) | 2,315 | 13,442* | 5,798 | 6,155 | 1,313 | 7,287 |
| Glasgow Shettleston<br>*Frank McAveety (Lab) | 1,260 | 11,078* | 943 | 5,611 | 1,640 | 5,467 |
| Glasgow Springburn<br>*Paul Martin (Lab) | 1,293 | 14,268* | 1,288 | 6,375 | 1,141 | 7,893 |

HIGHLANDS AND ISLANDS

|  | Con | Lab | LDem | SNP | Other | Majority |
|---|---|---|---|---|---|---|
| Argyll & Bute<br>*George Lyon (LDem) | 5,312 | 6,470 | 11,226* | 9,169 |  | 2,057 |

## HIGHLANDS AND ISLANDS

|  | Con | Lab | LDem | SNP | Other | Majority |
|---|---|---|---|---|---|---|
| Caithness, Suth. & E. Ross<br>*Jamie Stone (LDem) | 2,167 | 6,300 | 10,691* | 6,035 | 836 | 4,391 |
| Inverness E, Nairn &<br>Lochaber<br>*Fergus Ewing (SNP) | 6,107 | 13,384 | 8,508 | 13,825* |  | 441 |
| Moray<br>*Margaret Ewing (SNP) | 8,595 | 8,889 | 3,056 | 13,027* |  | 4,138 |
| Orkney<br>*Jim Wallace (LDem) | 1,391 | 600 | 6,010* | 917 |  | 4,619 |
| Shetland<br>*Tavish Scott (LDem) | 872 | 2,241 | 5,435* | 1,430 |  | 3,194 |
| Ross, Skye & Inv'ss W<br>*John Farquhar Munro<br>(LDem) | 3,351 | 10,113 | 11,652* | 7,997 | 2,302 | 1,539 |
| Western Isles<br>*Alasdair Morrison (Lab) | 1,095 | 7,248* | 456 | 5,155 |  | 2,093 |

## LOTHIANS

|  | Con | Lab | LDem | SNP | Other | Majority |
|---|---|---|---|---|---|---|
| Edinburgh Central<br>*Sarah Boyack (Lab) | 6,018 | 14,224* | 6,187 | 9,598 | 1,385 | 4,626 |
| Edinburgh E & M'burgh<br>*Susan Deacon (Lab) | 4,600 | 17,086* | 4,100 | 10,372 | 831 | 6,714 |
| Edinburgh N & Leith<br>*Malcolm Chisholm (Lab) | 5,030 | 17,203* | 4,039 | 9,467 | 907 | 7,736 |
| Edinburgh Pentlands<br>*Iain Gray (Lab) | 11,458 | 14,343* | 5,029 | 8,770 |  | 2,885 |
| Edinburgh South<br>*Angus MacKay (Lab) | 6,378 | 14,869* | 8,961 | 9,445 | 482 | 5,424 |
| Edinburgh West<br>*Margaret Smith (LDem) | 10,578 | 8,860 | 15,161* | 6,984 |  | 4,583 |

LOTHIANS

|  | Con | Lab | LDem | SNP | Other | Majority |
|---|---|---|---|---|---|---|
| Linlithgow<br>*Mary Mulligan (Lab) | 3,158 | 15,247* | 2,643 | 12,319 | 415 | 2,928 |
| Livingston<br>*Bristow Muldoon (Lab) | 3,014 | 17,313* | 2,834 | 13,409 |  | 3,904 |
| Midlothian<br>*Rhona Brankin (Lab) | 2,544 | 14,467* | 3,184 | 8,942 | 618 | 5,525 |

MID-SCOTLAND AND FIFE

|  | Con | Lab | LDem | SNP | Other | Majority |
|---|---|---|---|---|---|---|
| Dunfermline East<br>*Helen Eadie (Lab) | 2,931 | 16,576* | 2,275 | 7,877 |  | 8,699 |
| Dunfermline West<br>*Scott Barrie (Lab) | 2,981 | 13,560* | 5,591 | 8,539 |  | 5,021 |
| Fife Central<br>*Henry McLeish (Lab) | 1,918 | 18,828* | 1,953 | 10,153 |  | 8,675 |
| Fife North-East<br>*Iain Smith (LDem) | 8,526 | 5,175 | 13,590* | 6,373 | 2,277 | 5,064 |
| Kirkcaldy<br>*Marilyn Livingstone<br>(Lab) | 2,907 | 13,645* | 2,620 | 9,170 |  | 4,475 |
| North Tayside<br>*John Swinney (SNP) | 12,594 | 5,727 | 2,948 | 16,786* |  | 4,192 |
| Ochil<br>Richard Simpson (Lab) | 4,151 | 15,385* | 3,249 | 14,082 |  | 1,303 |
| Perth<br>*Roseanna Cunningham<br>(SNP) | 11,543 | 8,725 | 3,558 | 13,570* |  | 2,027 |
| Stirling<br>*Sylvia Jackson (Lab) | 9,158 | 13,533* | 3,407 | 9,552 | 155 | 3,981 |

NORTH-EAST SCOTLAND

|  | Con | Lab | LDem | SNP | Other | Majority |
|---|---|---|---|---|---|---|
| Aberdeen Central<br>*Lewis Macdonald (Lab) | 3,655 | 10,305* | 4,403 | 7,609 | 523 | 2,696 |

NORTH-EAST SCOTLAND

|  | Con | Lab | LDem | SNP | Other | Majority |
|---|---|---|---|---|---|---|
| Aberdeen North <br> *Elaine Thomson (Lab)** | 2,772 | 10,340* | 4,767 | 9,942 | | 398 |
| Aberdeen South <br> *Nicol Stephen (LDem)** | 6,993 | 9,540 | 11,300* | 6,651 | 206 | 1,760 |
| Aberdeenshire West & <br> Kincardine <br> *Mike Rumbles (LDem)** | 10,549 | 4,650 | 12,838* | 7,699 | | 2,289 |
| Angus <br> *Andrew Welsh (SNP)** | 7,154 | 6,914 | 4,413 | 16,055* | | 8,901 |
| Banff & Buchan <br> *Alex Salmond (SNP)** | 5,403 | 4,321 | 5,315 | 16,695* | | 11,292 |
| Dundee East <br> *John McAllion (Lab)** | 4,428 | 13,703* | 2,153 | 10,849 | 530 | 2,854 |
| Dundee West <br> *Kate Maclean (Lab)** | 3,345 | 10,925* | 2,998 | 10,804 | 1,010 | 121 |
| Gordon <br> *Nora Radcliffe (LDem)** | 6,602 | 3,950 | 12,353* | 8,158 | 2,559 | 4,195 |

SOUTH OF SCOTLAND

|  | Con | Lab | LDem | SNP | Other | Majority |
|---|---|---|---|---|---|---|
| Ayr <br> *Ian Welsh (Lab)** | 14,238 | 14,263* | 1,662 | 7,291 | | 25 |
| Carrick, Cum'ck & <br> Doon Valley <br> *Cathy Jamieson (Lab)** | 8,123 | 19,667* | 2,441 | 10,864 | | 8,803 |
| Clydesdale <br> *Karen Gillon (Lab)** | 5,814 | 16,755* | 3,503 | 12,875 | | 3,880 |
| Cunninghame South <br> *Irene Oldfather (Lab)** | 3,229 | 14,936* | 1,717 | 8,395 | | 6,541 |
| Dumfries <br> *Elaine Murray (Lab)** | 10,447 | 14,101* | 6,209 | 7,625 | | 3,654 |

SOUTH OF SCOTLAND

| | Con | Lab | LDem | SNP | Other | Majority |
|---|---|---|---|---|---|---|
| East Lothian<br>*John Home Robertson<br>(Lab) | 5,941 | 19,220* | 4,147 | 8,274 | | 10,946 |
| Galloway & Upper<br>  Nithsdale<br>*Alasdair Morgan (SNP) | 10,672 | 7,209 | 3,562 | 13,873* | | 3,201 |
| Roxburgh & Berwickshire<br>*Euan Robson (LDem) | 7,735 | 4,102 | 11,320* | 4,719 | | 3,585 |
| Tweeddale, Ettrick &<br>  Lauderdale<br>*Ian Jenkins (LDem) | 6,491 | 7,546 | 12,078* | 7,600 | | 4,478 |

WEST OF SCOTLAND

| | Con | Lab | LDem | SNP | Other | Majority |
|---|---|---|---|---|---|---|
| Clydebank & Milngavie<br>*Des McNulty (Lab) | 3,688 | 15,105* | 4,149 | 10,395 | | 4,710 |
| Cunninghame North<br>*Allan Wilson (Lab) | 6,649 | 14,369* | 2,900 | 9,573 | | 4,796 |
| Dumbarton<br>*Jackie Baillie (Lab) | 5,060 | 15,181* | 4,035 | 10,434 | | 4,747 |
| Eastwood<br>*Ken Macintosh (Lab) | 14,845 | 16,970* | 4,472 | 8,760 | 349 | 2,125 |
| Greenock & Inverclyde<br>*Duncan McNeil (Lab) | 1,699 | 11,817* | 7,504 | 6,762 | 857 | 4,313 |
| Paisley North<br>*Wendy Alexander (Lab) | 2,242 | 13,492* | 2,123 | 8,876 | 1,007 | 4,616 |
| Paisley South<br>*Hugh Henry (Lab) | 2,433 | 13,899* | 2,974 | 9,404 | 1,946 | 4,495 |
| Renfrewshire West<br>*Patricia Godman (Lab) | 7,243 | 12,708* | 2,659 | 9,815 | 1,612 | 2,893 |
| Strathkelvin & Bearsden<br>*Sam Galbraith (Lab) | 6,934 | 21,505* | 4,144 | 9,384 | 423 | 12,121 |

## (ii) Regional Seats
### Additional Members Elected by Proportional Representation

*CENTRAL SCOTLAND*

Lyndsay McIntosh (Con)
Linda Fabiani (SNP)
Alex Neil (SNP)
Andrew Wilson (SNP)

Donald Gorrie (LDem)
Michael Matheson (SNP)
Gil Paterson (SNP)

*GLASGOW*

Bill Aitken (Con)
Dorothy-Grace Elder (SNP)
Nicola Sturgeon (SNP)
Tommy Sheridan (SSP)

Robert Brown (LDem)
Kenneth Gibson (SNP)
Sandra White (SNP)

*HIGHLANDS AND ISLANDS*

Jamie McGrigor (Con)
Rhoda Grant (Lab)
Peter Peacock (Lab)
Duncan Hamilton (SNP)

Mary Scanlon (Con)
Maureen MacMillan (Lab)
Winnie Ewing (SNP)

*LOTHIAN*

James Douglas-Hamilton (Con)
David Steel (LDem)
Kenny MacAskill (SNP)
Robin Harper (Scottish Green)

David McLetchie (Con)
Fiona Hyslop (SNP)
Margo Macdonald (SNP)

*MID-SCOTLAND AND FIFE*

Keith Harding (Con)
Brian Monteith (Con)
Bruce Crawford (SNP)
George Reid (SNP)

Keith Raffan (LDem)
Tricia Marwick (SNP)
Murdo Fraser (Con)

*NORTH-EAST SCOTLAND*

David Davidson (Con)
Ben Wallace (Con)
Richard Lochhead (SNP)
Shona Robison (SNP)

Alex Johnstone (Con)
Brian Adam (SNP)
Irene McGugan (SNP)

SOUTH OF SCOTLAND

Phil Gallie (Con)
Murray Tosh (Con)
Mike Russell (SNP)
Christine Grahame (SNP)

David Mundell (Con)
Alex Fergusson (Con)
Adam Ingram (SNP)

*WEST OF SCOTLAND*

Annabel Goldie (Con)
Ross Finnie (LDem)
Fiona McLeod (SNP)
Colin Campbell (SNP)

John Young (Con)
Lloyd Quinan (SNP)
Kay Ullrich (SNP)

# CHAPTER 12

# Profiles of Members of the
# Scottish Parliament (MSPs)

# Brian Adam (SNP)
## MSP (List) North-East Scotland

**Born:** Newmill, 1948

**Education:** Keith Grammar School; Aberdeen
University.

**Career: 1970–3:** Section Leader, QA Laboratory, Glaxo;
**1973–88:** Biochemist/Senior Biochemist, Aberdeen City Hospital;
**1988–99:** Senior/Principal Biochemist, Aberdeen Royal Infirmary;
**1988–99:** served as Councillor on Aberdeen District then Aberdeen
City Councils; **1999:** elected MSP.

**Profile:** He is married with four sons and one daughter. He is a
Mormon, the only representative of his church in the Parliament. Most
of his social views stem from his religious beliefs and tend to be on the
moral right. He was, with Winnie Ewing, prominent in the campaign
to resist the abolition of Section 28.

While a Councillor, he unsuccessfully contested Gordon, then Aberdeen
North in general elections of 1992 and 1997. He has applied his pharmaceutical expertise to good use, putting questions on the incidence of
meningitis in Scotland, the possibility of adverse reactions to the meningitis C vaccine and the history of clinical trials for the vaccine. On a
different tack, he joined Margo Macdonald's assault on the Executive
for rejecting much of the Audit Committee's report on the Holyrood
building. 'Re-stating the guff,' he said eloquently. He also supported
the idea of a tie-up scheme for fishermen, unsurprising given his origin.
He has proposed an early warning system for votes in the Chamber,
like the division bell at Westminster. Until then, no-one had put his
general quietness down to somnolence.

**Committees:** Finance.

**Contact:** 0131-348-5692  Fax 0131-348-5953 (Parliament)
          01224-623150  Fax 01224-623160 (Constituency)
          e-mail brian.adam.msp@scottish.parliament.uk

# Bill Aitken (CONSERVATIVE)
## MSP (List) Glasgow

**Born:** Glasgow, 1947

**Education:** Allan Glen's School, Glasgow;
Central College of Commerce.

**Career: 1965–70:** Insurance Clerk, Eagle Star;
**1970–8:** Property Insurance Underwriter, NEM Ltd;
**1978–82:** Property Superintendent; **1982–8:** Underwriter for
Scotland; **1988–98:** Sales Underwriter for Scotland;
**1976–99:** Councillor, City of Glasgow Council, twice Leader of the
Opposition, thrice Bailie; **1999:** elected MSP.

**Profile:** There is something very Glaswegian about Bill Aitken – small,
dapper, pawky, never stuck for a word. Despite his passionate attachment to his native city, he lists foreign travel among his recreations (as
well as football, reading, wining and dining with friends). Thailand is
a particular favourite. He seems to have discovered a new lease of life
in Parliament.

He joined the Conservative Youth wing in 1970 and was National
Chairman from 1975 to 1977. His twenty-three years as a Glasgow
councillor, only once in power, do not seem to have dimmed his
enthusiasm. After two heady years in charge of Glasgow in the late
1970s, when Aitken was Convenor of the Licensing Committee and
Vice-Convenor of the Personnel Committee, the Tories have practically
disappeared from the City Council. Aitken led the Tory group twice
during that decline and held his own seat while all about were losing
theirs. He is currently Conservative Deputy Business Manager. His
most effective moments in the Chamber have been when attacking
the Executive's Housing Bill for its alleged failure to deal with poor
housing stock, anti-social tenants and homelessness. If you are looking
for a punchy quote, Bill's your man.

**Committees:** Justice 2 (Deputy Convener).

**Contact:** 0131-348-5642 (Parliament)
         0141-810-5743 Fax 0141-810-5897 (Constituency)
         e-mail bill.aitken.msp@scottish.parliament.uk

**Wendy Alexander** (LABOUR)
**Minister for Enterprise, Transport and
Lifelong Learning
MSP Paisley North**

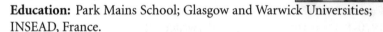

**Born:** Glasgow, 1963

**Education:** Park Mains School; Glasgow and Warwick Universities;
INSEAD, France.

**Career: 1987:** Parliamentary Assistant; **1987–8:** Editor, *Ledis*;
**1988–92:** Research Officer, Scottish Labour Party; **1994–7:** Senior
Associate, Booz, Allan & Hamilton Int.; **1997–8:** Special Adviser to
Secretary of State for Scotland; **1999:** elected MSP; **1999–2000:**
Minister for Communities.

**Profile:** Probably the brainiest of Scotland's ministers, certainly the
only one to have a degree from INSEAD, the college for European
high-flyers. She comes from a staunchly Labour family – her brother
Douglas is MP for Paisley South and confidant of Chancellor Gordon
Brown; her father the Rev. Douglas conducted Donald Dewar's funeral
service – but doesn't have much of a power base. She bubbles with ideas,
explains them in rapid-fire delivery, but may not always get her message across. She was picked up for her over-reliance on impenetrable
jargon when trying to encourage e-commerce and e-literacy.

She first came to the notice of Donald Dewar when she worked as
Research Assistant for the Scottish Labour Party and he subsequently
appointed her a Special Adviser when he became Secretary of State.
She was always assured of a place in his Scottish Cabinet and became
the first Minister for Communities. In that capacity her talent was clear
but so too was her comparative political inexperience. It fell to her to
introduce the clause to abolish Section 28 (2a in Scotland) and she
seemed to walk unsuspecting into a protest movement which – if not
representative of majority opinion – was certainly effective and shook the
Executive. She is better suited to her present department, Enterprise,
Transport and Lifelong Learning, though non-political Information
Officers have complained about her demands. She displayed her clout
by refusing to add the Water brief to her other responsibilities when
asked by McLeish, but slipped up badly when he resigned by first
indicating her intention to stand against Jack McConnell, then backing
out of a contest. She has lost some credibility, and much support. After

a threat to strip her department of Higher Education, McConnell has given her more functions (Transport and Planning) rather than fewer. Not shot, then – but submerged.

**Contact:** 0131-348-5752 (Parliament)
0141-561-5800 Fax 0141-561-5900 (Constituency)
e-mail wendy.alexander.msp@scottish.parliament.uk

## Jackie Baillie (LABOUR)
## MSP Dumbarton

**Born:** Hong Kong, 1964

**Education:** St Anne's School (Windermere);
Strathclyde and Glasgow Universities.

**Career: 1986–7:** Admin Assistant, Ruchill
Unemployed Workers Centre; **1987–90:** Co-ordinator, Gorbals
Unemployed Workers Centre; **1990–6:** Resources Central Manager,
Strathkelvin District Council; **1996–9:** Community Development
Manager, East Dunbartonshire Council; **1997–8:** Chair, Scottish
Labour Party; **1999:** elected MSP; **1999–2000:** Deputy Minister for
Communities; **2000–01:** Minister for Social Justice.

**Profile:** She is married with one daughter. Her warm and friendly
approach has brought her many admirers well beyond her own political
circle. Is she as nice and genuine as she seems? Almost certainly. She
developed her political conscience in Hong Kong, where her father was
a policeman and where she was struck by the contrast between private
or corporate wealth and public squalor.

She might have been an unknown outside Labour grassroots when
first appointed to the Executive, but no longer. In her original post of
Deputy Minister for Communities she was a practical associate for her
more cerebral senior colleague Wendy Alexander. She gave the
Executive's policies for social inclusion and equality a benevolently
human face. She was quietly effective in the Chamber and winningly
persuasive in the field, hence her translation to Minister for Social
Justice in her own right. She might not have been one of the Cabinet's
big hitters, but her open and approachable style was a considerable
electoral asset. Plainly, though, she was too identified with the old
regime and has been retired. She took her dismissal with characteristic
grace, although – since there is no love lost between her and the First
Minister – she no doubt saw it coming.

**Committees:** Education, Culture and Sport.

**Contact:** 0131-348-5905 (Parliament)
           01389-734214 (Constituency)
           e-mail jackie.baillie.msp@scottish.parliament.uk

## Scott Barrie (LABOUR)
## MSP Dunfermline West

**Born:** St Andrews, 1962

**Education:** Auchmuty High, Glenrothes; Edinburgh and Stirling Universities.

**Career: 1986–90:** Social Worker, Fife Regional Council; **1990–1:** Senior Social Worker; **1991–6:** Team Manager; **1996–9:** Team Leader, Fife Council; **1988–92:** Councillor, Dunfermline District Council; **1999:** elected MSP.

**Profile:** He has never strayed far from Fife, but then neither has Henry McLeish. And who needs to if, like Scott Barrie, your hobbies are football, hill-walking and real ale. He is a former social worker who has benefited from a reasonable local profile by acquiring a safe seat. He won his selection conference by a large majority.

He has not set the heather on fire, or anything else for that matter. He seems something of a Labour placeman, but even placemen have their day and he decided that he wanted to get anti-smacking legislation on the statute books. He did not proceed with the idea because the Executive is currently engaged in a consultation procedure on the issue and he keeps a watching brief. He maintains a strong interest in youth justice and children's issues, and has proposed a number of legislative amendments to ensure that children's voices can be heard in educational decisions. Some of his questions to ministers sound suspiciously planted.

**Committees:** Audit; Justice 2.

**Contact:** 0131-348-5849 (Parliament)
01388-731884 (Constituency)
e-mail scott.barrie.msp@scottish.parliament.uk

## Sarah Boyack (LABOUR)
## MSP Edinburgh Central

**Born:** Glasgow, 1961

**Education:** Royal High School, Edinburgh; Glasgow and Heriot Watt Universities.

**Career: 1986–8:** Planning Assistant, Brent; **1988–92:** Senior Planning Officer, Central Region; **1992–9:** Lecturer in Planning, Edinburgh College of Art/Heriot Watt; **1999:** elected MSP; **1999–2000:** Minister for Transport and the Environment; **2000–01:** Minister for Transport.

**Profile:** Recently married to her long-term partner, she lives a very private life with him, and two bicycles, in cosmopolitan Marchmont. She is the daughter of the late Jim Boyack, town planner and tireless campaigner for Scottish devolution, and it must have been richly rewarding for her to carry his torch into the new Scottish Parliament. At Glasgow University, she shared a flat with Wendy Alexander and, yes, she was the quiet one. Her mild, soft-spoken manner nevertheless belies her grasp and determination. Like her former flatmate, she is very much a child of feminism who cut her teeth in student politics. She is decidedly not a graduate of the municipal or trade union school of horse-trading. Nor is she a flashy performer, but she is honest and hard working.

Her first elected post, after years of backroom committee work, also brought her a front-bench job as Minister of Transport and the Environment. Despite having the right qualifications for the task – a planning background and cycling habit – things did not go well initially. Her road-toll experiment and workplace parking charges, now buried if not truly dead, brought a public outcry. Yet Donald Dewar, once privately considering his young ministers, said: 'in some ways, she is the steadiest of them all'. Henry McLeish must also have had some faith in her. Despite strong rumours that she was to be sacked, he reappointed her to the Executive, though in charge of Transport only. The opposition parties, the Lib Dems and the municipal tendency in her own party gave her a hard time over the tendering process for trunk-road maintenance, though the SNP failed in their vote of no confidence. Her performance in the Chamber did not, however, show sufficient command and her association with the previous administration meant that Jack McConnell had reason enough to sack her. His trusty lieutenant Andy Kerr was one of her fiercest critics and as she moved out of the Cabinet he moved in.

**Committees:** European.

**Contact:** 0131-348-5751 Fax 0131-348-5974 (Parliament)
0131-476-2539 Fax 0131-467-3574 (Constituency)
e-mail sarah.boyack.msp@scottish.parliament.uk

# Rhona Brankin (LABOUR)
## MSP Midlothian

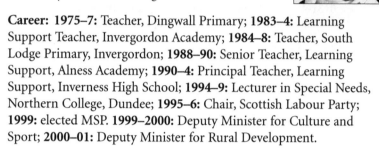

**Born:** Glasgow, 1950

**Education:** Jordanhill College School; Aberdeen
University, Northern College.

**Career: 1975–7:** Teacher, Dingwall Primary; **1983–4:** Learning
Support Teacher, Invergordon Academy; **1984–8:** Teacher, South
Lodge Primary, Invergordon; **1988–90:** Senior Teacher, Learning
Support, Alness Academy; **1990–4:** Principal Teacher, Learning
Support, Inverness High School; **1994–9:** Lecturer in Special Needs,
Northern College, Dundee; **1995–6:** Chair, Scottish Labour Party;
**1999:** elected MSP. **1999–2000:** Deputy Minister for Culture and
Sport; **2000–01:** Deputy Minister for Rural Development.

**Profile:** Married, with two daughters, she lives in Edinburgh with her
second husband Peter Jones, Scottish Correspondent of *The Economist*.
She is only one of several Labour luminaries whose partner is well
placed in the media. One of her daughters has spina bifida, and that
first led her into voluntary work with Riding for the Disabled. She also
helped found Ross-shire Women's Aid and set up a women's refuge in
Dingwall. That exposure to community affairs brought her into formal
politics, though she remains a fully paid-up member of the sisterhood.
Her poised, well-dressed appearance contrasts with a quiet, non-threatening manner. The frankness and dignity she showed when diagnosed
with cancer, undergoing mastectomy and breast reconstruction, made
her a role model beyond the confines of her own party.

In her initial foray into joined-up politics, if that is a fair description
of Ross and Cromarty District Council, she was the first person ever to
stand for Labour. She lost. She is a Blairite and owes her selection for
the Midlothian seat partly to the twinning arrangement which guar-
anteed equal representation for women in Labour's nominations. She
may not be reselected unless sitting women MSPs are protected against
the MCPs. She failed to make much of a public impact as Minister for
Culture and Sport, though she was ill for part of the time, but Henry
McLeish transferred her to Rural Development. In the negotiations
with the EC on fishing quotas she was able to get a less bad deal than
might have been expected, but walked straight into a substantial squall
with her compensation plan for fishermen. Her Executive motion was

lost when some Liberals failed to back the Executive and – even worse – the then Business Manager Tom McCabe failed to get the Labour vote out. A re-run later rescued the vote if not the argument. She was considered a good minister and it must be doubly galling for her to have lost her job to Allan Wilson.

**Contact:** 0131-348-5838 (Parliament)
0131-654-1585 Fax 0131-654-1586 (Constituency)
e-mail rhona.brankin.msp@scottish.parliament.uk

**Robert Brown** (LIBERAL DEMOCRAT)
**Scottish Parliament Corporate Body**
**MSP (List) Glasgow**

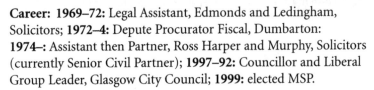

**Born:** Newcastle-upon-Tyne, 1947

**Education:** Gordon Schools, Huntly; Aberdeen
University.

**Career: 1969–72:** Legal Assistant, Edmonds and Ledingham,
Solicitors; **1972–4:** Depute Procurator Fiscal, Dumbarton:
**1974–:** Assistant then Partner, Ross Harper and Murphy, Solicitors
(currently Senior Civil Partner); **1997–92:** Councillor and Liberal
Group Leader, Glasgow City Council; **1999:** elected MSP.

**Profile:** He is married, with one son and one daughter, and lives in
Rutherglen. Most of his law career has been spent with the biggest law
firm in Scotland and one which boasted partners from all parties –
including Donald Dewar – and headed by the Tory stalwart Ross Harper.
At university he was, successively, Treasurer, Secretary and then
President of the Liberal Society. While a Councillor, he unsuccessfully
contested Rutherglen five times in general elections and rose to prominence in the Liberal (Democrat) hierarchy, being responsible for the
Manifestos for the UK election of 1997 and the Scottish election of
1999. He has considerable expertise in housing and is renowned for his
mastery of detail.

He may not be the most charismatic of MSPs but his constituency
reputation is sound, based on years of service as a councillor and as
chairman of the local Citizens' Advice Bureau. The quietly spoken,
mild-mannered Brown angered Glasgow Labour Leader, Councillor
Charles Gordon, by accusing him of treating ordinary people with
contempt over the closure of a local swimming pool without proper
consultation. Mr Gordon replied that his 'intervention in this matter . . . confirms my view that list MSPs are underemployed'. In fact,
together with seasoned representatives from each of the other three
main parties, Brown is a member of the Corporate Body which
oversees the administration of Parliament, in addition to his other
parliamentary responsibilities. He wants a railway station at Holyrood
to serve MSPs, Parliament staff, locals and tourists. The proposal has
been dismissed on all sides but – given Edinburgh's traffic problems,
and the likely congestion in that area – is it really such a silly idea?

**Committees:** Social Justice.

**Contact:** 0131-348-5792 (Parliament)
0141-243-2421 Fax 0141-243-2451 (Constituency)
e-mail robert.brown.msp@scottish.parliament.uk

## Bill Butler (LABOUR)
## MSP Glasgow Anniesland

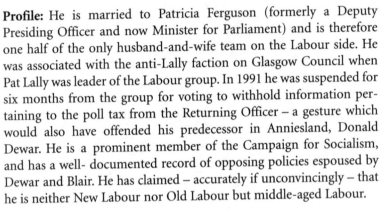

**Born:** Glasgow, 1956

**Education:** St Mungo's High School, Glasgow; Stirling University.

**Career: 1980–2000:** English teacher; **1987-2001:** Councillor, Glasgow City; **2000:** elected MSP (by-election).

**Profile:** He is married to Patricia Ferguson (formerly a Deputy Presiding Officer and now Minister for Parliament) and is therefore one half of the only husband-and-wife team on the Labour side. He was associated with the anti-Lally faction on Glasgow Council when Pat Lally was leader of the Labour group. In 1991 he was suspended for six months from the group for voting to withhold information pertaining to the poll tax from the Returning Officer – a gesture which would also have offended his predecessor in Anniesland, Donald Dewar. He is a prominent member of the Campaign for Socialism, and has a well- documented record of opposing policies espoused by Dewar and Blair. He has claimed – accurately if unconvincingly – that he is neither New Labour nor Old Labour but middle-aged Labour.

At his selection conference (to succeed Donald Dewar), he beat a good shortlist, including Donnie Munro. He is known to have strong reservations on the Executive's proposals for the transfer of Glasgow's housing stock to associations, but that issue was elided in the by-election campaign. Early in his parliamentary career, he was disciplined by the fearsome Tom McCabe (then Minister for Parliament) for voting against the Executive's wishes on an amendment to hurry the implementation of the Bill to abolish warrant sales. He also makes no secret of his opposition to PR for local government and his loyalty to the 'first past the post' system, which has led to the domination of many councils in Scotland by the people's party. It is to be hoped that his wife does not have occasion to discipline him, either in public or in private.

**Committees:** Enterprise and Lifelong Learning; Subordinate Legislation.

**Contact:** 0131-348-5771 (Parliament)
0141-944-9441 (Constituency)
e-mail bill.butler.msp@scottish.parliament.uk

## Colin Campbell (SNP)
## MSP (List) West of Scotland

**Born:** Paisley, 1938

**Education:** Paisley Grammar School; Glasgow University.

**Career: 1961–3:** History Teacher, Hillhead High School; **1963–7:** History Teacher, Paisley Grammar; **1967–73:** Principal Teacher, Greenock Academy; **1973–7:** Depute Head, Merksworth High; **1977–89:** Headteacher, Westwood Secondary; **1995–8:** part-time Tutor, Strathclyde University; **1995–9:** Councillor, West Renfrewshire; **1999:** elected MSP.

**Profile:** He is married, with three sons, four grandchildren, and lives in rustic Kilbarchan, where he enjoys gardening and is a pillar of the local community – church, Civic Society, Community Council. He sounds too nice a man to be the defence spokesperson, but his interest in military history is apparently sufficient to qualify him for that post. He is also co-authoring a book on the poets of the First World War. Surprisingly, he is the only Campbell in the Parliament, though there are two Macdonalds.

He joined the SNP in 1976 and has stood, unsuccessfully, in three general elections and two European elections. He served as National Secretary from 1997 to 1999 and remains a member of the National Executive. He has been defence spokesperson since 1995, but the SNP prefers not to have too much exposure on that front, except to complain about UK nuclear installations. Equally his other role as Principal in 'Reserved Matters' does not bring him centre stage in the Scottish Parliament. He's not one for the cut-and-thrust, and seems to belong to an earlier, softer age.

**Committees:** European; Subordinate Legislation.

**Contact:** 0131-348-5723 Fax 0131-348-5954 (Parliament)
01475-806020 Fax 01475-806021 (Constituency)
e-mail colin.campbell.msp@scottish.parliament.uk

**Dennis Canavan** (INDEPENDENT)
**MSP Falkirk West**

**Born:** Cowdenbeath, 1942

**Education:** St Columba's High School,
Cowdenbeath; Edinburgh University.

**Career: 1970–4:** Principal Teacher of Mathematics, St Modans High
School, Stirling; **1974:** Assistant Head, Holy Rood High School,
Edinburgh; **1973–4:** Councillor, then Leader, Stirling District
Council; **1974–83:** MP for Stirlingshire West, then **1983–2000:** MP
for Falkirk West; **1999:** elected MSP.

**Profile:** He is divorced, remarried and has three surviving children.
He has an unarguable reputation for being dogged, though some
would say stubborn. All the world loves a rebel, even if not all the
world understands the cause of his rebellion. Dennis is a rebel, and
glories in it, though he had good cause when the Scottish Labour Party
declined to allow him on their candidate's list for the Scottish Parliament. 'Not good enough,' said Donald Dewar, but Dennis suspected a
personal vendetta with many protagonists, including some in Downing
Street itself. He made it handsomely to the Scottish Parliament as an
independent MSP, with the biggest majority in any constituency. He
then upstaged Donald Dewar (whom he had beaten in the West
Stirlingshire selection conference twenty-five years before) by walking
across the Parliament floor with the outstretched hand of congratula-
tion, when Dewar was elected First Minister. He hates to be called an
'Independent', preferring 'the member for Falkirk West'.

There seemed to be a chance of his readmission to the Labour Party,
after Dewar's death, with Labour anxious to avoid a tricky Westminster
by-election. After making conciliatory noises, Canavan suddenly –
and with no convincing reason – changed his mind and resigned his
Westminster seat. Labour managed to hold it narrowly but are not
likely to forget. Such a strange about-turn also damaged Canavan's
reputation for consistency. In the Scottish Parliament, being a party of
one, he is called to speak more often than most ordinary members, but
Labour has curtailed his committee opportunities. He makes common
cause with the other 'loners' Tommy Sheridan and Robin Harper, and

some predict the formation of a Scottish Socialist Party with Canavan, Sheridan, Margo Macdonald and even Alex Neil.

**Committees:** European.

**Contact:** 0131-348-5629 (Parliament)
01324-825-922 Fax 01324- 823-972 (Constituency)
e-mail dennis.canavan.msp@scottish.parliament.uk

## Malcolm Chisholm (LABOUR)
**Minister for Health and Community Care**
**MSP Edinburgh North and Leith**

**Born:** Edinburgh, 1949

**Education:** George Watson's College, Edinburgh;
Edinburgh University.

**Career:** Teacher; **1992–7:** MP for Edinburgh Leith, then
**1997–2001:** MP for Edinburgh North and Leith; **1997:** Under-
Secretary, Scottish Office; **1999:** elected MSP; **2000–01:** Deputy
Minister for Health and Community Care.

**Profile:** A former Dux of George Watson's, and a classicist, he is married,
with two sons and one daughter. He is a man of quiet sincerity and
deep principle. Although next to Dennis Canavan in the alphabetical
list of MSPs, and not a million miles from him politically, Malcolm
Chisholm's conduct and demeanour has been diametrically different.
He chooses his words carefully and does not flirt with the media.

He succeeded the colourful (code for strange), deselected Ron Brown
at Westminster and quickly restored Labour's reputation in Leith. He
was made an Under-Secretary at the Scottish Office by Donald Dewar
after the 1997 general election but resigned only a few months later in
protest against cuts in single-parent benefits, the first minister to leave
the government. One of the few Scottish Labour MPs to decide to
stand for Holyrood, he did not win a post in the Scottish Executive
immediately. After his election as First Minister, Henry McLeish made
him deputy to Susan Deacon at Health, where his first big task was to
lead the development study for care of the elderly. His appointment
was a recognition of his talents but also a reward for loyal and sensible
behaviour. It meant another genuine left-winger was added to Team
McLeish. On McLeish's resignation, he threatened to stand against Jack
McConnell but didn't. He was given the Health brief in place of Susan
Deacon, who declined one step sideways and one step down.
Obviously the hard feelings McConnell extends towards others from
the McLeish cabinet do not apply to him. Chisholm has always seemed
too honest a man to make any kind of backstairs deal.

**Contact:** 0131-348-5908 (Parliament)
            0131-555-3636 Fax 0131-555-3737 (Constituency)
            e-mail malcolm.chisholm.msp@scottish.parliament.uk

# Cathie Craigie (LABOUR)
## MSP Cumbernauld and Kilsyth

**Born:** Stirling, 1954

**Education:** Kilsyth Academy.

**Career: 1984–96:** Councillor, Cumbernauld and Kilsyth District Council; **1995–9:** Councillor, North Lanarkshire Council; **1992–7:** Parliamentary Assistant; **1999:** elected MSP.

**Profile:** She is married with two children and lives in Kilsyth. She is a conscientious member but not a vociferous one. Although a loyalist, she did play a major role in the backbench revolt on warrant sales and supported Jack McConnell when he first stood against Henry McLeish for the leadership. In McConnell's second campaign, her mobile phone was used over and over again to record votes for him in a media opinion poll – not by her, she claims, but by an 'over-zealous assistant'. She reported the SNP 'List' member Andrew Wilson for calling himself the 'local MSP' when that is her proud boast.

She spent her last two years on Cumbernauld and Kilsyth Council as Leader. Subsequently, on North Lanarkshire Council, she was Chair of Environmental Services, a representative to CoSLA and criticised the ruling Motherwell clique. On both councils, she served on Housing Committees and she was Chair of the Cumbernauld Housing Partnership. This experience led her to introduce a Private Members' Bill (the first woman to do so) on Mortgage Rights. The Bill is intended to reduce repossessions, and therefore homelessness, and had wide support inside and outside the Scottish Parliament. Crucially, it had the backing of the Executive and was passed unanimously in June 2001. It is thought likely to have more impact than the abolition of warrant sales.

**Committees:** Social Justice.

**Contact:** 0131-348-5756 Fax 0131-348-5977 (Parliament)
01388-731884 (Constituency)
e-mail cathie.craigie.msp@scottish.parliament.uk

**Bruce Crawford** (SNP)
**MSP (List) Mid-Scotland and Fife**

**Born:** Perth, 1955

**Education:** Kinross High School; Perth High
School.

**Career: 1974–99:** Civil Servant, Scottish Office; **1996– :** Chairman,
Perth and Kinross Recreational Facilities Ltd: **1998– :** Chairman,
Kinross-shire Partnership Ltd; **1988–96:** Councillor, Perth and
Kinross District Council; **1995–9:** Councillor, then Leader Perth and
Kinross Council; **1999:** elected MSP.

**Profile:** He is married with three sons and lives near where he was
born and has spent most of his life. His professional experience, as a
civil servant, is in personnel management, but he also had a seat on
Perth Tourist Board, Scottish Enterprise Tayside and Perth College
board.

His skill in personnel management was harnessed as SNP Chief Whip
during the first year of the Scottish Parliament, but he did not seem
quite tough or nasty enough for the job. John Swinney then moved
him to Transport and the Environment, a key area in SNP campaigning
and one for which his geographical background suited him. He led the
opposition assault in the vote of confidence on Transport Minister
Sarah Boyack and her plans for trunk-road maintenance by private
companies. In Swinney's 2001 reshuffle, he lost the Transport half of
his brief to Andrew Wilson's Economy portfolio, more of a strategic
switch than a criticism. He is a popular figure in the SNP group.

**Contact:** 0131-348-5686 Fax 0131-348-5957 (Parliament)
        01577-863531 Fax 01577-863531 (Constituency)
        e-mail bruce.crawford.msp@scottish.parliament.uk

## Roseanna Cunningham (SNP)
### Deputy Leader of SNP
### MSP Perth

**Born:** Glasgow, 1951

**Education:** John Curtin High School, Australia;
Universities of Western Australia, Edinburgh and Aberdeen.

**Career: 1977–9:** Researcher, SNP; **1983–6:** Solicitor, Dumbarton
District Council; **1986–9:** Solicitor, Glasgow District Council;
**1989– :** Solicitor, Private Practice: **1990:** Called to the Advocate's Bar;
**1995–2001:** MP for Perth and Kinross, then Perth; **1999:** elected MSP.

**Profile:** She emigrated to Australia with her family at the age of eight,
and received all but her Law education there. She joined the Australian
Labor Party but also the SNP and is firmly on the left of the party. She
was a supporter of the '79 Group but was not one of those disciplined
when the Group was proscribed by Gordon Wilson. She is also a
Republican, which could have been a handicap in Perthshire, but
clearly not an insurmountable one. In fact her biggest battle was to get
the SNP nomination in the 1995 by-election – at least one of the
Ewing family led the campaign against her, but Alex Salmond stood
firmly by her then and later. She is stylishly dressed, highly articulate
and admits to loving argument, Australian wine, *Star Trek*, Celtic
music and cats.

She began the Scottish Parliament as SNP Spokesperson for Justice,
Equality and Land Reform, and Convenor of the Parliament's Justice
and Home Affairs Committee. She made such an impact that, after
the resignation of Alex Salmond, she was widely quoted as a potential
leader. In the end, the leadership went to John Swinney – Salmond's
established deputy and policy partner – while she was elected deputy.
She has kept her portfolio, though not the Convenership, and continues to shine in debate and in the media. In fact, she outshines her
leader, who is yet to shake off his bank-manager image and awkward
manner. If she can keep her cool and curb her occasional volatility, she
could yet assume the leadership.

**Contact:** 0131-348-5696 Fax 0131-348-5952 (Parliament)
        01738-444002 Fax 01738-444602 (Constituency)
        e-mail roseanna.cunningham.msp@scottish.parliament.uk

## Margaret Curran (LABOUR)
## Deputy Minister for Social Justice
## MSP Glasgow Baillieston

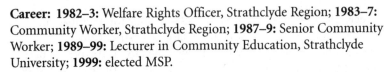

**Born:** Glasgow, 1958

**Education:** Our Lady of St Francis, Glasgow;
Glasgow University.

**Career: 1982–3:** Welfare Rights Officer, Strathclyde Region; **1983–7:** Community Worker, Strathclyde Region; **1987–9:** Senior Community Worker; **1989–99:** Lecturer in Community Education, Strathclyde University; **1999:** elected MSP.

**Profile:** Married with two sons. She was embroiled in the painful Westminster selection conference at Govan, as the third candidate to Mike Watson and Mohammed Sarwar. Eventually so shocked by behind-the-scenes manoeuvres, she dropped out of the re-run and became Mohammed Sarwar's agent. There then followed a painful eighteen months when Sarwar was investigated, accused, then acquitted of mal-practice. She herself was accused of irregularities in election expenses, though these charges were dropped and her reputation restored. Like many of her left-wing women colleagues, she is a fan of country and western music. Could it be the recurrent theme of all those tortured women and wayward men?

She was a popular and influential Convener of the Social Inclusion Committee in the first year of Parliament and also acted as co-convener of the Cross-party Group on Women. The controversial visit of Mike Tyson to Scotland gave her an opportunity to raise the issue of violence inflicted by men on women. In McLeish's reshuffle, her local activism made her an excellent choice as Deputy to the Social Justice Minister, with a particular brief on housing and including immediate responsibility for the transfer of Glasgow's municipal housing from Council control to housing associations. This is a delicate issue and will require all her can-do approach and persuasive skills, especially since her boss is no longer Jackie Baillie but Ian Gray, a reliable but quiet man from Edinburgh Pentlands.

**Contact:** 0131-348-5842  Fax 0131-348-5984 (Parliament)
0141-771-4844  Fax 0141-771-4877 (Constituency)
e-mail margaret.curran.msp@scottish.parliament.uk

# David Davidson (CONSERVATIVE)
## MSP (List) North-East Scotland

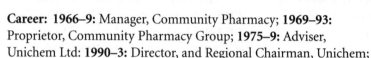

**Born:** Edinburgh, 1943

**Education:** St Serf's Prep; Trinity Academy, Edinburgh; Heriot Watt School of Pharmacy, Manchester Business School.

**Career: 1966–9:** Manager, Community Pharmacy; **1969–93:** Proprietor, Community Pharmacy Group; **1975–9:** Adviser, Unichem Ltd: **1990–3:** Director, and Regional Chairman, Unichem; **1990– :** Farmer; **1995–9:** Councillor, Stirling Council; **1999:** elected MSP.

**Profile:** Married with three sons and two daughters. His career in pharmacy developed towards the entrepreneurial side, ending up on the board of Unichem. In the 1990s, he also became managing director of a family farming business. Outwith his professional interests, he is a member of Stirling Enterprise and Stirling Business Works and is founder-chairman of the Association of Scottish Community Councils.

He is Deputy Tory Spokesperson on Industry, Economy and Finance but has made little impact on parliamentary proceedings. He is gentlemanly and slightly humourless. He did, however, act as reporter for the Finance Committee's consideration of the costs of the new Parliament building. He accused Parliament, which approved the costs at £195 million by just nine votes, of accepting a 'naive proposition'. He was naive if he thought the Executive would turn back, and the project has now had the 'cap' lifted, with the likelihood of costs reaching £230 million at least. The Tories, and Mr Davidson, will make much of it, though they do not seem to have any constructive proposal of their own and have declined to join the group monitoring the project. He has called for an urgent review of government funding for the treatment of eating disorders, after one of his daughters nearly died from anorexia. Many anxious parents will agree that provision for these conditions in Scotland is lamentably limited.

**Committees:** Audit (Deputy Convener); Finance.

**Contact:** 0131-348-5653 (Parliament)
e-mail david.davidson.msp@scottish.parliament.uk

## Susan Deacon (LABOUR)
## MSP Edinburgh East and Musselburgh

**Born:** Musselburgh, 1964

**Education:** Musselburgh Grammar School; Edinburgh University.

**Career: 1987–9:** Research Officer/Administrative Assistant, West Lothian District Council; **1990–2:** Senior Administrative Officer, East Lothian District Council; **1992–4:** Manager, East Lothian District Council; **1993–5:** Part-time Tutor, Open University; **1994:** Senior Consultant, Eglinton Management Centre; **1994–8:** MBA Director of Programmes, Heriot Watt University; **1998–9:** Self-employed Business and Marketing Consultant; **1999:** elected MSP; **1999–2000:** Minister for Health and Community Care.

**Profile:** She lives with her partner, BBC man John Boothman, and their daughter Claire, in her home town of Musselburgh, which she also represents. In an unscheduled moment at the opening of the Scottish parliament, Claire told the distinguished audience, 'That's my mummy.' Her mummy doesn't need much help in making a mark. Her career outside politics went from administrative assistant in local government to university teaching. Inside politics, she was a student activist, a member of Scottish Labour Action, and an opponent of paying the poll tax. This last stance, and her association with the neo-nationalist SLA, was probably the reason why she was at first denied a place on Labour's candidate list for the Scottish elections, before being one of the very few reinstated on appeal.

After she came so close to being refused selection, it surprised many that Donald Dewar gave her the Health portfolio rather than his old friend Sam Galbraith, himself a consultant. She had impressed Dewar in the election campaign by her cogent presentation and persuasive performance. She was widely considered to be one of the biggest successes of the administration, handling policy in the Chamber and politicking in her parish with equal dexterity. Her portfolio, and that of Jim Wallace, were the only two to remain intact and unchanged since the beginning of the Dewar administration. Her biggest challenge came from the new First Minister and his ambivalent approach to the Sutherland Report on care of the elderly. She was left by McLeish to present the Executive's agreed policy to a hostile chamber, only for him to abandon it later the same day in favour of free universal care, with considerable implications for the Scottish budget. Later, the then First Minister allowed a rumour to circulate that she was to be sacked. In the end the deed was done by Jack McConnell who offered her a lesser job, which she refused. Constructive dismissal by another name. Still, she expects another baby in 2002, so she can afford to be philosophical about her immediate fate. She'll be back, surely.

**Committees:** Standards.

**Contact:** 0131-348-5753 (Parliament)
0131-669-6446 Fax 0131-669-9162 (Constituency)
e-mail susan.deacon.msp@scottish.parliament.uk

# Lord James Douglas-Hamilton
(CONSERVATIVE)
MSP (List) Lothian

**Born:** Strathaven, 1942

**Education:** Eton; Oxford and Edinburgh Universities.

**Career: 1968–74:** Advocate and Interim Procurator Fiscal Depute at the Scottish Bar; **1974–97:** MP for Edinburgh West; **1976–9:** Scottish Conservative Whip; **1979–81:** Government Whip; **1987–95:** Under-Secretary of State for Scotland; **1995–7:** Minister of State, Scottish Office; **1999:** elected MSP.

**Profile:** Lord James or – to give him his full name – the Rt Hon Lord James Alexander Douglas-Hamilton, Baron Selkirk of Douglas, is married with four sons. He is probably the nicest of Scottish toffs, certainly the toffiest: his father was the 14th Duke of Hamilton and Brandon, his mother a Percy of Northumberland, his wife a Buchan of Tweedsmuir. He also fought a court battle with a relative so that his son and heir would be able to inherit the title of Earl of Selkirk (he disclaimed it himself). That apart, he is thoroughly decent and approachable, with an unaristocratic diffidence that disguises his ability. He was President of the Oxford Union and the Oxford University Conservative Association. He has written half a dozen books, mostly on pre-war and wartime flying and on Rudolph Hess, mirroring his father's connection with both.

He was Conservative Chief Whip and Business Manager in the Scottish Parliament for two sessions, and served in a similar capacity at Westminster. If, so polite and diffident, he seems an odd choice for such a tough job, it should be remembered that he was a boxing blue at Oxford (like his father before him). Where persuasion failed on wee hard men like Brian Monteith or Bill Aitken, there was always the threat of an elegantly straight left. He is now the justice spokesperson, a more moderate voice than his predecessor Phil Gallie. He is genuinely well liked on all sides of the house.

**Committees:** Standards; Justice 1.

**Contact:** 0131-348-5661 Fax 0131-348-5936 (Parliament)
0131-557-5158 Fax 0131-557-6682 (Constituency)
e-mail james.douglas-hamilton.msp@scottish.parliament.uk

## Helen Eadie (LABOUR)
## MSP Dunfermline East

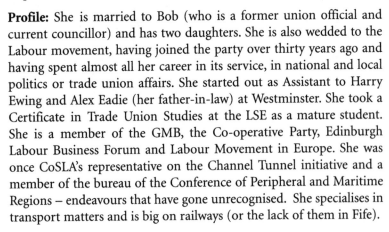

**Born:** Stenhousemuir, 1947

**Education:** Larbert High School; Falkirk Technical College; London School of Economics.

**Career: 1970–6:** MPs' Assistant; **1976–84:** Equal Opportunities and Political Officer, GMB Union; **1986–99:** Councillor and sometime Depute Leader, Fife Council; **1999:** elected MSP.

**Profile:** She is married to Bob (who is a former union official and current councillor) and has two daughters. She is also wedded to the Labour movement, having joined the party over thirty years ago and having spent almost all her career in its service, in national and local politics or trade union affairs. She started out as Assistant to Harry Ewing and Alex Eadie (her father-in-law) at Westminster. She took a Certificate in Trade Union Studies at the LSE as a mature student. She is a member of the GMB, the Co-operative Party, Edinburgh Labour Business Forum and Labour Movement in Europe. She was once CoSLA's representative on the Channel Tunnel initiative and a member of the bureau of the Conference of Peripheral and Maritime Regions – endeavours that have gone unrecognised. She specialises in transport matters and is big on railways (or the lack of them in Fife).

For such a loyal and assiduous party member, she made an inexplicable error in not turning up for the vote on the Executive's fishing package. She and a few other Labour MSPs (plus the naughty Lib Dems) suffered the wrath of the then Business Manager Tom McCabe, though he should probably have shouldered the blame himself for the Executive's defeat. She does have the reputation of being something of a loner.

**Committees:** European; Public Petitions (Deputy Convener).

**Contact:** 0131-348-5749 (Parliament)
01383-412856 Fax 01383-412855 (Constituency)
e-mail helen.eadie.msp@scottish.parliament.uk

## Dorothy-Grace Elder (SNP)
## MSP (List) Glasgow

**Born:** Undisclosed

**Education:** Undisclosed

**Career:** Journalist with several Scottish newspapers, starting out with D. C. Thomson. Later, a reporter and feature writer with the (then) *Glasgow Herald* and *Scottish Daily News*; and a freelance columnist with the *Scottish Daily Express* and *Scotland on Sunday*. Also periods with BBC Scotland and Scottish Television. **1995–6:** Olivier Award-winning columnist and British Reporter of the Year; **1996–7:** UK Press Awards. She is a Trustee of Children's Fund, Royal Hospital for Sick Children, Glasgow.

**Profile:** She lives in Glasgow with her husband and three children. Interestingly, for a journalist once engaged in investigative work, her entry on the Scottish Parliament website does not reveal her date or place of birth, details of education or dates of career changes. Her journalism, schooled by D. C. Thomson, speaks directly to Glasgow's wee wifies. She is the Mrs Mack of her trade, though more generous in spirit.

She is a hard-working and vociferous member of the Health and Community Care Committee of the Parliament and a member of cross-party groups on violence against women and children, epilepsy and animal welfare. Her assaults on the Executive in committee and in the Chamber, however, resemble attacks from a terrier – noisy, persistent, but creating nuisance rather than damage. No cause is too populist for her vocal support – 'Jings, crivvens, whit a scandal'. On the inaugural day of business of the new Parliament, she led the first public demonstration, on the issue of fuel prices. When Alex Salmond announced his resignation as leader, other parties mischievously started a 'draft Dorothy' campaign: 'It's Gottae Be Dottie.' A critic of the SNP leadership, she has announced that she will stand down at the next election. John Swinney said he was sorry about that and almost managed to sound as if he meant it.

**Committees:** Health and Community Care; Public Petitions

**Contact:** 0131-348-5682/5683 Fax 0131-348-5944 (Parliament)
0141-204-1749 Fax 0141-204-1762 (Constituency)
e-mail dorothy.elder.msp@scottish.parliament.uk

**Fergus Ewing** (SNP)
**MSP Inverness East, Nairn and Lochaber**

**Born:** Glasgow, 1957

**Education:** Loretto; Glasgow University.

**Career: 1979-81:** Apprentice Solicitor; **1981–5:**
Solicitor, Leslie Wolfson & Co.; **1985– :** Partner, Ewing & Co.;
**1999:** elected MSP.

**Profile:** Married to Margaret (MSP, Moray), who is some years his
senior, and son of Winnie (MSP, Highlands and Islands), who is the
senior member of the Scottish Parliament. He is a gifted amateur
pianist and, as his lean and lanky frame suggests, a keen runner and
walker. He is a senior member of a local mountain rescue team. In his
younger days he took adventurous and rather risky holidays in places
like Albania and Romania, which might just have persuaded him that
Scotland's lot wasn't quite so bad after all.

He is beginning to emerge from the shadows of the two other and more
experienced members of the Ewing dynasty. He is SNP spokesperson
on Rural Affairs and has been particularly vocal of the impact of high
fuel prices on the Highland economy. In 2001, his committee work on
the foot-and-mouth issue raised his profile. He is also recognised as a
expert on the problems of small businesses. He has the distinction of
having asked the largest number of written questions, the majority of
which have been on environmental topics of vital interest to his constituents. He is a formidable local campaigner and his victory in 1999
was the only SNP constituency 'gain' from Labour. He is taking on his
mother's role of champion of the Highlands.

**Committees:** Rural Development (Deputy Convener).

**Contact:** 0131-348-5731 Fax 0131-348-5737 (Parliament)
             01463-713004 Fax 01463-710194 (Constituency)
             e-mail fergus.ewing.msp@scottish.parliament.uk

# Margaret Ewing (SNP)
## MSP Moray

**Born:** Lanark, 1945

**Education:** Biggar High School; Glasgow and Strathclyde Universities; Jordanhill College.

**Career: 1968–70:** Teacher, Our Lady's High, Cumbernauld; **1970–3:** Teacher, St Modans High, Stirling; **1973–4:** Principal Teacher, St Modan's; **1974–9:** MP for Dumbarton East; **1979–81:** Freelance Journalist; **1981–7:** Co-ordinator, West of Scotland Certificate in Social Service Scheme; **1987–2001:** MP for Moray: **1999:** elected MSP.

**Profile:** She is married (for the second time) to Fergus, MSP for Inverness East, Nairn and Lochaber. She first came to prominence as the leggy, blonde bombshell Margaret Bain (she was then married to SNP research officer Donald Bain) elected to Westminster as one of the SNP's 'team' of successes in 1974. Almost all the team, including her, were wiped out in the post referendum election of 1979, but she bounced back in the 1980s to become the party's Senior Vice-Chairman and MP for Moray. Like many of her colleagues, she's a folk-singing buff, but takes a wider interest in the arts.

She stood against Alex Salmond for the National Convener's job in 1990 and was beaten more convincingly than had been anticipated. She was nevertheless Parliamentary Leader at Westminster, despite the presence of Alex Salmond, and in 1993 led the group into the lobby in support of the Tories over Maastricht in return for concessions on the European Committee of the Regions. It wasn't much of a deal. Her talents are now rather wasted as the SNP Parliamentary Group Convener in Edinburgh. She has made less impact in the Chamber than might have been expected and often looks far from happy. Yet, when McLeish castigated the SNP for being guilty of something nasty, beginning with H and ending with Y, it was she who had the wit to shout 'Henry'. (The correct answer was, of course, hypocrisy.)

**Committees:** Justice 2.

**Contact:** 0131-348-5705  Fax 0131-348-5857 (Parliament)
　　　　　01343-551111  Fax 01343-556355 (Constituency)
　　　　　e-mail margaret.ewing.msp@scottish.parliament.uk

**Winnie Ewing** (SNP)
**MSP Highlands and Islands**

**Born:** Glasgow, 1929

**Education:** Queen's Park Secondary School,
Glasgow; Glasgow University.

**Career: 1952–** Solicitor; **1954–6:** Lecturer in Law, Glasgow College
of Commerce: **1956– :** Solicitor, practising on her own account;
**1961–7:** Secretary, Glasgow Bar Association; **1967–70:** MP for
Hamilton; **1970–1:** President, Glasgow Bar Association;
**1974–9:** MP for Moray and Nairn; **1979–99:** MEP for Highlands and
Islands; **1999:** elected MSP.

**Profile:** She is married with two sons and one daughter (one son and
daughter-in-law are with her in the Scottish Parliament; her daughter
sits at Westminster). She joined the SNP in 1946, but literally burst onto the wider political scene in 1967 with a stunning by-election victory
in the safe Labour seat of Hamilton, which marked the beginning of
the modern Nationalist success. She lost that seat at the next general
election but came storming back in Moray and Nairn in 1974 to beat
the then Tory Secretary of State, the genteel and lairdly Gordon
Campbell. She complained bitterly of being badly treated in her first
stint at Westminster, especially by antagonistic Scottish Labour MPs,
though she has always been on a fairly short fuse herself. The
European Parliament, used to diversity and even eccentricity, was
more welcoming and dubbed her 'Madame Ecosse'. Her service as
MEP for the Highlands and Islands is immeasurable. She is President
of the SNP, an honour rather than a responsibility.

In recognition of her seniority, she was allowed to occupy the Chair at
the very first session of the Scottish Parliament, when the Parliament's
senior officers were elected. The honour fell to her to say: 'The Scottish
Parliament, adjourned on 25th March 1707, is hereby reconvened,' a
prosaic sentence loaded with historic significance. It was quite a
moment, particularly for a lifelong Nationalist, but she has been rather
quiet since – savouring the experience and letting the younger and less
traditional element in her party make the running. She will stand
down at the 2003 election. There was a flashback to her fiery youth

when the Taoiseach came to town and she demanded the removal of the Union Jack from its position alongside the Saltire and the Tricolour. There remains a guid conceit, too, as displayed when she made an ill-judged reference to 'St Donald Dewar'. By way of an enforced apology she explained: 'I'll probably be sanctified myself.' Well, an icon perhaps, but hardly a saint.

**Committees:** Public Petitions.

**Contact:** 0131-348-5726   Fax 0131-348-5947 (Parliament)
01463-713004 (Constituency)
e-mail winnie.ewing.msp@scottish.parliament.uk

## Linda Fabiani (SNP)
## MSP (List) Central Scotland

**Born:** Glasgow, 1956

**Education:** Hyndland Secondary School, Glasgow; Napier College, Edinburgh; Glasgow University.

**Career: 1975–82:** Secretarial Work; **1982–5:** Administration, Glasgow Housing Association; **1985–8:** Administration and Housing Officer, Clydebank Housing Association; **1988–94:** Development Manager, Bute Housing Association; **1994–9:** Director, East Kilbride Housing Association; **1999:** elected MSP.

**Profile:** She has been a housing administrator in Glasgow, Clydebank, Bute and East Kilbride, where she was Director of the EK Housing Association. She is active in promoting Third World issues, went to East Timor as a UN observer, and is a campaigner on behalf of asylum seekers. She has become a target for the anti-abortion group Precious Life because of her pro-choice views.

She is the Vice-Convener of the progress group on the new Parliament building, a bit of a poison chalice for any SNP representative, and has spoken supportively of its work thus far – for example, the appointment of consultants to advise on a strategy for art and design to be displayed within the Parliament. To the consternation of her SNP colleague Margo Macdonald, arch-critic of the new building, she predicted that it would be necessary to break the budget to be sure of getting a building of real quality. So it has proved. She is reported to be advising John Swinney on how to improve his image and dress sense with softer colours and more informal clothes . . . Fratini, Fahri, Fabiani.

**Committees:** Social Justice.

**Contact:** 0131-348-5698 Fax 0131-348-5943 (Parliament)
01357-523147 (Constituency)
e-mail linda.fabiani.msp@scottish.parliament.uk

# Patricia Ferguson (LABOUR)
**Minister for Parliament**
**Member, Scottish Parliamentary Bureau**
**MSP Glasgow Maryhill**

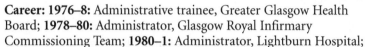

**Born:** Glasgow, 1958

**Education:** Garnethill Convent Secondary School, Glasgow; Glasgow College of Technology.

**Career: 1976–8:** Administrative trainee, Greater Glasgow Health Board; **1978–80:** Administrator, Glasgow Royal Infirmary Commissioning Team; **1980–1:** Administrator, Lightburn Hospital; **1981–3:** Assistant Administrator, Glasgow Dental School; **1983–5:** Secretary SE Glasgow Health Council; **1985–90:** Assistant Administrator, Lanarkshire Health Board; **1990–4:** Administrator, Scottish TUC; **1994–6:** Organiser, South-West Scotland, Scottish Labour Party; **1996–9:** Scottish Officer, Labour Party; **1999:** elected MSP; **1999–2001:** Deputy Presiding Officer.

**Profile:** She is married to Bill Butler, the former teacher who succeeded Donald Dewar as MSP for Anniesland. They are one of two married couples in Parliament (the other, Margaret and Fergus Ewing). Butler has always been openly hard-left but Ferguson has seemed to be quietly loyalist. History does not relate what they debate over the toast and marmalade. She is a highly experienced administrator, with twelve years in the health service and ten in the Labour movement.

Elected straight from Labour's Scottish headquarters, with all her administrative experience, her smart dress and pleasant manner, she must have seemed an excellent choice as Deputy Presiding Officer. She was often tentative and hesitant in the post, however, failing to impose her personality on the Chamber. Apparently she was not consulted by her Chair-colleagues Sir David Steel and George Reid when they decided to get tough with ministers who were leaking forthcoming policy statements to the press. She was one of Jack McConnell's closest supporters in his pursuit of the First Minister's job and she has been rewarded with a job of her own. Her experience in the Chair will surely be an advantage and she is certain to bring more tact and diplomacy to the post of Minister of Parliament than Tom McCabe could ever muster. She must, however, add a bit of flair to her grasp.

**Contact:** 0131-348-5311 (Parliament)
0141-946-1300 Fax 0141-946-1412 (Constituency)
e-mail patricia.ferguson.msp@scottish.parliament.uk

**Alex Fergusson** (CONSERVATIVE)
**MSP (List) South of Scotland**

**Born:** Leswalt, Wigtonshire, 1949

**Education:** Eton College; West of Scotland
Agricultural College.

**Career: 1970–1:** Farm Management Consultant; **1971– :** Farmer;
**1999:** elected MSP.

**Profile:** Married with three sons. He combines the simplest of cvs
with the most exotic educational background – Eton and Auchencruive,
morning suits to nickie-tams. He farmed in South Ayrshire until
recently, ran a restaurant and was President of the Blackface Sheep-
breeders Association (presumably they did see the humour of the
title). He spent two teenage years in New Zealand and retains a love of
rugby, as well as curling, country dance music and public speaking,
which he now has ample opportunity to practise.

He is the Tories' spokesman on Rural Development. He has made some
sound points during debates on the crisis in the farming industry. He
is a pleasant, sociable man, well liked by his colleagues. He is a Tory
wet, with little ideological baggage.

**Committees:** Rural Development (Convener).

**Contact:**   0131-348-5636 Fax 0131-348-5932 (Parliament)
             0800-731-9590 FREEPHONE (Constituency)
             e-mail alex.fergusson.msp@scottish.parliament.uk

**Ross Finnie** (LIBERAL DEMOCRAT)
**Minister for the Environment and**
**Rural Development**
**MSP (List) West of Scotland**

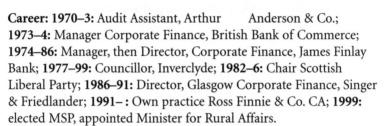

**Born:** Greenock, 1947

**Education:** Greenock Academy.

**Career: 1970–3:** Audit Assistant, Arthur      Anderson & Co.;
**1973–4:** Manager Corporate Finance, British Bank of Commerce;
**1974–86:** Manager, then Director, Corporate Finance, James Finlay
Bank; **1977–99:** Councillor, Inverclyde; **1982–6:** Chair Scottish
Liberal Party; **1986–91:** Director, Glasgow Corporate Finance, Singer
& Friedlander; **1991– :** Own practice Ross Finnie & Co. CA; **1999:**
elected MSP, appointed Minister for Rural Affairs.

**Profile:** He is married with a son and a daughter and still lives in
Greenock, where he was born and educated. He is James Ross Finnie II,
named after his father, the Town Chamberlain – a splendid local-government office now in abeyance. Through his business interests and
his long-standing membership of Inverclyde Council, he is quite simply the best-known Liberal in the west of Scotland. Thanks to him and
a few others, Greenock was for decades an island of Liberalism in a
hostile sea. His basso profundo voice (rivalling the great Willie Ross),
constant good humour and affable manner make him a popular and
appealing personality. His nickname is 'Captain Mainwaring', but it is
applied with affection.

He and Jim Wallace are the two Lib Dems in senior ministerial positions in the Executive. Finnie was well respected by Donald Dewar and
the feeling was mutual. He has fought the Executive's corner hard
against the malcontents in his own party. There was surprise that the
Rural Affairs' brief went to an urban representative with no farming
background, especially with an ex-President of the NFU (George
Lyon) also on the Lib Dem benches. Finnie's warm but no-nonsense
approach has gone down reasonably well in the farming community,
even when the message isn't always palatable. He has tried to be the
farmers' friend without being their prisoner and was congratulated for
putting Scotland ahead of England and Wales by his willingness to lift
the 'beef on the bone' ban before Nick Brown had got round to it. With

foot and mouth disease coming so soon after the BSE crisis, his mettle has been thoroughly tested. In a no-win situation, he certainly hasn't lost. McLeish added Environment to his portfolio and McConnell has confirmed him in that larger role. His timely paper outlining *A Forward Strategy for Scottish Agriculture* was well received in all quarters.

**Contact:**  0131-348-5783  Fax 0131-348-5966 (Parliament)
0131-805-020  Fax 01475-805-021 (Constituency)
e-mail ross.finnie.msp@scottish.parliament.uk

# Brian Fitzpatrick (LABOUR)
## MSP Strathkelvin and Bearsden

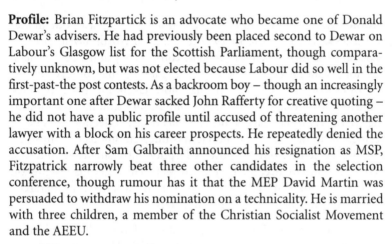

**Born:** Arisaig, 1961

**Education:** Bellarmine Secondary, Glasgow; Glasgow University.

**Career: 1983– :** Solicitor, then Advocate; **1991–6:** Director, Head Injuries Trust; **1999–2000:** Adviser then Head of Policy Unit to First Minister; **2001:** elected MSP (by-election).

**Profile:** Brian Fitzpartick is an advocate who became one of Donald Dewar's advisers. He had previously been placed second to Dewar on Labour's Glasgow list for the Scottish Parliament, though comparatively unknown, but was not elected because Labour did so well in the first-past-the post contests. As a backroom boy – though an increasingly important one after Dewar sacked John Rafferty for creative quoting – he did not have a public profile until accused of threatening another lawyer with a block on his career prospects. He repeatedly denied the accusation. After Sam Galbraith announced his resignation as MSP, Fitzpatrick narrowly beat three other candidates in the selection conference, though rumour has it that the MEP David Martin was persuaded to withdraw his nomination on a technicality. He is married with three children, a member of the Christian Socialist Movement and the AEEU.

When Henry McLeish succeeded Donald Dewar, Fitzpatrick's contract as Head of the Policy Unit was not renewed. Effectively, with Dewar's other confidants like Press Chief David Whitton, he was sacked. He is a close friend of the Alexanders (once working in the same leading law firm as Douglas) and, therefore, in the Gordon Brown camp. He is also close to the Solicitor General, Neil Davidson. His election victory, however, was a little less than glorious, and he took 22 per cent of the vote less than Galbraith. His main opponent was a single-issue candidate fighting to save Stobhill Hospital, and who started campaigning only twenty days before polling day.

**Committees:** Enterprise and Lifelong Learning.

**Contact:** 0131-348-5913 (Parliament)
0141-942-9662 (Constituency)
e-mail brian.fitzpatrick.msp@scottish.parliament.uk

**Murdo Fraser** (CONSERVATIVE)
**MSP (List) Mid-Scotland and Fife**

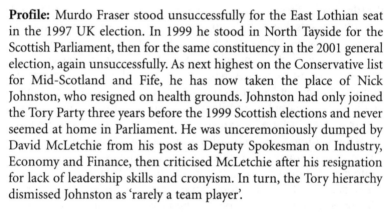

**Born:** Inverness, 1965

**Education:** Inverness Royal Academy; Aberdeen University.

**Career: 1987–2001:** Solicitor; **1989–91:** Chairman, Scottish Young Conservatives; **1991:** Chairman UK Young Conservatives; **2001:** elected MSP.

**Profile:** Murdo Fraser stood unsuccessfully for the East Lothian seat in the 1997 UK election. In 1999 he stood in North Tayside for the Scottish Parliament, then for the same constituency in the 2001 general election, again unsuccessfully. As next highest on the Conservative list for Mid-Scotland and Fife, he has now taken the place of Nick Johnston, who resigned on health grounds. Johnston had only joined the Tory Party three years before the 1999 Scottish elections and never seemed at home in Parliament. He was unceremoniously dumped by David McLetchie from his post as Deputy Spokesman on Industry, Economy and Finance, then criticised McLetchie after his resignation for lack of leadership skills and cronyism. In turn, the Tory hierarchy dismissed Johnston as 'rarely a team player'.

Fraser, who is married, can be expected to behave with more loyalty. He has solid, if distinctly right-wing, credentials. He was the first Scot to be Chairman of the UK Young Conservatives. He is a member of the Tuesday Club, like Brian Monteith, and of the Conservative Christian Fellowship. He is a keen walker and climber, and a Rangers supporter. Like his leader, he is an Edinburgh lawyer, but his closest relationship will be with Monteith, who does need a few friends.

**Committees:** Subordinate Legislation.

**Contact:** 0131-348-5645 (Parliament)
01592-612511 Fax 01592-612259 (Constituency)
e-mail murdo.fraser.msp@scottish.parliament.uk

## Phil Gallie (CONSERVATIVE)
## MSP (List) South of Scotland

**Born:** Portsmouth, 1939

**Education:** Dunfermline High School; Rosyth and Kirkcaldy Technical Colleges.

**Career: 1955–60:** Apprentice Electrical Fitter, Rosyth Dockyard; **1960–4:** Electrical Engineer, Merchant Navy; **1964–92:** Power Station operative, then Power Station Manager; **1980–4:** Councillor, Cunninghame District Council; **1992–7:** MP for Ayr; **1999:** elected MSP.

**Profile:** He is married with one son and one daughter. Despite being brought up a Fifer, he has made Ayrshire his home and his political base. After losing his seat at Westminster in 1997, he became a business adviser to Ayrshire Enterprise and started his own company PG Business Advice. He's keen on sport (a member of Ayr Rugby Club), walking and after-dinner speaking, though he is by no means a great orator. He's a pretty unsophisticated law-and-order man, but strikes a chord with some. He is certainly a willing quotesman and broadcaster, whose engineering background makes him a reliable occupant of remote, unmanned studios which can often baffle the technically challenged.

He first succeeded the urbane and gifted George Younger as MP for Ayr – there could scarcely be a more dramatic contrast in Tory circles. Subsequently, he has gained from the wipe-out of the Conservative Party in Scotland at Westminster and Holyrood. One of the few Tories on the Mound with parliamentary experience, he was initially given the Home Affairs brief, but effectively demoted in 2001 to Constitutional Affairs. As a list MSP, he had the chance to run again for the Ayr constituency when Labour MSP Ian Welsh stood down, but he chose instead to hang on to the Conservative nomination for the Westminster seat. So keen was he to get re-elected in 2001 that he and his team put up election posters before Parliament had been dissolved and were asked to desist. He also lost the contest. He challenged David McLetchie for the leadership of the Scottish Conservatives in 1998 but has since behaved like a loyal, if limited, lieutenant. He is rather excitable but not afraid to speak his mind. In 2003 he will be standing down.

**Committees:** Public Petitions.

**Contact:** 0131-348-5665 (Parliament)
01292-263991 Fax 01292-280480(Constituency)
e-mail phil.gallie.msp@scottish.parliament.uk

**Kenneth Gibson** (SNP)
**MSP (List) Glasgow**

**Born:** Paisley, 1961

**Education:** Bellahouston Academy, Glasgow;
Stirling University.

**Career: 1982–6:** Systems Development Officer,
British Steel; **1987–8:** Product Development Adviser, Glasgow Garden
Festival; **1988–99:** Sales Representative and Trainer, pharmaceutical
industry; **1992–9:** Councillor, Glasgow City Council;
**1998–9:** Opposition Leader, Glasgow City Council; **1999:** elected MSP.

**Profile:** He is married with two sons and one daughter. When he was
elected to the Scottish Parliament, his mother Iris took over as
Councillor for the Mosspark ward he had represented for seven years.
A boy can always trust his mammy. He is amusing and well liked and
was 'Kenny' until recently, but has now decided that 'Kenneth' has
more resonance.

He is the SNP's spokesman on Social Justice, Housing and Urban
Regeneration, promoted from the local-government brief after the
2001 election. He is also a member of a range of cross-party groups
on health and mental health and convener of the group on tobacco
control. He is a fierce critic of the Glasgow housing stock transfer and
a leading opponent of warrant sales. In the year 2000, he was the MSP
who asked the most questions in Parliament – a total of 611. Does he
know the difference between persistence and pertinence?

**Committees:** Social Justice (Deputy Convener).

**Contact:** 0131-348-5924  Fax 0131-348-5943 (Parliament)
0141-204-1753  Fax 0141-204-1754 (Constituency)
e-mail kenneth.gibson.msp@scottish.parliament.uk

# Karen Gillon (LABOUR)
## MSP Clydesdale

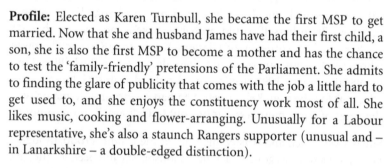

**Born:** Edinburgh, 1967

**Education:** Jedburgh Grammar School; Birmingham University.

**Career: 1991–5:** Project worker, Youth Centre, Blantyre; **1995–7:** Community Education Worker; **1997–9:** Personal Assistant to the Labour Minister Helen Liddell MP; **1999:** elected MSP.

**Profile:** Elected as Karen Turnbull, she became the first MSP to get married. Now that she and husband James have had their first child, a son, she is also the first MSP to become a mother and has the chance to test the 'family-friendly' pretensions of the Parliament. She admits to finding the glare of publicity that comes with the job a little hard to get used to, and she enjoys the constituency work most of all. She likes music, cooking and flower-arranging. Unusually for a Labour representative, she's also a staunch Rangers supporter (unusual and – in Lanarkshire – a double-edged distinction).

Despite being one of six UNISON-sponsored MSPs and representing a seat in deepest Labour Lanarkshire, she has impressed colleagues of all parties with her independent stance and capacity for hard work. It was her activism in Unison that led to her appointment as PA to the formidable Helen Liddell, and surviving it must say something for her strength of character. She got a bad press initially for being one of several backbenchers who fed the Executive with blatantly planted interventions, made with less than oratorical panache. Since then, however, she has given a dogged and effective performance in the Standards Committee, especially during the Lobbygate hearings, and in the Committee on Education, Culture and Sport. She has replaced Mary Mulligan as Convener of the latter Committee and questioned the larger-than-expected grant to Scottish Opera. She's tipped as possible ministerial material and her plain speaking would make her a natural for the Whip's office.

**Committees:** Education, Culture and Sport (Convener).

**Contact:** 0131-348-5822/5823 (Parliament)
01555-660-526  Fax 01555-660-528 (Constituency)
e-mail karen.gillon.msp@scottish.parliament.uk

**Trish Godman** (LABOUR)
**MSP Renfrewshire West**

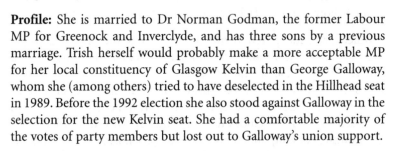

**Born:** Glasgow, 1939

**Education:** St Gerard's Secondary School, Glasgow;
Jordanhill College.

**Career:** Social Worker; Councillor; Strathclyde Region; Councillor,
Glasgow City Council; **1999:** elected MSP.

**Profile:** She is married to Dr Norman Godman, the former Labour
MP for Greenock and Inverclyde, and has three sons by a previous
marriage. Trish herself would probably make a more acceptable MP
for her local constituency of Glasgow Kelvin than George Galloway,
whom she (among others) tried to have deselected in the Hillhead seat
in 1989. Before the 1992 election she also stood against Galloway in the
selection for the new Kelvin seat. She had a comfortable majority of
the votes of party members but lost out to Galloway's union support.

She is a well-liked and trusted member of the Labour group, though –
now that Dewar has gone – lacking a sponsor. She has been an effective
Convenor of the Local Government Committee since its inception, but
has made not made much impact in the Chamber for someone who
was considered to be a candidate for office. Her finest hour was when
the Section 28/2a controversy came before the Local Government
Committee and she dealt calmly and competently with the controversy
and the strong views within her committee. The majority opinion, and
hers too, was in favour of repeal. She was minded to put her name forward for the vacancy as Deputy Presiding Officer, a job she would have
done with some style. The First Minister let it be known he wanted
Cathy Peattie instead, thereby ensuring that a Tory man (Murray Tosh)
was elected rather than a Labour woman.

**Committees:** Local Government (Convener).

**Contact:** 0131-348-5837 (Parliament)
01475-805537 Fax 01475-805458 (Constituency)
e-mail trish.godman.msp@scottish.parliament.uk

# Annabel Goldie (CONSERVATIVE)
## MSP (List) West of Scotland

**Born:** Glasgow, 1950

**Education:** Greenock Academy; Strathclyde University.

**Career: 1978– :** Partner, law firm Donaldson, Alexander, Russell & Haddow; **1992–8:** Successively, Vice-Chairman, Deputy Chairman, Chairman, and Deputy Leader of the Scottish Conservative Party; **1999:** elected MSP, confirmed Deputy Leader Scottish Conservative Party.

**Profile:** Annabel Goldie is a glutton for charitable and unpaid work – Prince's Scottish Youth Business Trust, Strathclyde University Court, Salvation Army Advisory Board. She's also an elder in the Church of Scotland (indeed she shares a pew with Wendy Alexander at Bishopton, where Alexander's father is minister), a Deputy Lord Lieutenant, a member of the National Trust for Scotland, the RSPB and the Scottish Wildlife Trust. If that makes her sound boringly earnest, nothing could be further from the truth. She's quick-witted and entertaining, with an optimistic outlook and an appetite for work – just what's needed in the reconstruction of the Scottish Tory Party. She is one of several MSPs who attended Greenock Academy, something of a factory for politicians of all persuasions.

She's had a successful initial spell as deputy leader and spokesperson for Industry, Economy and Finance. Her good-humoured jousts with the late Donald Dewar were a highlight of sometimes dull parliamentary debates. She has also taken on pew-mate Wendy Alexander with disarming wit: 'as one spinster to another'. She does a lot of unglamorous work touring constituencies, trying to revive the Tory vote. She has considerable support in the grassroots of the party but is probably too nice to kill for the leader's post, even if she wanted it. Her genuine popularity outside her own ranks might, however, make her the strongest candidate for the post of Presiding Officer when Sir David Steel steps down. Her reputation for niceness took a slight dent when she told a couple of gey coorse jokes to a Businesswomen's function; at least, they were blue, but not – she says – as blue as had been reported.

**Committees:** Enterprise and Lifelong Learning (Deputy Convener).

**Contact:** 0131-348-5662 (Parliament)
01463-713004 (Constituency)
e-mail annabel.goldie.msp@scottish.parliament.uk

# Donald Gorrie (LIBERAL DEMOCRAT)
## MSP (List) Central Scotland

**Born:** India, 1933

**Education:** Oundle; Hurst Grange, Stirling; Oxford University.

**Career: 1957–60:** Master, Gordonstoun School; **1960–6:** Director of Physical Education, Marlborough School; **1966–9:** Adult Education Lecturer; **1969–75:** Director of Research, then Administration, Scottish Liberal Party; **1976–9:** Small Businessman; **1971–97:** served as Liberal Councillor for Corstorphine throughout 26 years, in Lothian Region and Edinburgh City Councils, leading the Liberal group for most of that period; **1997–2001:** served as MP for Edinburgh West, at the fifth attempt; **1999:** elected MSP.

**Profile:** He is married with two sons, lives in Edinburgh but lost the local nomination to Margaret Smith. His biography is the longest on the Scottish Parliament website, running to twice the length of most others. That may be because he has a more extensive and varied history or because he is somewhat self-regarding – perhaps both: a do-gooder who does good. His considerable voluntary activity extends from sport to drama, with an emphasis on youth and community work. He is President of Corstorphine AAC, President of Salveson Boys' Club, President of Edinburgh City Youth Café and Convenor of Diverse Attractions, a community drama centre. He initiated the last two projects and still had time to found two after-school clubs and a community sports centre. Among his personal interests he lists 'music, books and theatre'. Perhaps he should have added 'committees' since – apart from the foregoing – he sits on five others, not including his parliamentary duties. If he has the slim, spare shape of a middle-distance runner, that's because he was – and a Scottish record holder forbye.

Gorrie is an archetypal Liberal, jealous of the purity of the party. He was one of the minority who opposed partnership with the Labour Party to form the Scottish Executive, describing Labour as a bunch of liars. He has continued to pursue an independent line – not least over the plans for the Holyrood Parliament building, which he has (with Margo Macdonald) criticised and opposed at every stage – and was first recipient of the Scottish Media Group award for the Backbencher of the Year. His failure to vote for the Executive's fishing compensation deal shows that he's still on form. His latest initiative is a Bill to outlaw sectarian harassment: admirable, but perhaps not workable.

**Committees:** Finance; Justice 1; Procedures.

**Contact:**  0131-348-5795/5796 Fax 0131-348-5963 (Parliament)
          e-mail donald.gorrie.msp@scottish.parliament.uk

## Christine Grahame (SNP)
## MSP (List) South of Scotland

**Born:** Burton-on-Trent, 1944

**Education:** Boroughmuir Secondary School, Edinburgh; Edinburgh University; Moray House College of Education.

**Career: 1966–82:** Secondary Teacher, Woodmill High School, Whithorn Secondary School, Douglas Ewart High School; **1985–99:** Solicitor, Alan Dawson Simpson and Hampton WS, J. & R. A. Robertson WS, Dickson McNiven & Dunn WS; **1999:** elected MSP.

**Profile:** She was elected as Christine Creech, has two sons and is now divorced. Her mid-life change of career from teaching to the law speaks volumes for her determination and application. For recreation, she claims to be able to garden and drink malt whisky simultaneously – there are no photographs of her garden.

She began as SNP spokesperson for Older People and then became Shadow Minister for Social Security, though that's an area reserved to Westminster and there is no Scottish minister to shadow. It is, in short, a licence to make mischief. In the reshuffle after the 2001 election, Swinney followed the logic of the devolution settlement and gave the portfolio to Annabelle Ewing at Westminster. Ms Grahame was not best pleased, to put it mildly, because it also meant the loss of her Shadow Cabinet seat. She was placated, if not wholly satisfied, with the promise of nomination for the Convenership of the important Justice 1 Committee. Indeed, that is her area of expertise and, during the Ruddle affair, she gave the Executive a hard time. She has a reputation for the lawyer's mastery of detail. She was formerly regarded as a critic of the SNP leadership, seemed to have drifted with the tide back into the centre, but – after the demotion – who knows?

**Committees:** Justice 1 (Convener).

**Contact:** 0131-348-5729  Fax 0131-348-5943 (Parliament)
            01896-759575  Fax 01896-759579 (Constituency)
            e-mail christine.grahame.msp@scottish.parliament.uk

## Rhoda Grant (LABOUR)
### MSP (List) Highlands and Islands

**Born:** Stornoway, 1963

**Education:** Plockton High School; Inverness College; Open University.

**Career: 1987–92:** Highland Regional Council, Clerical Assistant; **1991–2:** ESF Accounts Assistant; **1992–3:** Administrative Assistant; **1993–9:** UNISON, Administrator; **1999:** elected MSP.

**Profile:** Rhoda Grant is married. She has an Honours degree from the Open University in Social Sciences. A Gaelic speaker, she is a member of the parliamentary cross-party groups on Gaelic and on the Scots language.

Rhoda is the Labour group representative on the Scottish Executive of the Labour Party. She is not one of the most frequent speakers in Parliament, to put it mildly. In fact she is virtually anonymous. She was prominent in Scotland Forward, but has got lost in the corridors of the Assembly Hall. She does campaign on women's issues and is close to her fellow Labour 'list' MSP Maureen Macmillan.

**Committees:** Public Petitions; Rural Development.

**Contact:** 0131-348-5766 Fax 0131-348-5767 (Parliament)
0134 9-867650  Fax 01349-867762 (Constituency)
e-mail rhoda.grant.msp@scottish.parliament.uk

# Iain Gray (LABOUR)
## Minister for Social Justice
## MSP Edinburgh Pentlands

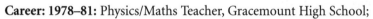

**Born:** Edinburgh, 1957

**Education:** Inverness Royal Academy; George Watson's; Edinburgh University.

**Career: 1978–81:** Physics/Maths Teacher, Gracemount High School; **1982–3:** Escola Basica Agraria, Chokwe Mozambique; **1984–6:** Inveralmond High School; **1986–99:** Scottish Campaigns Manager, Oxfam; **1999:** elected MSP; **1999–2000:** Deputy Minister for Community Care; **2000–01:** Deputy Minister for Justice.

**Profile:** He is married, for the second time, and has one daughter and two stepdaughters. He is regarded by many (women) as the handsomest man in Parliament, a sort of George Clooney on the Mound. To add to the romance, he spent time teaching in Mozambique and has a proven interest in the developing world. He runs hard, walks hills and supports Hibs. He was a sound choice for Edinburgh Pentlands, well spoken, well mannered and well dressed. Oddly, he lost the Westminster nomination for Pentlands to Lynda Clark, probably his most embarrassing moment in politics thus far.

He became Deputy Minister for Justice in the McLeish reshuffle of 2000, after a respectable spell at the same level in Community Care. His main task was to co-ordinate and present the Executive's policies on drug abuse. He came over as hard-working and sincere but not as someone who would have blasted or dazzled his way to a senior ministry. He slipped into his new post as Minister for Social Justice when Susan Deacon (and Kate Maclean) declined to accept it. In some ways he's an odd choice since his first major challenge will be to persuade Glasgow's tenants to accept the transfer of council house stock to housing agencies. He's quiet and assiduous, but he may need his deputy Margaret Curran to hold his hand in Glasgow.

**Contact:** 0131-348-5754 (Parliament)
0131-477-4511 Fax 0131-477-2816 (Constituency)
e-mail iain.gray.msp@scottish.parliament.uk

## Duncan Hamilton (SNP)
## MSP (List) Highlands and Islands

**Born:** Troon, 1973

**Education:** Bearsden Academy; Glasgow, Edinburgh and Harvard Universities.

**Career: 1998–9:** Assistant to Chief Executive, SNP; **1999:** elected MSP.

**Profile:** He is the youngest member of the Scottish Parliament, a fact he never tires of repeating. Rather like Charles Kennedy, he has entered the great race of politics without trying the training run of life. Charles Kennedy does have the advantage of having been brought up in the community he represents. Duncan Hamilton is, for all that, a personable and promising young man with an excellent educational record, climaxed by a spell as a Kennedy Scholar at Harvard's Kennedy School of Government. He won the World Debating Championships in 1994 and worked very briefly for Proctor and Gamble before joining SNP headquarters' staff.

He is the SNP's deputy spokesman on Enterprise and Lifelong Learning (including Highlands and Islands). His column in the Glasgow *Evening Times* probably causes as much of a stir as anything he does in the Chamber. Not unnaturally perhaps, he uses it to discomfit the Labour Party but undoubtedly went too far when he described Labour's women MSPs as 'overweight, inarticulate, and an embarrassment to their party'. The arrogance of gilded youth. He has some way to go, but is a good bet for a very senior job. He needs to find and develop an expertise like his friend Andrew Wilson, the SNP's Economy spokesman, to add to his articulate charm.

**Committees:** Enterprise and Lifelong Learning

**Contact:**  0131-348-5700 Fax 0131-348-5737 (Parliament)
0131-571359 Fax 01631-571630 (Constituency)
e-mail duncan.hamilton.msp@scottish.parliament.uk

## Keith Harding (CONSERVATIVE)
## MSP (List) Mid-Scotland and Fife

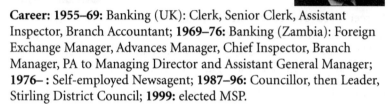

**Born:** Chipping Norton, 1938

**Education:** Chipping Norton Grammar School; Oxford College of Further Education.

**Career: 1955–69:** Banking (UK): Clerk, Senior Clerk, Assistant Inspector, Branch Accountant; **1969–76:** Banking (Zambia): Foreign Exchange Manager, Advances Manager, Chief Inspector, Branch Manager, PA to Managing Director and Assistant General Manager; **1976– :** Self-employed Newsagent; **1987–96:** Councillor, then Leader, Stirling District Council; **1999:** elected MSP.

**Profile:** He is married with a grown-up family. After a career in banking in the UK and abroad, he resettled in Stirling to become a shopkeeper. Ultimately he owned three newsagent's shops, one sub-post office, a pet shop and a wholesale confectionery business. He has since down-sized to one shop in order to concentrate on politics. Apart from the stereotypical connection between shopkeepers and the Conservative Party, many of his political attitudes stem from his personal experience. He is interested in palliative care, for example, because his wife Anne suffered from breast cancer and he lost both parents at a young age from leukaemia. He is a keen ornithologist and is trying to start a 'twitchers' club in the Scottish Parliament.

He is the Conservative spokesman on Local Government and Housing, but his party is out of step with the others on reform of local government. He made his reputation as a hard-working leader of Stirling Council, one of the most marginal in Scotland, and he has promised – despite criticism from members from other parties – to keep his dual mandate and complete his term as a councillor. His most appreciated contribution to Scottish life may be his proposed Bill on dog fouling, which had the second highest number of MSPs' signatures of any Bill so far. He is a dog-lover but is appalled by the lack of responsibility shown by some dog owners. All those who have had nervous cause to check the soles of their shoes will wish more power to his scooper. The Bill will be introduced in the session 2001–02.

**Committees:** Local Government.

**Contact:**  0131-348-5643 (Parliament)
             01592-612511 Fax 01592-612259 (Constituency)
             e-mail keith.harding.msp@scottish.parliament.uk

## Robin Harper (GREEN)
## MSP (List) Lothian

**Born:** Thurso, 1940

**Education:** St Marylebone Grammar School; Elgin
Academy; Aberdeen and Heriot Watt Universities.

**Career: 1962–3:** Teacher, Crookston Castle, Glasgow; **1964–8:**
Teacher, Braehead School; **1968–70:** Teacher, Kilanya School, Kenya;
**1970:** Teacher, Braehead School; **1971–2:** Actor; **1972–99:** Teacher,
Boroughmuir School, Edinburgh; **1999:** elected MSP.

**Profile:**  He is married with one stepson. Although a teacher for most of
his career, he did have a brief spell at acting and it has to be admitted
that, with his long multi-coloured scarf, he could be cast as Dr Who.
With the other two independent MSPs (Canavan and Sheridan), he
has made an impact on the Scottish political scene and, with him at
least, you never feel he's a poser. He is a truly rounded man – music
teacher, guitarist, former member of Lothian Health Council and
Lothian Children's Panel. He is currently Rector of Edinburgh University (2001–03) and highlights student hardship at every opportunity.

As the first Green Party member to be elected to any British Parliament,
he has become the environmental conscience of Holyrood. He is conducting public consultation on his private member's Bill on organic
farming and food, a move that has been given added impetus by foot
and mouth. He is also constantly monitoring plans for the new Parliament building to ensure that all materials used, particularly timber,
are environmentally friendly and from sustainable resources. He was
outraged – not the only one by any means – when Henry McLeish
decided not to replace Sam Galbraith directly with a new Environment
minister. Although he had personal talks with McLeish, he was not
able to effect a change and Jack McConnell, too, has left things as they
were. The leadership and profile of the Scottish Green Party has altered
considerably over the years, but Robin Harper is a constant.

**Committees:** Transport and the Environment.

**Contact:**  0131-348-5927  Fax 0131-348-5972 (Parliament)
            0131-478-7895  Fax 0131-478-7891 (Constituency)
            e-mail robin.harper.msp@scottish.parliament.uk

# Hugh Henry (LABOUR)
## Deputy Minister for Health and Community Care
## MSP Paisley South

**Born:** Glasgow, 1952

**Education:** St Mirin's Academy, Paisley; Glasgow University; Jordanhill College.

**Career: 1973–5:** Accountant IBM; **1976–9:** Teacher, Strathclyde Region; **1979–84:** Welfare Rights Officer; **1984–93:** Senior Welfare Rights Officer; **1984–99:** Councillor, then Leader, Renfrew Council; **1993–6:** Community Care Manager; **1999:** elected MSP.

**Profile:** He is married with two daughters and a son. His professional career has been varied – accountant, teacher, social worker – and his political direction has also been subject to change. He spent fifteen years on Renfrew Council, where he was leader, but was at one time a Militant supporter. He abandoned his Trotskyist roots to pursue the parliamentary road.

He was COSLA's spokesman on Europe for three years before being elected to Parliament and, once there, he was given the Convenership of the European Committee. To the outsider, it sounds like a cushy number, but he has operated well in the chair. There was a moment, though, when he and Dennis Canavan nearly came to blows in Committee – just like home in Renfrew, the rowdiest council in the land. The SNP opposition in Renfrew were an angry bunch who clamed there was malpractice by the Labour group and – if Henry knew – he ought to have stopped it and – if he didn't know – he was equally culpable. Hugh Henry has failed to make much impact on Parliament thus far. Perhaps it's too genteel for him. But Jack McConnell has given him his big chance as a junior Health Minister and he must re-invent himself again, though he and his twin Health junior, Mary Mulligan, would hardly be described as the Dynamic Duo.

**Contact:** 0131-348-5929 (Parliament)
0141-848-7361 Fax 0141-848-7361 (Constituency)
e-mail hugh.henry.msp@scottish.parliament.uk

## John Home Robertson (LABOUR)
## MSP East Lothian

**Born:** Edinburgh, 1948

**Education:** Ampleforth College; West of Scotland
Agricultural College.

**Career: 1975– :** Farmer; **1974–8:** Councillor, Berwickshire District
Council; **1978–83:** MP for Berwick and East Lothian, then
**1983–2001:** MP for East Lothian; **1999:** elected MSP.
**1999–2000:** Deputy Minister for Rural Affairs.

**Profile:** He is married with two sons, and is distantly related to the
Douglas-Homes. A laird with a family history back to the Border raids,
he seems an unlikely Labour representative. In his youth he campaigned for David Steel but was converted to the Labour cause by the
late Professor John P. Mackintosh, whose seat he inherited. He is rather
modest and diffident, with some un-lairdly traits. He has a Class 1
Heavy Vehicle Driver's Licence and fishing rights in the Tweed, which
he personally declines to exercise. He has handed over the family home,
with its expensive furnishings and extensive parkland, to the Paxton
Trust.

He lost his ministerial post in the McLeish reshuffle of 2000, probably
due to a failure to make any real impact rather than any sin of commission. He blamed this on the fact that – as a landowner with a
possible conflict of interest – he was not allowed to speak on farming
issues. He was compensated with the Deputy Convenership of the
European Committee and the leadership of the progress group overseeing the cost and construction of the new Parliament building. With
this latter appointment comes an architect's model of a poisoned
chalice. He probably feels at home in a Lib–Lab coalition, since he
retains a number of attitudes that are more Lib than Lab – like being
passionately pro-Europe and pro-PR.

**Committees:** European (Deputy Convener).

**Contact:** 0131-348-5839 (Parliament)
        01368-863-679 (Constituency)
        e-mail john.home.robertson.msp@scottish.parliament.uk

## Janis Hughes (LABOUR)
## MSP Glasgow Rutherglen

**Born:** Glasgow, 1958

**Education:** Queen's Park School, Glasgow; Glasgow
Western School of Nursing.

**Career: 1980–6:** Nurse; **1986–8:** Medical Researcher;
**1988–99:** Clinical Administrator, Glasgow Royal Infirmary;
**1999:** elected MSP.

**Profile:** She is divorced with one son. Her progress from nurse to NHS
administrator, trade union representative and now MSP is a model of
single-parent achievement. Her ten-year spell as administrator in the
Renal Unit of Glasgow Royal Infirmary must have given her stark
experience of NHS problems and priorities.

Making sensible use of her expertise (not always the case), Labour have
now put her on the Health Committee and many of her cross-party
committees also have a medical bias. She is one of a group of Labour
women who sit three rows back in the Chamber, with their handbags
on the desk and a bag of sweeties at the ready. She has yet to make her
mark in the Chamber, though her committee work is better, and there
are apparently local rumours that her role as Rutherglen's representative may not be long sustained.

**Committees:** Health and Community Care.

**Contact:**    0131-348-5820 (Parliament)
                0141-647-0707 Fax 0141-647-0102 (Constituency)
                e-mail janis.hughes.msp@scottish.parliament.uk

# Fiona Hyslop (SNP)
**Member, Scottish Parliamentary Bureau**
**MSP (List) Lothian**

**Born:** Irvine, 1964

**Education:** Ayr Academy; Glasgow University; Scottish Textile College.

**Career: 1986–99:** Sales and Marketing, Standard Life Assurance Company, latterly Marketing Manager; **1999:** elected MSP.

**Profile:** She is married with one son and one daughter. If there were to be a beauty contest for Ms Scottish Parliament (perish the thought), she would be one of the favourites. Sometimes, however, she seems to have gone to the SNP School of Unsmiling Severity, where Nicola Sturgeon was top of the class.

She is a powerful member of the SNP hierarchy, appointed after the 2001 election to the key role of Shadow Parliament Minister with responsibility for scrutinising government strategy. She is a member of both the National Council and the National Executive, and is a close confidante of John Swinney. When she was Deputy Convenor of the Social Inclusion Committee she accused the (then) Convenor Margaret Curran of allowing the Executive to see and alter the agreed Committee Report on housing stock transfers. It was a bitter little spat, with no clear outcome, but both fought their corner well. As policy co-ordinator, she was behind the new-look *Cosmopolitan*-style SNP manifesto for the 2001 campaign, aimed at the aspirational twenty- and thirty-somethings and designed in *Cosmo* fashion to 'turn them on' to the different nationalist positions in politics. If election results are the measure, it didn't really do the trick.

**Committees:** Procedures.

**Contact:**  0131-348-5920  Fax 0131-348-5943 (Parliament)
0131-525-8916 (Constituency)
e-mail fiona.hyslop.msp@scottish.parliament.uk

## Adam Ingram (SNP)
## MSP (List) South of Scotland

**Born:** Kilmarnock, 1951

**Education:** Kilmarnock Academy; Paisley College.

**Career: 1971–6:** Manager A. H. Ingram & Sons, Bakers; **1985–6:** Senior Economic Assistant, Manpower Services Commission; **1987–8:** Lecturer, Paisley College; **1989–99:** self-employed Economic Development Consultant; **1999:** elected MSP.

**Profile:** He is married with three sons and one daughter. He ran the family bakery business before specialising in economic research and consultancy, including work for the European Union.

He is one of the few remaining old-style fundamentalists in the SNP parliamentary group. They seem to be a dying breed. He supported Alex Neil against John Swinney in the leadership election and, as with all of that faction, his light – never bright – is now distinctly dim.

**Committees:** Transport and the Environment.

**Contact:** 0131-348-5720 Fax 0131-348-5735 (Parliament)
01292-290611 (Constituency)
e-mail adam.ingram.msp@scottish.parliament.uk

## Gordon Jackson (LABOUR)
## MSP Glasgow Govan

**Born:** Saltcoats, 1948

**Education:** Ardrossan Academy; St Andrews University.

**Career: 1971–9:** Solicitor, Private Practice; **1979– :** Advocate; **1987–90:** Advocate Depute; **1989:** Member of the English Bar; **1990:** made QC; **1999:** elected MSP.

**Profile:** He is married with one son and two daughters. Although he began his career as a solicitor, he made his name as an advocate involved in some of Scotland's most prominent criminal trials. He built a lucrative practice at the Bar, one year earning over a quarter of a million pounds in legal aid fees alone. His parliamentary salary is £41,255 (in 2001).

Opposition parties objected to his membership of the Justice Committee's deliberations on the grounds that he should not be shaping law from which he stands to benefit financially. He was a high-earner at the Bar, allegedly spending more time in the Courts than his MSP duties should allow. It was also claimed that he was often missing from debates only to arrive in time to vote at Decision Time. He was nicknamed 'Crackerjack' because he always seemed to appear at 5 p.m. All of these allegations could apply to a large number of MPs at Westminster but perhaps that's precisely the point – the Scottish Parliament is meant to be different. He was also rebuked by a judge for failing to turn up in a case where he was scheduled to appear for the defence. Lord Bonomy eventually accepted that he had been legitimately attending to his parliamentary duties, but for Mr Jackson this was the final straw and he decided (in May 2001) to leave the legal profession and concentrate on Parliament. To Labour, he is a valued advocate and he was entrusted with the crucial task of speaking in support of the Executive in the vital 2000 debate on the costs of the new Parliament building. In the event, it was not his finest hour though the government case was narrowly carried. It is a surprise that this talented man, with his colourful reputation, has not yet found a post in government.

**Committees:** Justice 1 (Deputy Convener); Subordinate Legislation.

**Contact:**  0131-348-5899 (Parliament)
              0141-427-7047 Fax 0141-427-9374 (Constituency)
              e-mail gordon.jackson.msp@scottish.parliament.uk

# Dr Sylvia Jackson (LABOUR)
## MSP Stirling

**Born:** Gainsborough, 1946

**Education:** Brigg High School for Girls, Lincolnshire; Hull and Stirling Universities.

**Career:** Chemistry Teacher; Research Fellow; Adviser in Education to Lothian Region and Edinburgh District; Lecturer, Faculty of Education, Edinburgh University; **1999:** elected MSP.

**Profile:** She is widowed with two sons. Fiercely intellectual, she has two undergraduate degrees, a PGCE and a PhD. Her association with Central Region Labour Party – having served as Secretary and Chairperson – and her constituency work have brought her considerable respect in the Stirling area and she gets a good press locally.

She has been a member of the Scottish Policy Forum and held the chair of Labour's Local Government Committee in Scotland. A thoughtful backbencher, she has initiated a number of member's debates, most notably the first examination of Cornton Vale prison and a discussion on how to regulate the body-piercing industry. She tends to operate on her own. Although she is not a star in the Chamber, she performs intelligently there and elsewhere, and – for a newcomer to an elected role – very promisingly.

**Committees:** Local Government (Deputy Convener).

**Contact:**  0131-348-5742 (Parliament)
01786-446515 (Constituency)
e-mail sylvia.jackson.msp@scottish.parliament.uk

**Cathy Jamieson** (LABOUR)
**Minister for Education and Young People**
**MSP Carrick, Cumnock and Doon Valley**

**Born:** Kilmarnock, 1956

**Education:** James Hamilton Academy, Kilmarnock;
Glasgow School of Art; Goldsmiths College;
Glasgow and Glasgow Caledonian Universities.

**Career: 1980–1:** Strathclyde Regional Council, Trainee Social
Worker; **1983–6:** Social Worker; **1986–8:** Community Intermediate
Treatment Worker; **1988–92:** Senior Intermediate Treatment Worker;
**1992–9:** Principal Officer, Who Cares? Scotland; **1999:** elected MSP.

**Profile:** She is married with one son. Despite her qualifications in art
therapy, she retrained in social work and became a senior IT worker.
She was then appointed Principal Officer of Who Cares? Scotland,
developing policy and legislation for young people in care. She was
also a member of the inquiry team which investigated child abuse in
Edinburgh's children's homes. Throughout, she has also managed to
be active at all levels of the Labour Party, including being elected to the
Scottish and National Executive. She does have a recreation, equally
consuming. She follows Kilmarnock Football Club – Cathy for Killie.

She is Deputy Leader of the Scottish Labour Party in Parliament. She is
absolutely not New Labour – in fact a member of the hard left Campaign
for Socialism – and is uncomfortable with the idea of coalition. She
played a key role in organising the process of finding a new First
Minister in 2001, though there had been rumours that she might run
up a left-wing flag herself. She is a surprise choice as Education
Minister and some cynics smell a deal. In fact, she has plenty of experience in the field, though rather less in office, and has decided to leave
the day-to-day running of schools to her deputy Nicol Stephen, while
she concentrates on the wider aspects of her portfolio.

**Contact:**  0131-348-5776 (Parliament)
         01290-422990 (Constituency)
         e-mail cathy.jamieson.msp@scottish.parliament.uk

# Margaret Jamieson (LABOUR)
## MSP Kilmarnock and Loudoun

**Born:** Kilmarnock, 1953

**Education:** Grange Academy; Kilmarnock; Ayr College.

**Career: 1969–74:** Cook, Ayrshire and Arran Health Board; **1974–5:** Cook, Welch Margetson; **1975–9:** Cook, Strathclyde Region; **1979–99:** Regional Officer, NUPE now UNISON; **1999:** elected MSP.

**Profile:** She is married with one daughter. A former cook in the NHS, she graduated to being a full-time union official and was the first woman to be so appointed by UNISON. She has chaired Scottish Labour's Women's Committee.

She is a member of the Health Committee and is often critical of Executive policy in that area, though she is otherwise loyal and rather quiet. She did lobby hard for the completion of the M77 link, which will add to her popularity at home in Ayrshire.

**Committees:** Audit; Health and Community Care (Deputy Convener).

**Contact:** 0131-348-5774 (Parliament)
01563-520267  Fax 01563-539439 (Constituency)
e-mail margaret.jamieson.msp@scottish.parliament.uk

**Ian Jenkins** (LIBERAL DEMOCRAT)
**MSP Tweeddale, Ettrick and Lauderdale**

**Born:** Rothesay, 1941

**Education:** Rothesay Academy; Glasgow University.

**Career: 1964–70:** Teacher, Clydebank High School;
**1970–99:** Principal Teacher, Peebles High School;
**1999:** elected MSP.

**Profile:** He is married and lives in the Borders. In a long teaching career, he held only two posts, which suggests deep commitment or lack of ambition. The former seems the more likely since he has also been a close supporter of David Steel for nearly thirty years, and chairman of Steel's local party for six of them.

He is Liberal spokesperson for Education, Culture and Sport, not simply because he is an ex-teacher, language scholar and rugby watcher. He is a rare bird in the Liberal flock – he seems loyal to the party leadership and constructive towards the coalition. He does make his views felt on policy towards education, on which he is so well qualified, but otherwise he is one of the quiet ones.

**Committees:** Subordinate Legislation (Deputy Convener); Education, Culture and Sport.

**Contact:** 0131-348-5802  Fax 0131-348-5964 (Parliament)
01896-831011  Fax 01896-831011 (Constituency)
e-mail ian.jenkins.msp@scottish.parliament.uk

**Alex Johnstone** (CONSERVATIVE)
**MSP (List) North-East Scotland**

**Born:** Stonehaven, 1961

**Education:** Mackie Academy, Stonehaven.

**Career: 1980– :** Self-employed, partner in family
farm; **1993– :** Principal partner; **1999:** elected MSP.

**Profile:** He is married with one son and one daughter. He is a real son
of the Mearns, with farming in the blood. He was active in the Young
Farmers movement at both local and national level, and is an elder of
the Kirk. He is a popular figure in the Chamber.

He was the Conservative spokesperson on Rural Affairs and Convener
of the Parliament's Rural Development Committee until June 2001
when he was promoted to become the Tories' Business manager and
Chief Whip. All three cross-party groups he attends have an agricultural bias. He handled himself well in the chair of the Rural
Development Committee when it considered the Bill on fox-hunting,
its most time-consuming and controversial business, although he did
use his casting vote at the crucial meeting when a Labour member was
absent. The Bill was rejected by the Committee as unworkable in its
present form, but Parliament nevertheless gave its approval in principle. He is a voice of moderation and good sense on the Conservative
benches and fully deserved his promotion.

**Contact:** 0131-348-5649 (Parliament)
        01589-740248 Fax 01589-741248 (Constituency)
        e-mail alexander.johnstone.msp@scottish.parliament.uk

**Andy Kerr** (LABOUR)
**Minister for Finance and Public Services**
**MSP East Kilbride**

**Born:** East Kilbride, 1962

**Education:** Claremont High School, East Kilbride;
Glasgow College.

**Career: 1987–90:** Research and Development Officer, Strathkelvin
District Council; **1990–3:** Managing Director, Achieving Quality
(Consultancy); **1993–9:** Strategy and Development Manager, Land
Services, Glasgow City Council; **1999:** elected MSP.

**Profile:** He is married with three daughters. He looks older than his
years, perhaps because of a taxing career in local-government services
or perhaps it's simply the hairstyle. Before entering local government,
he was a full-time officer with the National Union of Students. He
has proven organisational skills at both the professional and political
level and is in with the bricks of Lanarkshire Labour. He is a Rangers
supporter who worked with Frank McAveety, a Celtic supporter, in
Glasgow Council. It must have made for interesting conversations at
least four times a year.

He has been secretary of the East Kilbride Labour Party, Election
Agent for MP Adam Ingram, and is a member of UNISON. That solid
party background must have seemed to make him ideal for the
Convenership of the Transport and Environment Committee, but he
has been trouble for the Executive. He championed the case for
planning restrictions on mobile phone masts. He also led the opposition to Sarah Boyack's plans to switch trunk-road maintenance from
local authorities to private contractors after tendering. He later
maintained it was not the person but the process he disliked, though
observers could be forgiven for thinking it was both. Since he was successively secretary of the UK and the Scottish Association of Direct
Labour Organisations, it is clear where he was coming from. Until Jack
McConnell became First Minister, it was less clear where he was going
to. He was McConnell's campaign organiser (both in 2000 and in
2001) and was suitably rewarded. No-one would have been surprised
if he had become Business Manager – he's a superb fixer – but the
post of Finance Minister may prove a step too far. Still, Jack has done

the job himself and needs a 'trusty' to do for him what Angus Mackay did for Henry McLeish.

**Contact:** 0131-348-5902 (Parliament)
01355-606223  Fax 01355-806434 (Constituency)
e-mail andy.kerr.msp@scottish.parliament.uk

## Johann Lamont (LABOUR)
## MSP Glasgow Pollok

**Born:** Glasgow, 1957

**Education:** Woodside Secondary School, Glasgow; Glasgow and Strathclyde Universities; Jordanhill College.

**Career: 1979–99:** Teacher of English and History; **1999:** elected MSP.

**Profile:** She is married, to the Glasgow Councillor Archie Graham, with one son and one daughter, and is a constant campaigner for women's rights and representation. With Margaret Curran, she helped found the Scottish Labour Women's Caucus. She was one of those in the former Hillhead constituency who tried to deselect George Galloway. She taught history in Glasgow and Rothesay and is identified with community projects in Education and Social Work in Castlemilk in particular. She speaks Gaelic and was the first person to use it in debate. She likes country music and runs long distances.

She is a former Chairperson of the Scottish Labour Party but was voted off the Executive in a right-wing purge instigated, it was thought, by the then Shadow Scottish Secretary, George Robertson. During the heated debate on the Bill to abolish warrant sales, sponsored by Tommy Sheridan, she made an impassioned and effective plea for the Executive not to ignore the strength of support for the Bill on Labour's backbenches. In the reorganisation of ministries and committees after Henry McLeish's election as First Minister, she became a deputy whip to Tom McCabe and Convener of the Social Justice Committee. That gave her a crucial role in the consideration of the Housing Bill and she was an invaluable ally for her close friend and colleague Margaret Curran, the Deputy Minister who saw the bill through. Johann Lamont has pursued the issue of sexual violence against women and redoubled her efforts after Lord Abernethy delivered himself of the debatable conclusion that 'sex without consent is not in itself rape'.

**Committees:** Social Justice (Convener).

**Contact:**  0131-348-5846 (Parliament)
0141-621-1213 Fax 0141-621-0606 (Constituency)
e-mail johann.lamont.msp@scottish.parliament.uk

## Marilyn Livingstone (LABOUR)
## MSP Kirkcaldy

**Born:** Kirkcaldy, 1949

**Education:** Viewforth Secondary School, Kirkcaldy; Fife College.

**Career:** Head of Business School, Fife College; Councillor, Fife; **1999:** elected MSP.

**Profile:** Her entry on the Scottish Parliament website and in other publications giving the barest biographical details. What secrets lie behind this sparsity? In fact, she suffered a long period of illness last year and has not yet been seen at her best.

She is Convener of the Labour group and, though Cathy Jamieson as Deputy Leader now shares the responsibility, she is a channel for communicating grassroot concerns and preoccupations. She is thought to have carried the cleft stick during the warrant sales debate, bearing the message that the backbenches were in favour of abolition. She is a close friend of Henry McLeish and was a trusted intermediary during his period as First Minister. She served on the Kerley Committee on local government democracy and, with Sandra Osborne (MP for Ayr), wrote a minority report dissenting from the recommendation that proportional representation be introduced to local-government elections. She argued for the direct link between councillor and ward that comes from first past the post.

**Committees:** Enterprise and Lifelong Learning.

**Contact:** 0131-348-5744 (Parliament)
01592-564114 Fax 01592-561085 (Constituency)
e-mail marilyn.livingstone.msp@scottish.parliament.uk

# Richard Lochhead (SNP)
## MSP (List) North-East Scotland

**Born:** Paisley, 1969

**Education:** Williamwood High School, Clarkston; Stirling University.

**Career: 1987–9:** Clerical Trainee, SSEB; **1994–8:** Office Manager for Alex Salmond; **1998–9:** Economic Development Officer, Dundee City Council; **1999:** elected MSP.

**Profile:** He went later to university, then added an HNC in Business Studies (from Glasgow College of Commerce) to his politics degree from Stirling. His first job was running Alex Salmond's office, so he knows where the bodies are buried and the causes of death.

He is the SNP's fisheries spokesperson and, though he had his moments during the Great Fishing Fiasco, he was not unnaturally overshadowed by Swinney and Salmond when the Nats trained their big guns on the Executive's disorganised defences. He is quietly spoken, works tirelessly and efficiently behind the scenes but needs to brush up and brighten his public performances. His application has been rewarded by the likelihood that he will lead the SNP's attack on the Executive's plans for the water industry. Step forward, Richard, this is your big chance.

**Committees:** Rural Development.

**Contact:** 0131-348-5713  Fax 0131-348-5737 (Parliament)
01224-632150 (Constituency)
e-mail richard.lochhead.msp@scottish.parliament.uk

**George Lyon** (LIBERAL DEMOCRAT)
**MSP Argyll and Bute**

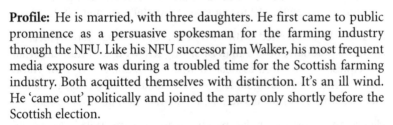

**Born:** Rothesay, 1956

**Education:** Rothesay Academy.

**Career: 1972–92:** Family farming business;
**1987:** Nuffield Scholar, New Zealand;
**1992– :** Own farming business; **1996–7:** Vice-President Scottish NFU;
**1997–9:** President Scottish NFU; **1999:** elected MSP.

**Profile:** He is married, with three daughters. He first came to public prominence as a persuasive spokesman for the farming industry through the NFU. Like his NFU successor Jim Walker, his most frequent media exposure was during a troubled time for the Scottish farming industry. Both acquitted themselves with distinction. It's an ill wind. He 'came out' politically and joined the party only shortly before the Scottish election.

He did not, as some expected, get the Rural portfolio in the Coalition Executive – no doubt on the grounds that he was too close to the farming community. He is Convenor of the Lib Dem group and speaks on Agriculture, Home Affairs and Land Reform. Unlike some of his LibDem colleagues, he seems able to cope with being part of a coalition without deep offence to his political principles, partly because he hates the Nats. He has held the Executive to account on the ferry services to the Isles on which his constituents depend. On the other hand, he has defended the Coalition's policy on the fishing industry when some of his colleagues deserted the cause. In the run up to the general election of 2001, he began to take a much more critical line on the performance of Labour ministers, accusing them of paying more attention to their own advancement than their portfolios. Deep disenchantment or plain electioneering? Whichever, it was a little rich from a man who does not disguise his own ambition or good opinion of himself. He looks and sounds like a candidate for office even though he pronounces hyperbole (not a word in the Liberal lexicon) as if it was the venue for an American football match.

**Committees:** Justice 2.

**Contact:** 0131-348-5787 Fax 0131-348-5807 (Parliament)
        01700-504237 (Constituency)
        e-mail george.lyon.msp@scottish.parliament.uk

## John McAllion (LABOUR)
### MSP Dundee East

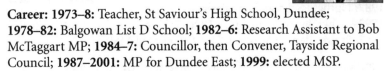

**Born:** Glasgow, 1948

**Education:** St Augustine's, Glasgow; St Andrews
University.

**Career: 1973–8:** Teacher, St Saviour's High School, Dundee;
**1978–82:** Balgowan List D School; **1982–6:** Research Assistant to Bob
McTaggart MP; **1984–7:** Councillor, then Convener, Tayside Regional
Council; **1987–2001:** MP for Dundee East; **1999:** elected MSP.

**Profile:** He is married with two sons. Unlike the stereotypical St
Andrews graduate, he is a man of strong left-wing and humanitarian
principles. He has been associated with CND, Shelter, War on Want,
Medical Aid for Nicaragua, Defence of Cuba – a collection of causes
that speak volumes for his activist credentials and personal credo.

He was an opposition spokesman between 1994 and 1996 but resigned
over Tony Blair's policy for a two-question referendum on Scottish
devolution. His home rule convictions have always been unshakeable,
and he joined Scotland United in the dark days of the 1980s when the
cause seemed lost and when many in his own party were ambivalent if
not downright hostile. He also supports another constitutional cause
with few adherents in the Labour Party – electoral reform. In debates in
the Scottish Parliament he has often found himself in agreement with
the awkward squad – Canavan and Sheridan (McAllion and Alex Neil
co-sponsored Sheridan's Warrant Sales Bill) – but he so far seems to be
tolerated by Labour as an honest doubter rather than a troublemaker.
He has put his name to a Bill to provide universal free school meals,
also sponsored by Sheridan and Neil, and that may result in action
against him by the Labour Whips. As a strong believer in the need for
Parliament to be open to the electorate, he was an ideal choice as
Convener of the Committee on Public Petitions, though it was a more
junior position than someone of his experience might have expected.
He would have stood for the leadership himself in 2001, but could not
find enough names for his nomination.

**Committees:** Public Petitions (Convener); Health and Community Care.

**Contact:** 0131-348-5931 (Parliament)
          01382-207000 Fax 01382-221280 (Constituency)
          e-mail john.mcallion.msp@scottish.parliament.uk

## Kenny MacAskill (SNP)
## MSP (List) Lothian

**Born:** Edinburgh, 1958

**Education:** Linlithgow Academy; Edinburgh University.

**Career:** Senior Partner, Edinburgh Solicitors; Director, Legal Services Agency; **1999:** elected MSP.

**Profile:** He is married, with two sons. He has one of the loudest and least mellifluous voices in the Scottish Parliament – the kind of voice that would rally a Scottish football crowd behind the national team. At least it would if he got as far as the stadium without being taken into custody for having drunk too well from the cup of patriotism, a fate that befell him on a recent trip to Wembley. Of course, it was all a misunderstanding and he was released after the match.

He has held several senior posts in the SNP, and stood for election at every level, despite having been something of a conspirator in his early years in the party. In those days he was close to Alex Salmond and – as a member of the '79 Group – was expelled with him from the SNP. The relationship seems to have cooled since those heady days. Certainly he lacks Salmond's subtlety. He led the SNP's campaign against the poll tax in the late 1980s, an odd involvement for a lawyer, but his brash and impetuous style offered many a hostage to fortune. He is now the SNP's spokesperson on Tourism, Transport and Telecommunications, and is clearly trying to develop a more constructive line. He has accepted Swinney's lead with apparent enthusiasm, despite being narrowly defeated by Roseanna Cunningham for the Deputy's job. He brings colour and passion to the front bench, but when he speaks you sense the leadership have their fingers crossed under the desk.

**Committees:** Enterprise and Lifelong Learning.

**Contact:** 0131-348-5722 Fax 0131-348-5737 (Parliament)
            0131-525-8916 (Constituency)
            e-mail kenny.macaskill.msp@scottish.parliament.uk

# Frank McAveety (LABOUR)
## MSP Glasgow Shettleston

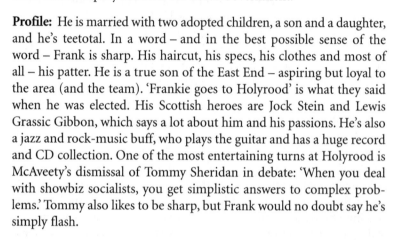

**Born:** Glasgow, 1962

**Education:** All Saints Secondary, Glasgow; Strathclyde University.

**Career: 1984–94:** Teacher, Glasgow; **1994–9:** Teacher, Renfrewshire; **1988–99:** Councillor, Glasgow District then Glasgow City; **1997–9:** Leader, Glasgow City Council; **1999:** elected MSP; **1999–2000:** Deputy Minister for Local Government.

**Profile:** He is married with two adopted children, a son and a daughter, and he's teetotal. In a word – and in the best possible sense of the word – Frank is sharp. His haircut, his specs, his clothes and most of all – his patter. He is a true son of the East End – aspiring but loyal to the area (and the team). 'Frankie goes to Holyrood' is what they said when he was elected. His Scottish heroes are Jock Stein and Lewis Grassic Gibbon, which says a lot about him and his passions. He's also a jazz and rock-music buff, who plays the guitar and has a huge record and CD collection. One of the most entertaining turns at Holyrood is McAveety's dismissal of Tommy Sheridan in debate: 'When you deal with showbiz socialists, you get simplistic answers to complex problems.' Tommy also likes to be sharp, but Frank would no doubt say he's simply flash.

He was the youngest ever leader of Glasgow Council, when the Labour Party picked him to rescue the city from the bitter, internecine feud between the Strathclyde faction (led by Robert Gould) and the Glasgow faction (led by Pat Lally). He was rewarded – with the post of Deputy Minister for Local Government, though some say he didn't buckle down and work as hard as he ought. When Donald Dewar died, he unwisely declared for Jack McConnell in the leadership election, before changing his mind and switching to Henry McLeish. If he had stuck to his guns, McLeish might have worried that dropping him looked too much like petty revenge. At any rate, he was sacked and – if Labour lose their battle to transfer Glasgow housing away from municipal control – it will partly be because McAveety wasn't there to argue for it in his inimitable hustling style. It was thought that McConnell might have picked him for just that role – but he must wait a bit longer to come back. However, come back he will.

**Committees:** Education, Culture and Sport (Deputy Convener); Procedures; Standards.

**Contact:** 0131-348-5906 (Parliament)
0141-764-0175 (Constituency)
e-mail frank.mcaveety.msp@scottish.parliament.uk

# Tom McCabe (LABOUR)
## MSP Hamilton South

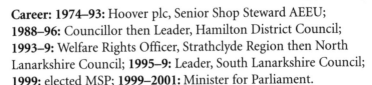

**Born:** Hamilton, 1954

**Education:** St Martin's School, Hamilton; Bell
College of Technology.

**Career: 1974–93:** Hoover plc, Senior Shop Steward AEEU;
**1988–96:** Councillor then Leader, Hamilton District Council;
**1993–9:** Welfare Rights Officer, Strathclyde Region then North
Lanarkshire Council; **1995–9:** Leader, South Lanarkshire Council;
**1999:** elected MSP; **1999–2001:** Minister for Parliament.

**Profile:** He is divorced and recently split from his long-term partner
Lorraine Davidson, Political Editor of the *Scottish Mirror*. The number of
Labour figures with a media relationship is probably unsurprising in a
country like Scotland, with such a small political elite, but it does not
pass unnoticed by opponents when the going gets tough. Tom McCabe
is tough enough himself to take criticism and lob it back. With the
demise of Hoover, he made a career change into social work and – his
local-government role already well established – conducted the dual
role of which Mrs Thatcher so heartily disapproved: working in local
government while also an elected representative.

His was the first seat to declare in the Scottish elections, so he was the
first MSP to be confirmed. With his reputation made in the rough –
and not problem-free – arena of Lanarkshire politics, he was a sound
if not inspired choice as Minister for Parliament. Every administration
needs someone like Tom McCabe to hold things together. Donald
Dewar declared him one of the successes of the Executive, but his luck
and his patience have recently run out. He was involved in a bad-tem-
pered (on his part) spat with Sir David Steel when the Presiding
Officer took exception to the Executive's growing habit of explaining
policy to the press before Parliament. He also attacked Sir David for
exercising his casting vote in favour of the opposition in a debate on
fishing when he (McCabe) had failed to deliver the number of Labour
MSPs needed to carry the day. He was openly contemptuous of his Lib
Dem partners – some of them are indeed unwhippable – and seemed
not always able to distinguish between his responsibilities to
Parliament and his role in the Executive. He was pressing Henry
McLeish for a move to a spending department which – since he is

often disappointingly inarticulate and frequently performs poorly in the Chamber – might just have been a job too far. In any event, with the demise of Henry, Tom was also considered expendable and the new First Minister replaced him with an altogether less abrasive personality, Patricia Ferguson.

**Committees:** Finance.

**Contact:** 0131-348-5830 Fax 0131-348-5562 (Parliament)
01698-454018 (Constituency)
e-mail tom.mccabe.msp@scottish.parliament.uk

## Jack McConnell (LABOUR)
### First Minister
### MSP Motherwell and Wishaw

**Born:** Irvine, 1960

**Education:** Arran High School; Stirling University.

**Career: 1983–92:** Maths Teacher, Lornshill Academy;
**1984–93:** Councillor, finally Leader, Stirling District Council;
**1992–8:** General Secretary, Scottish Labour Party; **1998:** Chief
Executive, Public Affairs Europe Ltd; **1999:** elected MSP;
**1999–2000:** Minister for Finance; **2000–01:** Minister for Education,
Europe and External Affairs.

**Profile:** He is married with one son and one daughter. In his progress
to the First Minister's post, he volunteered the admission of a past
affair with a Labour Party colleague. The nickname, though hardly
original, is 'Jack the Lad' and in some senses it fits. He is a hustling,
hail-fellow, no-nonsense operator who likes to convey the impression
that what you see is what you get. In fact, the operation is a great deal
more sophisticated and self-interested than is immediately apparent.
He likes to be in charge, he wants to be in charge, and now he is. For
him more than almost anyone else, however, Donald Dewar's departure seemed to have come too early. He swithered momentarily about
competing for the leadership, but only momentarily. When he
decided to run, to lay down his ambitious marker, he campaigned
with a speed and vigour that made Henry McLeish look slow and over-
confident.

He had a sticky start to his Executive career with 'Lobbygate' and –
though he was cleared of impropriety – he was damaged and took
time to recover. None of his Cabinet colleagues backed him in his leadership challenge (or his second), but his performance was so surprisingly good that he left the new First Minister with a problem – how to
recognise him but neutralise him. Henry McLeish offered him
Education – a big ministry with major outstanding problems, including the reform of the SQA and implementation of the McCrone
Report. He reached a settlement with the teachers on McCrone, which
– though an expensive one – might be a new start for Scottish education. The SQA is improved but still has some way to go. To claim the
ultimate prize, he just had to do his job well and hope that Henry

failed to excel in his. And that's exactly what happened, give or take a few details. He had no competitors for the First Minister's job and, as with his predecessor, the greatest threat comes from himself.

Always a risk-taker, he swept obvious McLeish supporters and some talented politicians from his administration and replaced them with ministers whose loyalty to him is greater than their experience, including some who have gone directly to senior Cabinet portfolios. In some lights, it looks unnecessarily triumphalist and vindictive; in others, it suggests an end to internal bickering and factionalism – till the election of 2003, at least. When he let it be known that he wanted Cathy Peattie for Deputy Presiding Officer, Parliament gave its verdict on his approach to personnel management: it moved, not against Cathy Peattie, but against him, and elected Murray Tosh. So the presiding panel has no Labour members and no women. There's a lesson there that he needed to learn.

**Contact:**  0131-348-5831 (Parliament)
          01698-303040  Fax 01698-303060 (Constituency)
          e-mail jack.mcconnell.msp@scottish.parliament.uk

**Dr Lewis Macdonald** (LABOUR)
**Deputy Minister for Enterprise, Transport and
Lifelong Learning**
**MSP Aberdeen Central**

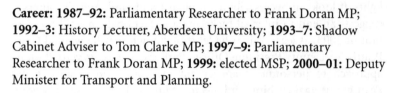

**Born:** Stornoway, 1957

**Education:** Inverurie Academy; Aberdeen University.

**Career: 1987–92:** Parliamentary Researcher to Frank Doran MP;
**1992–3:** History Lecturer, Aberdeen University; **1993–7:** Shadow
Cabinet Adviser to Tom Clarke MP; **1997–9:** Parliamentary
Researcher to Frank Doran MP; **1999:** elected MSP; **2000–01:** Deputy
Minister for Transport and Planning.

**Profile:** He is married, with two daughters. He is a son of the manse,
born on Lewis, but brought up and educated in Aberdeen since the age
of eleven. In addition to his experience as a political researcher, he has
a PhD – completed in Lagos and in Aberdeen – on malnutrition in
Nigeria during the civil war. He was the first post-graduate at
Aberdeen University to get a doctorate in African Studies.

He's a member of Labour's Scottish Executive and gave an intelligent
performance as a backbencher on the Mound, never acting like a party
patsy who has lodged his brains with the Whip's office, and making
conspicuous contributions in Committee. His solid Convenership of
the Holyrood Progress Group brought its reward when Sam Galbraith
resigned and he was given a ministerial post in McLeish's redistribu-
tion of functions. He became Deputy Minister to Sarah Boyack in
Transport and Planning and, safe and sound, he performed competently rather than outstandingly. With Wendy Alexander, he may have
to improve on that.

**Contact:** 0131-348-5915 (Parliament)
            01224-647846 (Constituency)
            e-mail lewis.macdonald.msp@scottish.parliament.uk

## Margo Macdonald (SNP)
## MSP (List) Lothian

**Born:** Hamilton, 1944

**Education:** Hamilton Academy; Dunfermline College.

**Career: 1963–5:** Teacher; **1965–73:** Barmaid, wife and mother; **1973–4:** MP Glasgow Govan; **1974–8:** Writer/Broadcaster; **1978–81:** Director, Shelter Scotland; **1981–3:** Broadcaster, Radio Forth; **1983–5:** Editor, Topical Programmes; **1985–91:** Reporter/Presenter, current affairs and politics programmes; former Chief Executive, Network Scotland; **1999:** elected MSP.

**Profile:** She is married, for the second time, to ex-MP Jim Sillars. They have four grown-up children between them, and live – two red refugees from the west of Scotland – in south Edinburgh. Margo is an ex-gym teacher and beauty queen who helped out behind the bar of her first husband's pub when their children were small. She must have been its greatest asset. In 1973, with vigorous idealism and winning personality, she took Govan in a by-election from the enfeebled grasp of the moribund local Labour organisation. Unlike the other SNP heroine, Winnie Ewing, she was popular at Westminster for the year she was there, but lost her seat in the subsequent general election. She was Deputy Leader of the SNP from 1974 to 1979 – effectively its champion at home – during the party's best ever representation in the House of Commons, but what might have happened had she remained at Westminster? In the intervening years, though still a popular figure, she left the party for a decade after the suspension of the leaders of the '79 Group. Since then, political power has eluded her and she seems disillusioned, even bitter, that she has not had her due.

She has no Shadow Cabinet role in the SNP, but still commands the attention of Parliament when she speaks from her slightly isolated seat at the back of the Chamber. Like her husband Jim Sillars – now outside the party hierarchy but never outside politics – she believes the present leadership cannot be trusted to pursue independence with absolute dedication. In fact, it's hard to know whom she trusts these days. Her unceasing campaign against the site, design and cost of the new Parliament building is a measure of her conviction that Scotland is still being run by a parcel of rogues. There are suggestions that she might join Canavan and Sheridan in a Scottish Socialist alliance, but perhaps she wants the distinction of being the lone voice in the wilderness, the voice of the people, La Reine Margo.

**Committees:** Subordinate Legislation (Convener).

**Contact:** 0131-348-5715 Fax 0131-348-5716 (Parliament)
0131-525-8916 (Constituency)
e-mail margo.macdonald.msp@scottish.parliament.uk

## Jamie McGrigor (CONSERVATIVE)
## MSP (List) Highlands and Islands

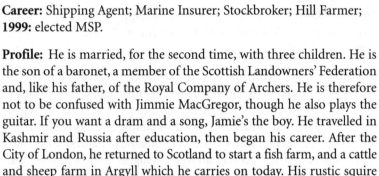

**Born:** London, 1949

**Education:** Cladich School, Argyll; Eton College; Neuchatel University, Switzerland.

**Career:** Shipping Agent; Marine Insurer; Stockbroker; Hill Farmer; **1999:** elected MSP.

**Profile:** He is married, for the second time, with three children. He is the son of a baronet, a member of the Scottish Landowners' Federation and, like his father, of the Royal Company of Archers. He is therefore not to be confused with Jimmie MacGregor, though he also plays the guitar. If you want a dram and a song, Jamie's the boy. He travelled in Kashmir and Russia after education, then began his career. After the City of London, he returned to Scotland to start a fish farm, and a cattle and sheep farm in Argyll which he carries on today. His rustic squire appearance should not mislead the innocent observer. His involvement in local affairs in Loch Awe is more than *noblesse oblige*, though his membership of the Crofters Union must give rise to a joke or two.

He is the Conservative's Deputy Spokesperson on Rural Affairs, with special responsibility for fishing. In the great fishing debate of 2001, he allowed himself to be persuaded to accept an SNP amendment in favour of a tie-up scheme when his own decommissioning motion was the more sound proposal. Opposition determination to gub the government seemed to overcome good argument. He did, however, speak boldly for the uncompensated West Coast scallop fisherman. As an angler himself, he feels a bond.

**Committees:** Equal Opportunities; Rural Development.

**Contact:** 0131-348-5648 (Parliament)
01546-606586 Fax 01546-606387 (Constituency)
e-mail jamie.mcgrigor.msp@scottish.parliament.uk

**Irene McGugan** (SNP)
**MSP (List) North-East Scotland**

**Born:** Angus, 1952

**Education:** Forfar Academy; Robert Gordon's
Institute, Aberdeen; Dundee University.

**Career: 1985–96:** Social Worker, Tayside Region;
**1996–9:** Childcare Manager, Social Work, Angus Council;
**1999:** elected MSP.

**Profile:** She is married with one son and one daughter. She did Voluntary Service Overseas in a rural school in India and then voluntary work on her return to Scotland before resuming her studies. She began with a social work qualification before obtaining an advanced certificate in child protection studies. Although she lives in Forfar, where she went to school, she has been a leading campaigner in Skye Bridge tolls. It may seem a long way from loon toon, but it's the principle. She is a Kirk elder and has probably been in the Assembly Hall wearing a different hat (and allowed keep to keep it on her head).

She is a keen campaigner for the use of the Scots language in Parliament. A newcomer to the business of elected responsibility, she has made a quietly effective start without turning any heads. She is often confused with her friend Fiona MacLeod, but asks more questions.

**Committees:** Education, Culture and Sport.

**Contact:**  0131-348-5711 Fax 0131-348-5944 (Parliament)
01224-623150 (Constituency)
e-mail irene.mcgugan.msp@scottish.parliament.uk

# Kenneth Macintosh (LABOUR)
## MSP Eastwood

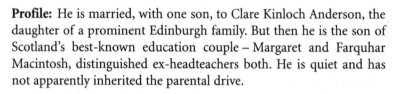

**Born:** Inverness, 1962

**Education:** Royal High School, Edinburgh;
Edinburgh University.

**Career: 1987–99:** BBC News and Current Affairs Producer;
**1999:** elected MSP.

**Profile:** He is married, with one son, to Clare Kinloch Anderson, the daughter of a prominent Edinburgh family. But then he is the son of Scotland's best-known education couple – Margaret and Farquhar Macintosh, distinguished ex-headteachers both. He is quiet and has not apparently inherited the parental drive.

On the Finance Committee in 2000, he was appointed reporter for the investigation into the (then) true cost of the new Holyrood Parliament building. Fortunately, no-one suggested shooting the messenger. Earlier in the Parliament, he had a tendency to ask questions that were loyal almost to the point of sycophancy. He has the right stuff but will have to find another way of endearing himself.

**Committees:** Enterprise and Lifelong Learning; Procedures (Deputy
Convener); Standards.

**Contact:**  0131-348-5897 (voicemail only) (Parliament)
0141-644-3330 (all telephone enquiries) (Constituency)
e-mail kenneth.macintosh.msp@scottish.parliament.uk

**Lyndsay McIntosh** (CONSERVATIVE)
**MSP (List) Central Scotland**

**Born:** Glasgow, 1955

**Education:** Duncanrig Secondary, Glasgow;
Langside College; Abertay University.

**Career: 1973–5:** Legal Secretary; **1975–84:** Civil Servant;
**1984–96:** Housewife/mother; **1996–9:** Business Consultant;
**1999:** elected MSP.

**Profile:** She is married with one son and one daughter. She is a late developer in personal and career terms, starting out as a legal secretary then progressing to a post-graduate diploma in management studies. Her website entry tells us that 'she lived in Saudi Arabia for two years and then joined the Ladies Circle, PTA and the Tory Party', though it doesn't say if that was the right order. Who says travel does not broaden the mind?

She was the Conservative's Deputy Spokesperson on Home Affairs, with specific responsibility for drugs policy, and is now their spokesperson on Social Justice. Her views on law and order are chillingly close to Anne Widdecombe's, so it should be an enlightening experience for all of us, and she looks such a homely body, too. She would like the Tory Party to be more conspicuously Scottish.

**Committees:** Social Justice.

**Contact:**  0131-348-5639 Fax 0141-348-5655 (Parliament)
01236-426667 Fax 01236-434856 (Constituency)
e-mail lyndsay.mcintosh.msp@scottish.parliament.uk

# Angus MacKay (LABOUR)
## MSP Edinburgh South

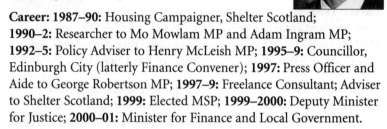

**Born:** Edinburgh, 1964

**Education:** St Augustine's High School, Edinburgh; Edinburgh University.

**Career: 1987–90:** Housing Campaigner, Shelter Scotland; **1990–2:** Researcher to Mo Mowlam MP and Adam Ingram MP; **1992–5:** Policy Adviser to Henry McLeish MP; **1995–9:** Councillor, Edinburgh City (latterly Finance Convener); **1997:** Press Officer and Aide to George Robertson MP; **1997–9:** Freelance Consultant; Adviser to Shelter Scotland; **1999:** Elected MSP; **1999–2000:** Deputy Minister for Justice; **2000–01:** Minister for Finance and Local Government.

**Profile:** He is presentable, modest, intelligent and married. Apart from being a former employee of Shelter, he's also a member of Amnesty International (and the RSPB), so sensitive and principled can be added to the list of epithets. In fact, he seems a thoroughly decent bloke with a cv heavy on New Labour credentials, though is said to be a shade lazy.

He was one of the small band for whom a dazzling future was predicted on election to Parliament and he hasn't disappointed. He distinguished himself in his first post, as Deputy to Jim Wallace at Justice, where he looked after drugs policy among other things. In the reshuffle when McLeish became First Minister, he was promoted to the top job in Finance and Local Government, for which his Edinburgh City Council experience suited him. It is, however, a job in which enemies can be made just as easily as friends, so it represented a true test of his political skills as well as his prowess at sums. He was also building the bonfire of the quangos, though that had been a modest conflagration thus far. His review of the Executive's finances and spending commitments, though ritually criticised by opponents, looked sound enough and seemed to have found the money for the package on care of the elderly. He had been Henry McLeish's campaign manager and was critical of Jack McConnell, so took his dismissal on the chin. He's able and should make a comeback.

**Committees:** Transport and the Environment.

**Contact:** 0131-348-5025 (Parliament)
0131-348-5025 Fax 0131-348-5576 (Constituency)
e-mail angus.mackay.msp@scottish.parliament.uk

# Kate Maclean (LABOUR)
## MSP Dundee West

**Born:** Dundee, 1958

**Education:** Craigie High School, Dundee.

**Career: 1988–99:** Councillor, Dundee District then Dundee City Council; **1990–2:** Chief Whip, Dundee District; **1992–9:** Leader of Administration, Dundee District then Dundee City Council; **1996–9:** Vice-President, CoSLA; **1999:** elected MSP.

**Profile:** She is divorced with one daughter and one son. She honestly and bravely admitted to the Big Issue that she had once smoked cannabis. The Labour Party didn't like it (her public admission that is) but she was unrepentant, having cleared it first with her children rather than the Whips. She has managed a dual role as single mother and elected representative since she became a councillor in the late 1980s.

Like her Dundee and left-wing comrade John McAllion, she might have assumed that her experience would be put to good use in the administration. She claims, however, to be happy as a backbencher and not to be tempted by office. In fact, she was offered the Social Justice brief by Jack McConnell and declined. She thinks the high proportion of women in the Scottish Parliament means that a wider range of subjects are debated. Thanks to the Committee system, the legislative scope is also wider. She is Convener of the Equal Opportunities Committee, which has a wide remit and can in many ways set the tone for modern Scotland. She says that's the most rewarding part of her work, but there must be a grudging feeling that she hasn't quite made the grade.

**Committees:** Equal Opportunities (Convener).

**Contact:** 0131-348-5758 (Parliament)
            01382-207007 Fax 01382-206714 (Constituency)
            e-mail kate.maclean.msp@scottish.parliament.uk

# Henry McLeish (LABOUR)
## MSP Fife Central

**Born:** Methil, 1948

**Education:** Buckhaven High School; Heriot Watt University.

**Career: 1973–4:** Planning Officer, Glenrothes Development Corporation; **1974–5:** Research Officer, Edinburgh Social Work Department; **1974–7:** Councillor, Kirkcaldy District Council; **1975–85:** Planning and Employment Officer, Dunfermline District Council; **1977–87:** Councillor, then Leader, Fife Regional Council; **1985–7:** Employment Co-ordinator; **1973–87:** Part-time Lecturer, Heriot Watt University; **1984–7:** Part-time Consultant on employment matters; **1987–2001:** MP for Central Fife; **1997–9:** Minister of State, Scottish Office; **1999:** elected MSP; **1999–2000:** Minister for Enterprise and Lifelong Learning; **2000–01:** First Minister.

**Profile:** The First Minister is married, for the second time, and has a son and daughter, plus a stepson and stepdaughter. His first wife died tragically young, but he rebuilt his personal and political life. As a young man, he played professional football for East Fife and he has turned this passable prowess to political advantage. It's a solid point of contact with the electorate, together with his humble background. He is built like a bustling midfielder, more application than flair, and that also describes his general characteristics. He is immensely hard working and undoubtedly ambitious. His close-quarter work is impressive, but he's a poor public speaker, whose verbal gaffes and facial muscles betray nerves under pressure.

McLeish's previous ability to keep out of trouble – like avoiding any fallout from the Jason Campbell affair or the SQA fiasco – deserted him in the top job. His determination to make a break from the Dewar regime – in style as well as content – resulted in uncertainty in public perception. His confused stance over personal care for the elderly, in which he surrendered to a vote in Parliament and seemed not to back his own health minister, typified his performance. He often took the populist but expensive option and sometimes failed to back his ministers publicly. After the 2001 election, he made deeply unflattering remarks about Brian Wilson and John Reid while still wearing a radio microphone and had to grovel apologetically. Despite this record, and increasing disquiet amongst some of his colleagues, the Opposition failed to land a serious blow on him until details of his office expenses – claimed when he was an MP at Westminster – began to be made public in dribs and reluctant drabs. The relentless prosecution by David McLetchie of the Conservatives, the piecemeal and unconvincing explanations by the First Minister himself, and the increasing hostility of the media combined to force McLeish's resignation. In a dignified personal statement he announced his decision to return to the backbenches, barely a year after his election as First Minister of Scotland.

**Contact:** 0131-244-5213 Fax 0131-244-6915 (Parliament)
01592-755540 Fax 01592-610325 (Constituency)
e-mail henry.mcleish.msp@scottish.parliament.uk

## Fiona McLeod (SNP)
## MSP (List) West of Scotland

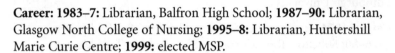

**Born:** Glasgow, 1957

**Education:** Bearsden Academy; Edinburgh, Glasgow and Strathclyde Universities.

**Career: 1983–7:** Librarian, Balfron High School; **1987–90:** Librarian, Glasgow North College of Nursing; **1995–8:** Librarian, Huntershill Marie Curie Centre; **1999:** elected MSP.

**Profile:** She is married with one son. Her wide experience as a librarian have given her a particular speciality – an interest in information technology. Every one thinks it is a good thing, but Fiona McLeod proves in debate that she actually understands it and its importance.

She appeared to come from nowhere to make the SNP list, and has not made much of a stir so far, except in her IT interventions and her objections to the subsidies for Hampden Park. Like her friend Irene McGugan, she is a supporter of the Scots language.

**Committees:** Transport and the Environment.

**Contact:**  0131-348-5670  Fax 0131-348-5957 (Parliament)
        01475-806020  Fax 01475-806021 (Constituency)
        e-mail fiona.mcleod.msp@scottish.parliament.uk

**David McLetchie** (CONSERVATIVE)
**Leader, Scottish Conservative Party**
**MSP (List) Lothian**

**Born:** Edinburgh, 1952

**Education:** George Heriot's School, Edinburgh;
Edinburgh University.

**Career: 1974–6:** Apprentice Solicitor, Shepherd & Wedderburn;
**1976–80:** Solicitor, Tods Murray; **1980– :** Partner, Tods Murray;
**1994–7:** President, Scottish Conservative and Unionist Association;
**1998:** Elected Leader, Scottish Conservative Candidates Group;
**1999:** elected MSP, Leader of the Scottish Conservative Party.

**Profile:** He is married, for the second time after being widowed, and
has one son. He has been in and around the Conservative Party and its
councils for all his adult life, starting as a Young Conservative and in
student politics. He spoke at grown-up conferences even then, sounding
like a young fogey (Scottish style) before the phrase was invented. He
was measured and avuncular, very much as he is today. That's not to
say he hasn't changed at all; he has learned many tricks along the way
and there are some who say the avuncular touch is misleading – he's
not half as nice as he seems.

His progress through the ranks of the Conservative Party was so extra-
ordinarily well timed, it is tempting to assume it wasn't accidental. He
was Vice-President, then President of the Association over five years
until 1997, from which platform he was elected as leader of the party's
candidates in 1998. On election, he became party leader and has since
acted with wit and guile without ever threatening to do real damage
until McLeish's 'Officegate'. In fairness, his group of nineteen (eighteen
elected from regional lists) is undistinguished and there is widespread
concern in senior Tory circles that they may be selected unchallenged
for the next election. There is also criticism on policy grounds. In an
effort to give the party a distinctive and appropriate Scottish voice, the
parliamentary group has supported some very un-Tory spending commitments rather than simply defend the faith and the taxpayer. Yet,
after his highly successful if slightly sanctimonious pursuit of Henry
McLeish, his own position is unassailable.

**Contact:**  0131-348-5659  Fax 0131-348-5935 (Parliament)
          0131-557-5168  Fax 0131-557-6682 (Constituency)
          e-mail david.mcletchie.msp@scottish.parliament.uk

## Michael McMahon (LABOUR)
### MSP Hamilton North and Bellshill

**Born:** Lanark, 1961

**Education:** Our Lady's High School, Motherwell; Glasgow Caledonian University.

**Career: 1977–92:** Welder, Terex Equipment Ltd; **1992–6:** full-time student; **1996–9:** Researcher; **1999:** elected MSP.

**Profile:** He is married with one son and two daughters. After leaving school, he was a welder for fifteen years before taking the brave decision of going to university. He graduated with an Honours degree in Politics and Sociology from Glasgow Caledonian. Since the start of his welding career he has been an active trade unionist, and chaired the youth committees of both the GMB and the STUC. He was once his union branch's equality officer and sits on Parliament's Equal Opportunities Committee. Old habits obviously die hard since he is the only MSP who has a photograph of his assistant on his parliamentary website entry. Her name is Nicole, and very nice she is, too.

On the Education Committee, he pushed hard to have the importance of marriage recognised in the legislation to abolish Section 28. His amendment was defeated but he was one of a group of Lanarkshire Labour and Catholic MSPs who were thought to be too receptive to the views of the hierarchy instead of helping the Executive rid the statute book of prejudice. He seemed also to agree with the late Cardinal Winning's description of homosexuality as 'perverted'.

**Committees:** Equal Opportunities; Local Government.

**Contact:** 0131-348-5828 (Parliament)
01698-304501 Fax 01698-300223 (Constituency)
e-mail michael.mcmahon.msp@scottish.parliament.uk

**Maureen Macmillan** (LABOUR)
**MSP (List) Highlands and Islands**

**Born:** Oban, 1943

**Education:** Oban High School; Edinburgh
University.

**Career: 1965–76:** wife/mother; **1976–83:** supply/ part-time Teacher;
**1983–99:** English Teacher, Senior Teacher, Millburn, Inverness;
**1999:** elected MSP.

**Profile:** She is married with two daughters and two sons. Like her colleague Rhona Brankin, she was involved in the formation of Ross-shire Women's Aid and is still a member of the Highland Domestic Abuse Forum. Her political involvement goes back over twenty-five years. Not everyone can star in the debating chamber or committee room, and Maureen Macmillan is one of those who does her work quietly. In debates on domestic violence, however, she has made striking contributions. She was also the prime mover in the development of the 'Protection from Abuse' Bill which will be the first 'committee' Bill to go though Parliament.

She is soft spoken but effective, and one of only three Labour list MSPs, all three from the Highlands. The others are her friend Rhoda Grant and the minister Peter Peacock. It was she who provided a tearful talking point after the McLeish resignation. 'Murder,' she said. 'It was murder by the media.'

**Committees:** Justice 1; Transport and the Environment.

**Contact:**   0131-348-5766 Fax 0131-348-5767 (Parliament)
              01349-867650  Fax 01349-867762 (Constituency)
              e-mail maureen.macmillan.msp@scottish.parliament.uk

## Duncan McNeil (LABOUR)
**MSP Greenock and Inverclyde**

**Born:** Greenock, 1950

**Education:** The Mount School, Greenock; Reid Keir College, Paisley.

**Career: 1965–79:** Shipyard boilermaker; **1979–81:** Co-ordinator, Unemployed Workers' Centres; **1981–99:** Full-time Trade Union Official, GMB; **1999:** elected MSP.

**Profile:** He is married with one son and one daughter. He went straight from school into the shipyards, apprenticed in the Cartsdyke yard. He graduated through union activism to a full-time post with the GMB as Regional Organiser. Given the precarious state of shipbuilding on the Clyde, he became a familiar media figure when representing the interests of his members. It is reassuring that Labour remembered people like him when slicing the cake.

The position of his local football team, Morton, is also precarious, parlous even, and he has taken a keen interest in what happened to the public money that the club has received over the years in various grants. There is no record of how the money was spent in the club's accounts and he wants monitoring procedures to ensure that any grant to any club is spent as the donor intended. He has also done good work in the campaign for asbestos victims. With his background in trade unions, he is a useful man to have around in the Labour Party these days. Even as a whip, he has remained popular and respected. No mean feat.

**Committees:** Deputy Member of the Scottish Parliamentary Bureau.

**Contact:** 0131-348-5912 (Parliament)
01475-791696  Fax 01475-791036 (Constituency)
e-mail duncan.mcneil.msp@scottish.parliament.uk

## Pauline McNeill (LABOUR)
## MSP Glasgow Kelvin

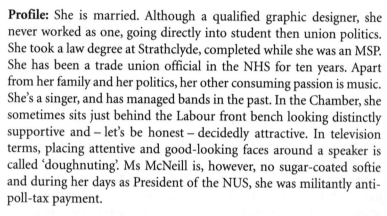

**Born:** Paisley, 1962

**Education:** Our Lady's High School, Cumbernauld;
Glasgow College of Building and Printing;
Strathclyde University.

**Career: 1986–8:** Full-time President, National Union of Students,
Scotland; **1988–99:** Regional Organiser GMB; **1999:** elected MSP.

**Profile:** She is married. Although a qualified graphic designer, she
never worked as one, going directly into student then union politics.
She took a law degree at Strathclyde, completed while she was an MSP.
She has been a trade union official in the NHS for ten years. Apart
from her family and her politics, her other consuming passion is music.
She's a singer, and has managed bands in the past. In the Chamber, she
sometimes sits just behind the Labour front bench looking distinctly
supportive and – let's be honest – decidedly attractive. In television
terms, placing attentive and good-looking faces around a speaker is
called 'doughnuting'. Ms McNeill is, however, no sugar-coated softie
and during her days as President of the NUS, she was militantly anti-
poll-tax payment.

As Convener of one of the Justice Committees, she has led moves to
have the law on rape amended so that conviction does not depend on
the use of violence. Her main parliamentary focus has been on women's
issues and she has also done work on stalking, harassment and the
need for more women judges. She is a loyalist, though not slavishly so,
and is considered a good bet for promotion to office in the future. In
the meantime, she has a pivotal role as Deputy Convener of the Parliamentary Labour Group, a point of contact between the backbenches
and the Executive. Under McLeish and McConnell, greater emphasis
has been placed on keeping the party informed and listening to its views.

**Committees:** Justice 2 (Convener).

**Contact:**  0131-348-5910 (Parliament)
              0141-304-4534 (Constituency)
              e-mail pauline.mcneill.msp@scottish.parliament.uk

## Des McNulty (LABOUR)
**Member, Scottish Parliament Corporate Body**
**MSP Clydebank and Milngavie**

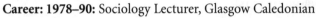

**Born:** Stockport, 1952

**Education:** St Bede's College, Manchester;
York and Glasgow Universities.

**Career: 1978–90:** Sociology Lecturer, Glasgow Caledonian
University; **1990–1:** Senior Lecturer; **1990–6:** Councillor, Strathclyde
Region; **1991–7:** Asst Head, Social Sciences, Glasgow Caledonian;
**1996–9:** Councillor, Glasgow City; **1997–9:** Strategic Planning
Officer, Glasgow Caledonian; **1999:** elected MSP.

**Profile:** He is married with two sons. He had a wide range of experience as a councillor – Chair of Glasgow 1999 Festival and Design,
Member of Glasgow University Court, Member of the Kemp
Commission on the Voluntary Sector in Scotland, Chair of the Healthy
Glasgow Partnership, Chair of the COSLA taskforce on non-elected
public bodies, Member of the Lighthouse Trust, assessor to the Board
of Scottish Opera, non-executive director of Greater Glasgow Health
Board – displaying a degree of public spiritedness that would shame
lesser men. In addition to the normal MSP's e-mail address, he can
also be reached at Des.Direct@scottish.parliament.uk – a model of
accessibility.

This man of many committees is tailor-made for the Scottish Parliament
Corporate Body, a team of four experienced but worthy MSPs who
supervise the administration of Parliament. He probably expected
more, but it is now unlikely that he will advance further. For such an
important occasion, he made a poor and uninspiring speech on behalf
of the Corporate Body when Parliament finally decided to lift the 'cap'
on the cost of the new Holyrood building. If minds had not already
been made up, his performance would not have helped.

**Committees:** Enterprise and Lifelong Learning; Finance (Convener);
Transport and the Environment.

**Contact:** 0131-348-5918  Fax 0131-348-5978 (Parliament)
0141-952-7711 (Constituency)
e-mail des.mcnulty.msp@scottish.parliament.uk

## Paul Martin (LABOUR)
## MSP Glasgow Springburn

**Born:** Glasgow, 1967

**Education:** All Saints Secondary School, Glasgow; Barmulloch College, Glasgow.

**Career: 1993–9:** Councillor, Glasgow District then Glasgow City Council; **1999:** elected MSP.

**Profile:** He is the son of Michael Martin MP, Speaker of the House of Commons, and – when he was first elected as the District Councillor for Alexandra Park at the age of twenty-six – there were accusations of nepotism by Scottish Militant Labour, who contested the seat. Now that he and his father are MSP and MP respectively for the same constituency, that accusation still no doubt lingers. Perhaps more germane is that, despite wide experience in council affairs, politics does seem to have been his only career from an early age. He is married.

He has sensibly concentrated on Springburn and Glasgow matters as an MSP and led a conspicuous campaign against the plans of Greater Glasgow Health Board to site a secure unit in his constituency at Stobhill Hospital. He exposed the lack of local consultation and forced a reconsideration of the project. A triumph for community politics – except the reconsideration produced the same conclusion: the best site for the unit is still Stobhill.

**Committees:** Audit; Justice 1.

**Contact:**  0131-348-5844 (Parliament)
           0141-564-1364 Fax 0141-564-1112 (Constituency)
           e-mail paul.martin.msp@scottish.parliament.uk

# Tricia Marwick (SNP)
## MSP (List) Mid-Scotland and Fife

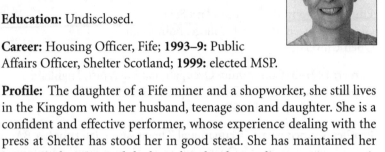

**Born:** Cowdenbeath, 1953

**Education:** Undisclosed.

**Career:** Housing Officer, Fife; **1993–9:** Public Affairs Officer, Shelter Scotland; **1999:** elected MSP.

**Profile:** The daughter of a Fife miner and a shopworker, she still lives in the Kingdom with her husband, teenage son and daughter. She is a confident and effective performer, whose experience dealing with the press at Shelter has stood her in good stead. She has maintained her interest in housing and the homeless, but her parliamentary responsibilities for the SNP are now much wider, having made a conspicuously good start to her elected career. Some people have taken to Parliament like ducks to water, but this one's a swan. One panel of political experts chose her as 'Politician to Watch'.

She was the SNP's Deputy Business Manager to Mike Russell from the opening of Parliament and succeeded him as Business Manager after a year, also representing the SNP on the Parliamentary Bureau. She now has the Local Government brief and remains in the Shadow Cabinet. From the outset, she has also been Deputy Convener of the Standards Committee and made a strong impact in the 'Lobbygate' hearings. On the private member's level, she is co-sponsor with Labour's Mike Watson of the Bill on fox-hunting, a measure which has probably swollen her mailbag with praise and condemnation in equal measure. She sees it as an opportunity to rid Scotland of an offensive practice, but not her main political objective.

**Committees:** Local Government; Standards (Deputy Convener).

**Contact:** 0131-348-5680  Fax 0131-348-5708 (Parliament)
01592-750500 (Constituency)
e-mail tricia.marwick.msp@scottish.parliament.uk

# Michael Matheson (SNP)
## MSP (List) Central Scotland

**Born:** Glasgow, 1970

**Education:** John Bosco Secondary School, Glasgow; Queen Margaret College, Edinburgh; Open University.

**Career: 1991–3:** Community Occupational Therapist, Highland Region; **1991–7:** C.O.T., Central Region; **1997–9:** C.O.T. Stirling Council; **1999:** elected MSP.

**Profile:** Trained as an Occupational Therapist, he later took a BA in Social Sciences from the Open University. He is a keen mountaineer and a member of the Ochils Mountain Rescue Team. He and Fergus Ewing run exhaustingly long distances for charity and claim to enjoy it. He acted as election agent for Roseanna Cunningham in her campaign for the post of Deputy Leader.

He has been the Deputy Shadow Minister for Justice and Equality since the opening of the Parliament, and his impact has been more substantial than shadowy. He speaks well, in confident and pointed interventions, and shows what can be done if you apply yourself. He is popular in the party and looks set for promotion.

**Committees:** Justice 1.

**Contact:** 0131-348-5672 Fax 0131-348-5895 (Parliament)
01698-266312 (Constituency)
e-mail michael.matheson.msp@scottish.parliament.uk

## Brian Monteith (CONSERVATIVE)
## MSP (List) Mid-Scotland and Fife

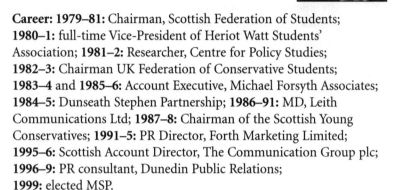

**Born:** Edinburgh, 1958

**Education:** Portobello High School; Heriot Watt University.

**Career: 1979–81:** Chairman, Scottish Federation of Students; **1980–1:** full-time Vice-President of Heriot Watt Students' Association; **1981–2:** Researcher, Centre for Policy Studies; **1982–3:** Chairman UK Federation of Conservative Students; **1983–4** and **1985–6:** Account Executive, Michael Forsyth Associates; **1984–5:** Dunseath Stephen Partnership; **1986–91:** MD, Leith Communications Ltd; **1987–8:** Chairman of the Scottish Young Conservatives; **1991–5:** PR Director, Forth Marketing Limited; **1995–6:** Scottish Account Director, The Communication Group plc; **1996–9:** PR consultant, Dunedin Public Relations; **1999:** elected MSP.

**Profile:** He is married with twin sons. He and his family are long-time season-ticket holders at Hibernian, which speaks of a loyalty bordering on masochism. He is a founder-member of Hands On Hibs, which tries to promote greater investment in the club. He is also a supporter of the rights of smokers, a truly lost cause but in keeping with his libertarian principles; he is also a member of SPUC, which isn't obviously so. He had mixed fortunes in his business career, one of his companies going bust. He launched a campaign to have the Presiding Officer impose a smart dress code in the Scottish Parliament, though his own suits would probably be described as sharp rather than elegant.

He is an unrepentant Thatcherite, well on the right of the Conservative Party (especially in his student days when he was practically out of sight), and arouses strong opinions across the board. Despite his cheery ebullience, it is fair to say that he is not the most popular MSP even within his own party. He is thought, however, to be close to Scottish leader David McLetchie and to Lord (Michael) Forsyth of Drumlean. In 1978 he founded Students against the Devolution Act; in 1987 Conservatives against Apartheid and, in 1996, the right-wing Scottish Conservative dining group, the Tuesday Club. Then, in 1997, with QC Donald Findlay (but not many others in public) he ran the colourful but comprehensively unsuccessful anti-devolution Referendum campaign Think Twice. He must wish he had. He is now the party's parliamentary spokesperson on Education, Culture and Sport.

**Committees:** Education, Culture and Sport.

**Contact:** 0131-348-5644 (Parliament)
01786-461200 (Constituency)
e-mail brian.monteith.msp@scottish.parliament.uk

# Alasdair Morgan (SNP)
## MSP Galloway and Upper Nithsdale

**Born:** Aberfeldy, 1945

**Education:** Breadalbane Academy, Aberfeldy; Glasgow and Open Universities.

**Career: 1973–4:** Teacher, Newton Stewart; **1974–80:** Computer analyst, Shell Oil; **1980–4:** GEC; **1984–6:** Computer Systems Team Leader, Fife Regional Council; **1986–97:** Lothian Region then West Lothian Council; **1997–2001:** MP for Galloway and Upper Nithsdale; **1999:** elected MSP.

**Profile:** He is married with two daughters. He stayed only briefly in teaching before forging a career in computers. He served the SNP as National Treasurer for seven years, Senior Vice-Convener for two, National Secretary for a further five, and then Vice-President. Morgan is the very model of a highly competent loyalist. He was the old guard's favourite to stand in the Perth and Kinross by-election in 1995, but Roseanna Cunningham was selected and won well. He also clashed with Ms Cunningham at the 1997 Party Conference when she called for the abolition of the monarchy in an independent Scotland. It did seem an unnecessary diversion, but that's Roseanna. That's Alasdair, too: very low key and non-threatening.

He is SNP spokesman on Finance – a job he also did in the House of Commons and which brings him into the Shadow Cabinet. He was previously spokesman on Rural Affairs and Deputy Convener of the Rural Affairs Committee. He was particularly assiduous in pursuing the Executive during the foot and mouth outbreak, which fell within his constituency and his (then) portfolio, though the SNP lost his old Westminster seat in the 2001 general election. He is, as they say, a safe pair of hands, but rather dull.

**Committees:** Finance.

**Contact:**  0131-348-5728 Fax 0131-348-5954 (Parliament)
01556-611956 (Constituency)
e-mail alasdair.morgan.msp@scottish.parliament.uk

## Alasdair Morrison (LABOUR)
## MSP Western Isles

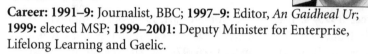

**Born:** North Uist, 1968

**Education:** Nicolson Institute, Stornoway; Glasgow
Caledonian University.

**Career: 1991–9:** Journalist, BBC; **1997–9:** Editor, *An Gaidheal Ur*;
**1999:** elected MSP; **1999–2001:** Deputy Minister for Enterprise,
Lifelong Learning and Gaelic.

**Profile:** He is married with one daughter and was the youngest minister in a fairly young Executive when first appointed in 1999 at the age
of just thirty. Despite that, he is well connected. His brother is John
Morrison, the BBC Scotland correspondent, and his mentor is Brian
Wilson MP, Minister of State at Trade and Industry. The son of a Free
Presbyterian minister, his support for the abolition of Clause 28 did
not meet with universal approval at home in the Western Isles. He's a
handsome chiel, always well dressed, with a healthy almost cherubic
complexion. He is a native Gaelic speaker and a champion of the language, and led the first parliamentary debate in his native language. In
his official capacity as Highland and Gaelic Minister, he opened the
annual Mod. This seemed to be enough to persuade the Free
Presbyterian Church of Scotland not to baptise his child. After all, at
the Mod people sing, dance, drink and – for all we know – fornicate.

Until 2001, Alasdair Morrison had not put a foot wrong, working first
for Henry McLeish and then for Wendy Alexander, earning himself
unofficial recognition as the Minister for the Highlands and Islands.
He had other responsibilities which he carried out with energy and
efficiency, including tourism in its worst ever crisis because of the foot
and mouth outbreak. He worked hard to persuade tourists and locals
alike that Scotland was still open for business, before nipping off for a
pre-planned family holiday in Tuscany. It was a crass misjudgement
and the Scottish press went for him as only the Scottish press can. His
career did not seem to have suffered permanently, but Jack McConnell
decided he could do without his particular mix of qualifications. What
the Gaedhealtacht thinks is unprintable.

**Committees:** Justice 2; Rural Development.

**Contact:** 0131-348-5760 (Parliament)
            01851-704684 (Constituency)
            e-mail alasdair.morrison.msp@scottish.parliament.uk

## Bristow Muldoon (LABOUR)
## MSP Livingston

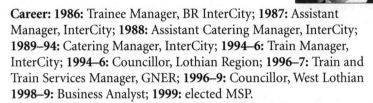

**Born:** Glasgow, 1964

**Education:** Cumbernauld High School; Strathclyde and Open Universities.

**Career: 1986:** Trainee Manager, BR InterCity; **1987:** Assistant Manager, InterCity; **1988:** Assistant Catering Manager, InterCity; **1989–94:** Catering Manager, InterCity; **1994–6:** Train Manager, InterCity; **1994–6:** Councillor, Lothian Region; **1996–7:** Train and Train Services Manager, GNER; **1996–9:** Councillor, West Lothian **1998–9:** Business Analyst; **1999:** elected MSP.

**Profile:** Bristow Muldoon is married with three sons. He is not, as his name might suggest, a musical-hall artist or a bare-knuckle prize-fighter. He belongs to a much rarer group, less regarded even than politicians, the railway manager. He was brought up in one New Town and now represents another, something of a novelty if not a distinction.

He has been a councillor in both Lothian Region and West Lothian Council, as well as Robin Cook's agent. He is very New Labour – middle class, middle management, always smartly dressed and on message. Nothing particularly wrong with that, except it seems a little unadventurous for a man called Bristow Muldoon.

**Committees:** Subordinate Legislation; Transport and the Environment (Convener).

**Contact:** 0131-348-5760 (Parliament)
01506-497961 Fax 01506-497962 (Constituency)
e-mail bristow.muldoon.msp@scottish.parliament.uk

# Mary Mulligan (LABOUR)
**Deputy Minister for Health and Community Care**
**MSP Linlithgow**

**Born:** Liverpool, 1960

**Education:** Notre Dame High School, Liverpool; Manchester University.

**Career: 1981–2:** Trainee then Assistant Staff Manager, BHS; **1982–8:** Assistant Manager, Edinburgh Woollen Mill Ltd; **1988–96:** Edinburgh District Council; **1996–9:** Edinburgh City Council; **1999:** elected MSP.

**Profile:** Ms Mulligan is married with two sons and a daughter. She's extremely earnest, even at the risk of dullness.

On the strength of her five-year stint as Chairman of Housing in Edinburgh, she was made the first Convener of Education, Culture and Sport. A number of important issues came before the Committee during her period in the chair – the SQA crisis, the debacle over Hampden Park and the funding problem at Scottish Opera – and her handling of them was not thought to have been distinguished. She became PPS to Henry McLeish. Given her lack of success in the Convener's role, the move was hardly promotion and ended abruptly when the First Minister resigned. She might have had to content herself with a career on the backbenches, like her former boss, but Jack McConnell plucked her from potential obscurity and – as one of his many surprises – made her a junior Health Minister.

**Contact:**  0131-348-5779 (Parliament)
01506-636555 (Constituency)
e-mail mary.mulligan.msp@scottish.parliament.uk

**David Mundell** (CONSERVATIVE)
**MSP (List) South of Scotland**

**Born:** Dumfries, 1962

**Education:** Lockerbie Academy; Edinburgh and
Strathclyde Universities.

**Career: 1984–96:** Councillor, Annandale and
Eskdale District; **1986–7:** Councillor, Dumfries and Galloway Region;
**1989–91:** Corporate Lawyer, Biggart Baillie; **1991–8:** Group Legal
Adviser, BT Scotland; **1998–9:** Head of National Affairs;
**1999:** elected MSP.

**Profile:** He is married with two sons and a daughter and lives in Moffat.
Apart from his legal qualifications and his MBA from Strathclyde
University Business School, he is also an accredited Mediator in Alternative Dispute Resolution – a cheaper and quicker method of solving
problems than going to law though (for obvious reasons) not all
lawyers like it. He was a member of the Management Board of the
International Teledemocracy Centre, which sounds very grand, a
member of the Institute of Management and the Institute of Directors,
and a Director of the Ayrshire Chamber of Commerce.

It became known after his election that he had retained a £10,000 per
year contract as an adviser to BT, and he was roundly criticised. He
resolved this dispute by taking the obvious alternative of giving up the
consultancy and sticking to the day job. He was Conservative Deputy
(to Brian Monteith) Spokesman on Education, Arts, Culture and Sport
but lost that post. For someone who was a high-flyer at BT, he has yet
to take off in Edinburgh.

**Committees:** Enterprise and Lifelong Learning.

**Contact:**  0131-348-5635 (Parliament)
0800-731-9590 FREEPHONE (Constituency)
e-mail david.mundell.msp@scottish.parliament.uk

## John Farquhar Munro (LIBERAL DEMOCRAT)
## MSP Ross, Skye and Inverness West

**Born:** Glen Sheil,1934

**Education:** Plockton High School; Sea Training
College, Sharpness.

**Career: 1951–61:** Merchant Navy; **1961–5:** Plant Fitter, Road
Construction; **1965–75:** Manager, Contracting Company;
**1966–99:** Councillor, Skye and Lochalsh and Highland Council;
**1971–97:** Crofter; **1975–93:** self-employed contractor;
**1999:** elected MSP.

**Profile:** He is married with one son and one daughter. Like many a
Highlander, he has done several jobs – some of them at the same time.
During over thirty years of unbroken service as a councillor, he has
also sat on innumerable committees in connection with the Highland
economy, transport system and cultural life. While in the chair of Skye
and Lochalsh Council during the construction of the Skye Bridge, he
bitterly opposed tolls and has been frustrated at the Executive's inability
to move on the issue. He is a native Gaelic speaker and an eloquent
advert for the language. He is also the MSP most often seen in the kilt,
which he wears 'in the traditional way. Modesty is not something I
subscribe to.'

He was one of only three Lib Dems who voted against entering the
coalition with Labour in 1999 and his subsequent support has been
somewhat unpredictable. With several colleagues, he voted against the
Executive's decommissioning deal for fishermen. He favours radical land
reform and regards the Executive's approach as too timid. Generally,
however, he has been quiet unless Highland interests are threatened.
He is a great champion of that neglected artery, the Kyle railway line.
He is the Lib Dems' spokesperson on Gaelic and Forestry.

**Committees:** Public Petitions; Rural Development.

**Contact:**   0131-348-5793 (Parliament)
              01463-714377 (Constituency)
              e-mail john.munro.msp@scottish.parliament.uk

## Dr Elaine Murray (LABOUR)
## Deputy Minister for Tourism, Culture and Sport
## MSP Dumfries

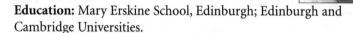

**Born:** Hitchin, 1954

**Education:** Mary Erskine School, Edinburgh; Edinburgh and Cambridge Universities.

**Career: 1979–81:** Research Fellow, Cavendish Laboratory; **1981–4:** Research Fellow, Royal Free Hospital; **1984–7:** Senior Scientific Officer, Institute of Food Research; **1990–3:** Assistant to Alex Smith MEP; **1992–9:** Associate Lecturer, Open University; **1994–6:** Councillor, Strathclyde Region; **1995–9:** Councillor, South Ayrshire Council; **1999:** elected MSP.

**Profile:** Dr Murray is married with two sons and a daughter, and is a seriously well-qualified lady, having worked at those world-renowned institutions, the Cavendish Laboratory and the Royal Free Hospital. She allies considerable charm to her formidable brain. She also rattles a mean keyboard.

She is probably more left wing than she appears. She worked for the former European Member for South of Scotland Alex Smith, who is no New Labourite. She was also one of those Labour MSPs, led by Andy Kerr, who bitterly opposed Sarah Boyack's plans to give private contractors the contracts for trunk-road maintenance rather than local authorities. She was on the Rural Development Committee and, during the foot and mouth outbreak, spoke up persuasively for her own hard-pressed constituents in Dumfries. After a nervous start in Parliament, she has clearly settled down and will enjoy her ministerial responsibility. She did raise some left eyebrows when – in the fox-hunting debate – she presented a complicated amendment which would effectively have killed Mike Watson's bill for abolition. Her amendment was defeated, but her rural constituents know she tried. Ironically, her senior minister, now, is the self-same Mike Watson.

**Contact:** 0131-348-5826 (Parliament)
    01387-279205 Fax 01387-279206 (Constituency)
    e-mail elaine.murray.msp@scottish.parliament.uk

# Alex Neil (SNP)
## MSP (List) Central Scotland

**Born:** Irvine, 1954

**Education:** Dalmellington High School; Ayr
Academy; Dundee University.

**Career: 1977–9:** General Secretary, Scottish Labour
Party (SLP); **1979–83:** Marketing Manager; **1983–7:** Cumnock and
Doon Enterprise Trust; **1987–93:** Chairman, Network Scotland Ltd;
**1993– :** Economic Consultant; **1999:** elected MSP.

**Profile:** He is married with one son. He first came to political prominence when, after working as a researcher with the Labour Party in
Glasgow, he joined his mentor Jim Sillars in the formation of the
breakaway Scottish Labour Party (SLP) at a meeting in the Grosvenor
Hotel, Glasgow, in 1976. The meeting was attended by almost as many
media people as potential members; indeed, some of the media people
were potential members. Neil was the General Secretary and struggled
hard to cleanse the party of 'entryists' from extreme left-wing groups.
After a couple of years, the SLP sank under the weight of its own
expectations. He is a slightly more hectoring version of Sillars, a fellow
Ayrshireman, and followed him into the SNP.

Like Sillars again, he has become a fundamentalist in the SNP, another
contradiction of his Labour roots. He has been Policy Vice-Convener
but his most public contribution to the campaign for independence
was probably the slogan 'Scotland Free by '93', later regarded as a silly
answer to the wrong question and a substantial hostage to fortune. He
was the party spokesperson on Social Security but resigned that role
when, after Alex Salmond's resignation as party leader, he and his
'fundie' allies lost out in the party leadership elections. He is now Convener of the Enterprise and Lifelong Learning Committee and performs
energetically as a backbencher. His most effective performance on the
floor of the House was his speech in support of Tommy Sheridan's
warrant sales Bill – a model of passionate Ayrshire socialist logic.

**Committees:** Enterprise and Lifelong Learning (Convener).

**Contact:**  0131-348-5703 Fax 0131-348-5716 (Parliament)
             01563-541314 (Constituency)
             e-mail alex.neil.msp@scottish.parliament.uk

# Irene Oldfather (LABOUR)
## MSP Cunninghame South

**Born:** Glasgow, 1954

**Education:** Irvine Royal Academy; Strathclyde University.

**Career: 1977–8:** Lecturer, Arizona University; **1980–90:** Researcher/ Policy Analyst, Glasgow City Council; **1990–7:** Political Researcher to MEP; **1994–8:** Freelance Journalist European Affairs; **1995–9:** Councillor, North Ayrshire Council; **1996–8:** Lecturer Paisley University; **1999:** elected MSP.

**Profile:** She is married with one son and one daughter. Her consuming interest in politics seems to be European affairs and she has a good working knowledge of French. She was North Ayrshire's European Spokesperson, Chair of the West of Scotland European Consortium, a member of the European Committee of the Regions and spent seven years working for Alex Smith MEP.

Given her background, it is no surprise to find her on the European Committee, now as its Convener. The SNP's *enfant célèbre* Duncan Hamilton included her in his condemnation of Labour women. Mistake. Big mistake. She's hard working and extremely well informed.

**Committees:** European (Convener).

**Contact:**  0131-348-5769 (Parliament)
01294-313078 Fax 01294-313605 (Constituency)
e-mail irene.oldfather.msp@scottish.parliament.uk

## Gil Paterson (SNP)
## MSP (List) Central Scotland

**Born:** Glasgow, 1942

**Education:** Possilpark Secondary School, Glasgow.

**Career: 1957–63:** Apprentice Radiotrician;
**1963–5:** Electrical Repair Technician, Singers;
**1965–70:** Sales and Smoke Control, Scottish Gas Board;
**1970–3:** Tech/Sales, Parsons Paint; **1973–99:** Proprietor, Gils Motor
Factors; **1975–8:** Councillor, Strathclyde Region; **1999:** elected MSP.

**Profile:** A product of the now defunct Possilpark Secondary, he is
divorced with one son. The garage business in Bishopbriggs came after
varied experience in industry. One of his most conspicuous contributions to the SNP was his company spray-painting campaign vehicles
during elections. He once took the Conservative government to the
European Court of Human Rights, claiming that Scots businessmen
were discriminated against by having to pay higher rates than in
England. He lost on a technicality .

A left-wing fundamentalist, he supported Alex Neil in the election for
leader and predicted that John Swinney would set the party back
twenty years. He made a good showing in committee in the early
days, most particularly duffing up Frank McAveety for being less than
forthcoming in a session on local government. He acts as Convener of
the cross-party group on Men's Violence against Women. He is a
friend of that other SNP old-timer and traditionalist Adam Ingram,
and either or both could be single-term parliamentarians.

**Committees:** Equal Opportunities.

**Contact:** 0131-348-5922 Fax 0131-348-5735 (Parliament)
0141-577-6370 (Constituency)
e-mail gil.paterson.msp@scottish.parliament.uk

## Peter Peacock (LABOUR)
**Deputy Minister for Finance and Public Services**
**MSP (List) Highlands and Islands**

**Born:** Edinburgh, 1952

**Education:** Hawick High School; Jordanhill College.

**Career: 1973–5:** Community Education Worker, Orkney; **1975–87:** Area Officer (Highlands and Islands) Citizens' Advice Bureaux; **1982–96:** Councillor, then Deputy Leader, Highland Regional Council; **1987–96:** Partner, The Apt Partnership; **1996–9:** Councillor and Leader, Highland Council; **1999:** elected MSP.

**Profile:** He is married with two sons. He has worked in public service almost all his career and his long stint as a councillor was conducted as an Independent. Donald Dewar, impressed by his performance at the head of the Highlands Council, was known to be delighted when Peacock decided to throw in his lot with the Labour Party. Some local Labour stalwarts were less than delighted that he was placed – probably at Dewar's insistence – at the top of the Regional List for Labour in the Highlands and Islands, making his election almost certain.

He was immediately given an Executive post, as Deputy Minister for Children and Education, and was subsequently moved at the same level to Finance and Local Government. He is recognised as a very safe pair of hands, persuasive if not dynamic. His lack of party political baggage means that he can make decisions sound reasoned and reasonable. Jack McConnell decided to keep him in post. Praise indeed.

**Contact:**  0131-348-5766 (Parliament)
0131-867650 (Constituency)
e-mail peter.peacock.msp@scottish.parliament.uk

## Cathy Peattie (LABOUR)
## MSP Falkirk East

**Born:** Stirling, 1951

**Education:** Beancross Primary; Moray Secondary
School, Grangemouth.

**Career: 1966–8:** Shop worker; **1968–9:** Factory worker;
**1970–5:** Training Supervisor; **1975–80:** Full-time mother and
volunteer with Scottish Pre-school Play Association;
**1980–6:** Field Worker and Training Officer SPPA; **1986–90:**
Development Worker, Volunteer Network; **1990–1:** Community
Development Worker; **1991–3:** Manager, Community Outreach;
**1993–9:** Director, Falkirk Voluntary Action Resource Centre;
**1999:** elected MSP.

**Profile:** Cathy is married with two daughters. She is one of those
people who seems to pack more than 24 hours into a day. Her career in
community work blossomed after her children grew up, accompanied
by increasing political activity. She has been Convener of the Council
of Voluntary Service in Scotland and Chair of Scottish Labour's
Women's Committee. She also sings like a lintie. Her unaccompanied
singing of Burns's 'Aye Waukin' was one of the many moving moments
of Donald Dewar's funeral in Glasgow Cathedral.

As a member of Labour's Scottish Executive, she voted in favour of the
two-question referendum on devolution. She is not a frequent speaker
in the Chamber but is an eager committee member. She is a member
of two parliamentary committees as well as sixteen cross-party groups,
with a handful of convener-, co-convener- and vice-convenerships. One
of her main interests is the maintenance of the Scots language. The
First Minister publicly backed her for the vacancy as Deputy Presiding
Officer – just the kind of heavy-handed support to ensure her defeat
in a secret ballot. She declared herself 'scunnered' by the whole affair.
Aye, Cathie, it wis a richt moger.

**Committees:** Equal Opportunities.

**Contact:** 0131-348-5747 (Parliament)
            01324-666026 Fax 01324-473951 (Constituency)
            e-mail cathy.peattie.msp@scottish.parliament.uk

# Lloyd Quinan (SNP)
## MSP (List) West of Scotland

**Born:** Edinburgh, 1957

**Education:** Holy Cross Academy; St Augustine's High School, Edinburgh; Leith Academy; Queen Margaret College, Edinburgh.

**Career: 1978–83:** Actor; **1982–9:** Theatre Director; **1989–99:** Freelance Producer/Director/TV Presenter; **1999:** elected MSP.

**Profile:** Whatever theatrical or political ambitions beat in the Quinan breast, he is still best remembered as the wee man who did the weather forecast on STV (and presented *Trial by Night*, a debate programme bravely placed by STV in the middle of the night). There is much more to him than that and – if we had ever seen his Hamlet – it might have been a different story.

He was Deputy Spokesman for Social Inclusion, Trade Unions and the Voluntary Sector in the first session of Parliament. He is firmly on the fundamentalist left of the party and resigned his Shadow post after the SNP disciplined Margo MacDonald for speaking to the media about 'confidential' party matters. The SNP is no less faction-ridden than the other parties and this gesture may have been sympathetic but was probably futile. He took a keen interest in the case of the late Anton Gecas, supporting his extradition to Lithuania on war crimes charges. He accused Labour's Dr Richard Simpson – a respected GP – of being in the pay of the drug companies when he (Simpson) defended the MMR vaccine. Dr Simpson had in fact been paid (and declared) £5,000 per year while a member of the Prostate Advising Forum, an educational group financed by a company with links to the producer of MMR. The matter was considered by the Standards Committee, which dismissed the complaint unanimously but was concerned that 'an SNP MSP' had leaked the complaint to the press. More successfully, Quinan argued well for a review of the law on cannabis for medical use. All in all, he's busy if somewhat erratic.

**Committees:** Audit; European.

**Contact:** 0131-348-5734 Fax 0131-348-5735 (Parliament)
        01475-806020 Fax 01475-806021 (Constituency)
        e-mail lloyd.quinan.msp@scottish.parliament.uk

**Nora Radcliffe** (LIBERAL DEMOCRAT)
**MSP Gordon**

**Born:** Aberdeen, 1946

**Education:** Bowmore and Peterculter Primary Schools; High School for Girls, Aberdeen; Aberdeen University.

**Career: 1967–73:** Management, Hotel and Catering Industry; **1973–88:** full-time wife and mother, various part-time jobs; **1988–98:** Grampian Health Board; **1988–92:** Councillor, Gordon District Council; **1999:** elected MSP.

**Profile:** She is married with one son and one daughter. When a councillor, she promoted one of the first Council Environmental Charters and set up an Environmental Forum. She has often brightened the parliamentary environment by wearing sweaters of vivacious style and vivid hue. She maintains that the Scottish Parliament has attracted people from 'ordinary backgrounds', bringing a whole new dimension to political deliberations. Some people may dismiss an interest in equal opportunities as politically correct, but to her it's common decency.

She is a speaker of great clarity and purpose. She made impressive contributions to the debates on the repeal of Section 28, where she defended the Executive's position, and on the local government cash settlement of 2000–01, where she did not, on the grounds that it disadvantaged efficient authorities like her own in Aberdeenshire while helping the inefficient. On the whole she has been supportive of the coalition without submerging her own point of view, and is not one of the Lib Dem awkward squad. She is currently the party's spokesperson on the Environment and Transport but has also spoken on Health and Social Services. In a small party, you have to be versatile, and she's certainly that.

**Committees:** European; Transport and the Environment (Deputy Convener).

**Contact:** 0131-348-5804 (Parliament)
01467-672220 Fax 01467-672267 (Constituency)
e-mail nora.radcliffe.msp@scottish.parliament.uk

# Keith Raffan (LIBERAL DEMOCRAT)
## MSP (List) Mid-Scotland and Fife

**Born:** Aberdeen, 1949

**Education:** Robert Gordon's College, Aberdeen; Trinity College, Glenalmond; Cambridge University.

**Career: 1970–4:** National Chairman, Pressure for Economic and Social Toryism (Rowntree) Trust Fellowship; **1974–6:** Freelance Journalist; **1976–9:** Diary columnist, *Sunday Express*; **1979–81:** Editorial writer, *Daily Express*; **1981–3:** Parliamentary Correspondent and sketch writer, *Daily Express*; **1983–92:** Conservative MP for Delyn North Wales; **1992–4:** International PR Consultant, New York; **1994–8:** TV Presenter/Interviewer HTV Wales; **1999:** elected MSP.

**Profile:** The raffish Mr Raffan was a Tory in another life – albeit a left-wing Tory and the Chairman of PEST, Pressure for Economic and Social Toryism, the precursor of the Tory Reform Group. He was elected as Tory MP for Delyn and sat on the Welsh Affairs Select Committee during his ten years in the House. He left the Tory Party and joined the Lib Dems, partly because of his support for devolution.

His political volatility has not diminished since came to the Scottish Parliament. He was the only Lib Dem not to vote for Donald Dewar in the election for First Minister – oddly he abstained – and he was one of the three (with Gorrie and Munro) to vote against the party joining a coalition with Labour to form the Executive. He was briefly his party's spokesperson on Health and Community Care but resigned over the issue of implementation of the Sutherland Report on care of the elderly. Maverick is an overused word, but sometimes it fits.

**Committees:** Audit.

**Contact:** 0131-348-5800 (Parliament)
0705000-97950 (Constituency)
e-mail keith.raffan.msp@scottish.parliament.uk

## George Reid (SNP)
### Deputy Presiding Officer
### MSP (List) Mid-Scotland and Fife

**Born:** Tullibody, 1939

**Education:** Dollar Academy; St Andrews University.

**Career: 1962–4:** Reporter, *Daily Express*; **1964–6:** Presenter, STV;
**1966–9:** Producer, Granada TV; **1969–74:** Head of News and
Current Affairs, STV; **1974–9:** MP for Clackmannan and East
Stirling; **1979–84:** Presenter, BBC Scotland; **1984–96:** Director,
Public Affairs, International Red Cross; **1996–9:** Freelance
Consultant; **1999:** elected MSP, subsequently Deputy Presiding
Officer.

**Profile:** He has a wife and two daughters and lives in Bridge of Allan.
He is a gifted linguist and was in his element at the Red Cross, where
he spent much of his time getting on and off planes in pursuit of international conflicts and natural disasters. His current post also offers
some opportunity for travel, but his boss, Presiding Officer Sir David
Steel, takes most of the plum trips. He is practically a chain smoker and
regularly nips out of the Parliament premises to an area now known
unofficially as Reid's Close. The smoking betrays a certain intensity,
not to say tension. He is probably a workaholic, who is happier on the
move than standing still.

Reid joined the SNP just before the 1974 election, which saw him
returned as one of their team of successes. In the political neutrality of
television journalism, he had been assumed to be Lib–Lab. He admits
that voting down the Callaghan government in 1979 was one of the
worst moments of his political life. He thought it would set back the
cause of self-government and lose him his seat, both of which it did.
He has made an excellent Deputy Presiding Officer, respected by most.
He would dearly love the job when Sir David steps aside, but will the
Labour Party be willing to support him, especially after his strong
stand against the leaking to the press of ministerial statements?
Annabel Goldie is said to be preferred by sections of the Labour
group. Within the SNP, Reid is seen by some as suspiciously gradualist
and was forbidden to chair the steering committee on the Holyrood

Parliament building for fear the SNP would be seen to be giving its blessing. He has championed the Civic Forum, linking Parliament to Scottish society at large.

**Contact:** 0131-348-5312 Fax 0131-348-5996 (Parliament)
01786-935900 Fax 01786-835901 (Constituency)
e-mail george.reid.msp@scottish.parliament.uk

## Shona Robison (SNP)
## MSP (List) North-East Scotland

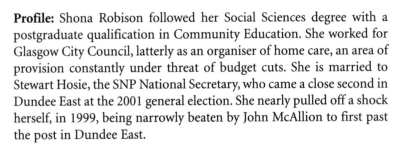

**Born:** Redcar, 1966

**Education:** Alva Academy; Glasgow University; Jordanhill College.

**Career: 1989–90:** Administrative Officer; **1990–3:** Community Worker; **1993–7:** Senior Community Worker; **1997–9:** Home Care Organiser; **1999:** elected MSP.

**Profile:** Shona Robison followed her Social Sciences degree with a postgraduate qualification in Community Education. She worked for Glasgow City Council, latterly as an organiser of home care, an area of provision constantly under threat of budget cuts. She is married to Stewart Hosie, the SNP National Secretary, who came a close second in Dundee East at the 2001 general election. She nearly pulled off a shock herself, in 1999, being narrowly beaten by John McAllion to first past the post in Dundee East.

She is a member of the SNP's National Executive, where she represents the trade union section and is Group Secretary of the parliamentary party. She also acts as Deputy Shadow Minister for Health. She works under Nicola Sturgeon, younger than she is but an object lesson in application. She should go far, but – like her colleague Nicola – could afford to lighten up a little.

**Committees:** Health and Community Care.

**Contact:**  0131-348-5707 (Parliament)
             01382-623200  Fax 01382-604767 (Constituency)
             e-mail shona.robison.msp@scottish.parliament.uk

**Euan Robson** (LIBERAL DEMOCRAT)
**Deputy Minister for Parliament**
**Member, Scottish Parliamentary Bureau**
**MSP Roxburgh and Berwickshire**

**Born:** Corbridge, Northumberland; 1954

**Education:** Trinity College, Glenalmond; Newcastle and Strathclyde Universities.

**Career: 1976–9:** Teacher, King Edward Vl School, Morpeth;
**1981–6:** Deputy Secretary, Gas Consumers' Northern Council;
**1981–9:** Councillor, Northumberland County Council;
**1986–99:** Scottish Manager, Scottish Gas Consumers' Council;
**1999:** elected MSP.

**Profile:** Nine years after graduating with an Honours degree in History, he took his Masters degree in Politics at Strathclyde. This coincided with a career change from teaching to looking after the interests of gas consumers. He is married with two daughters. Outside politics, he is an acknowledged expert on Scottish art and has publications to prove it.

He is the Liberal Democrat business manager and, as such, is also Deputy Minister for Parliament. He now works under Patricia Ferguson, not Tom McCabe, which must be something of a relief. His promotion was occasioned by the resignation of Tavish Scott over the Executive's fishing compensation package. Jim Wallace urgently had to find a Lib Dem who would not succumb to a sudden and unexpected rush of blood to the head.

**Contact:**   0131-348-5806 (Parliament)
        01573-225279 (Constituency)
        e-mail euan.robson.msp@scottish.parliament.uk

## Mike Rumbles (LIBERAL DEMOCRAT)
## MSP Aberdeenshire West and Kincardine

**Born:** South Shields, 1956

**Education:** St James School, Hebburn; Universities of Durham and Wales.

**Career: 1980–95:** Armed Forces;
**1995–9:** Team Leader, Business Management, Aberdeen College;
**1999:** elected MSP.

**Profile:** Like Paddy Ashdown, he spent a large part of his career in the Army before turning to politics. Unlike Action Man, he was in the education and training service and not regularly required to jump from amphibious vehicles at dead of night, dressed in black with a knife in his teeth. He is married with two sons.

He was Convener of the Standards Committee during the first session of Parliament and therefore chaired the hearings into 'Lobbygate'. After a shaky start, he acted with considerable skill, keeping the Executive at arm's length but restraining those who were determined to get a conviction whether or not the charges were proved. He was also his party's spokesman on rural affairs, a portfolio not without its controversies and where the lead minister is a Liberal Democrat, too. He resigned that post and returned to the backbenches, as did the fishing spokesman Jamie Stone, over the Executive's fishing compensation package. Both were among the Lib Dems who voted against the scheme on the first vote, apparently without warning, and caused a crisis in Lib–Lab relations.

**Committees:** Rural Development; Standards (Convener).

**Contact:**  0131-348-5798 (Parliament)
          01330-820268 Fax 01330-820106 (Constituency)
          e-mail mike.rumbles.msp@scottish.parliament.uk

# Michael Russell (SNP)
## MSP (List) South of Scotland

**Born:** Bromley, 1953

**Education:** Marr College, Troon; Edinburgh University.

**Career: 1974–7:** Creative Producer, Church of Scotland; **1977–81:** Director, Cinema Sgire, Western Isles; **1981–3:** Secretary-General, Association of Film and TV in Celtic Countries; **1983–91:** Chief Executive, Network Scotland; **1991– :** Director, Eala Bhan Ltd; **1994–9:** Chief Executive and Elections Director, SNP; **1999:** elected MSP.

**Profile:** Mike Russell is that rare beast in politics, a genuine intellectual. He writes books. His career has largely been spent straddling the creative fields of television, film and literature and the practical responsibilities of political administration. His twin interests have often come together in work for the Gaelic and Celtic film industry. He speaks Gaelic and is Vice-Convener of the cross-party group on the language. He was, until recently, the SNP's principal spokesman on Culture, Broadcasting and Gaelic. He is married with one son.

He has been a key figure in the machinery and strategy of the SNP for over a decade, working closely with Alex Salmond to modernise the party and generalise its message. That the party is now consistently the main opposition to Labour, and a serious contender for Scottish government, is due almost entirely to their work on organisation and policy. Now that Salmond has stepped aside from the leadership, Russell can be expected to take a more prominent public and parliamentary role. He has moved from Business Manager to Spokesperson on Children and Education. There may already have been a cooling in his relationship with Salmond, who had an uncharacteristically low-key election campaign in 1997. Russell ran the campaign and has subsequently admitted to tactical blunders – not the least of which was the 'Penny for Scotland' platform. He is very clever but – he should be warned – it is possible to be too clever and simply complicate the issues.

**Committees:** Education, Culture and Sport.

**Contact:** 0131-348-5678  Fax 0131-5944 (Parliament)
01292-290611  Fax 01292-290629 (Constituency)
e-mail michael.russell.msp@scottish.parliament.uk

# Mary Scanlon (CONSERVATIVE)
## MSP (List) Highlands and Islands

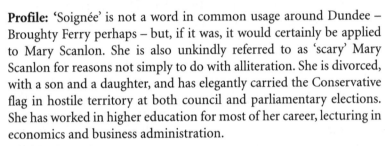

**Born:** Dundee, 1947

**Education:** Craigo School, Montrose; Dundee University.

**Career: 1969–72:** Civil Servant; **1972–83:** full-time mother, working part time and studying; **1983–8:** Lecturer, Perth College; **1988–94:** Dundee Institute of Technology; **1994–9:** Inverness College (UHI); **1999:** elected MSP.

**Profile:** 'Soignée' is not a word in common usage around Dundee – Broughty Ferry perhaps – but, if it was, it would certainly be applied to Mary Scanlon. She is also unkindly referred to as 'scary' Mary Scanlon for reasons not simply to do with alliteration. She is divorced, with a son and a daughter, and has elegantly carried the Conservative flag in hostile territory at both council and parliamentary elections. She has worked in higher education for most of her career, lecturing in economics and business administration.

She is the Tories' Principal Spokesperson on Health and Social Work, and a member of the Health and Community Care Committee. She made a particularly powerful speech when the Executive refused to be bound by all forty-five different recommendations of the Health Committee's unanimous report on care of the elderly. She accused the Executive – and she was not the only one – of misleading the electorate into thinking there was a definite commitment to free personal care for the elderly when there was none. 'Despicable' she called it. She worried the government even more when she rejected several offers of medical guidance from Mac Armstrong, the Chief Medical Officer, when compiling her report for the Health Committee on the MMR vaccine. 'Extraordinary' was the mildest word used about her by a government spokesperson. In the event, the Executive had to eat all its harsh words when she produced a report that was a model of balance and good sense. Mrs Scanlon sought, but is still waiting for, an apology for the way in which her work was traduced prior to publication.

**Committees:** Health and Community Care.

**Contact:** 0131-348-5650 (Parliament)
01463-233986 Fax 01463-714674 (Constituency)
e-mail mary.scanlon.msp@scottish.parliament.uk

# John Scott (CONSERVATIVE)
## MSP Ayr

**Born:** Irvine, 1951

**Education:** George Watson's College, Edinburgh;
Edinburgh University.

**Career:** Family farming firm, W. Scott and Son;
**1993–9:** Convener, Scottish NFU Hill Farming Committee;
**1994–6:** President Ayrshire Executive NFU; **2000:** elected MSP.

**Profile:** John Scott is a particularly successful Ayrshire farmer who diversified into fertiliser and catering enterprises, hygienically separated of course. His food business embraced 'Doorstep Dishes' (an allusion to delivery not scale) and 'Events in Tents'. He also founded Ayrshire Country Lamb and established Ayrshire Farmers Markets. You might wonder why he wants to bother with politics. He is an altogether quieter man than his Ayr colleague, the vociferous Phil Gallie. In 2000, he was tragically widowed. His wife had been a vital partner in his enterprise.

He stood for the Conservatives in the 1999 Scottish parliamentary campaign but unsurprisingly failed to get elected in Carrick, Cumnock and Doon Valley, though he did increase the Tory vote. When Ian Welsh, Labour MSP for marginal Ayr, resigned suddenly, it came at a time which suited Mr Welsh but not his party. Labour were in a slough at the time and John Scott, in March 2000, became the first Tory to be elected 'first past the post' to the Scottish Parliament rather than from a list by proportional representation. Phil Gallie, the list MSP for the area, might have stood but preferred to wait and try his luck again at the Westminster election – unsuccessfully as it turned out. As Phil Gallie went down a step in the Tory reshuffle of June 2001, John Scott went up one – to Spokesperson on the Environment.

**Committees:** Transport and the Environment.

**Contact:**  0131-348-5664 Fax 0131-348-5938 (Parliament)
01292-286251 Fax 01292-280480 (Constituency)
e-mail john.scott.msp@scottish.parliament.uk

**Tavish Scott** (LIBERAL DEMOCRAT)
**MSP Shetland**

**Born:** Inverness, 1966

**Education:** Anderson High School, Lerwick;
Napier College, Edinburgh.

**Career: 1989–90:** Parliamentary Researcher to Jim Wallace MP;
**1990–2:** Press Officer, Scottish Liberal Party; **1992–9:** Farmer;
**1994–9:** Councillor, Shetland Islands Council; **1997–9:** Director,
Shetland Islands Tourism; **1999:** elected MSP; **2000–1:** Deputy
Minister for Parliament.

**Profile:** Tavish Scott is married, with one son and one daughter, and
has long been marked out as one of the Lib Dems bright young men.
He worked for Jim Wallace and for party headquarters in Edinburgh
before returning to Shetland in 1992 to run the family farm, which
occupies a large part of Bressay. Once home, he was elected to the local
council and gained experience as Vice-Convener of Roads and
Transport, though there is only a modest amount of either on the
Islands. Shetland is a very well-run council.

Scott started off his parliamentary career as the Liberal Democrat
spokesperson for Transport and the Environment. He distinguished
himself by introducing and steering the first private member's Bill
through the Scottish Parliament. It was the Sea Fisheries (Shellfish)
(Amendment) Bill (amending thirty-year-old legislation), not headline grabbing stuff but an example of the useful work that was simply
left undone at Westminster but is promptly possible in Edinburgh. The
Bill aims to reduce tension between scallop farmers and fishermen, so
now you know. He was made Deputy Minister for Parliament in
November 2000 but resigned only five months later over the
Executive's compensation scheme for fishermen. He voted with the
Executive first time round, in keeping with collective responsibility,
then resigned and voted against after the second debate, in keeping
with the wishes of his constituents. It was, he said, 'the most difficult
decision' of his political career. It was also an honest decision, but there
is no doubt he will be back on the front benches ere long, and may
make it to the very top.

**Committees:** Enterprise and Lifelong Learning.

**Contact:** 0131-348-5815 (Parliament)
01595-690044 Fax 01595-690055 (Constituency)
e-mail tavish.scott.msp@scottish.parliament.uk

**Tommy Sheridan** (ssp)
**MSP (List) Glasgow**

**Born:** Glasgow, 1964

**Education:** Lourdes Secondary, Glasgow;
Stirling University.

**Career: 1980:** Sales Assistant, Burtons Menswear;
**1981:** Removals Labourer, Pickfords; **1982–5:** Health Instructor,
Dave Greenhills; **1985–6:** Hypothermia Programme Team Leader,
Community Programme Service; **1992– :** Councillor, Glasgow City
Council; **1999– :** National Convener, Scottish Socialist Party;
**1999:** elected MSP.

**Profile:** He is universally known as Tommy, and that's what he likes –
being universally known. He was expelled by Labour for being a leading
figure in the Militant Tendency. Self-publicist, full-time agitator and
part-time jailbird, he claims that he does everything for the cause of
Marxism and the working class. And it has to be admitted, even by
those who disapprove of him, that he does it very well. He has inspired
more column inches than any other MSP, save Donald Dewar and
Henry McLeish. In his youth he was an assistant in a men's clothiers and
a health instructor, which partly accounts for the sharp suits and the
permanent tan. Now he has the dual role of councillor and MSP,
donating half his salary – and all his journalistic earnings – to the
socialist movement and community causes. His spells in jail have been
for obstructing warrant sales and demonstrating at a nuclear installa-
tion (refusing to pay the fine in all three cases). He doesn't smoke or
drink but plays football with a passion. He recently married Gail, an
air hostess, in an RC Chapel before the honeymoon in Cuba.

As the sole member of the SSP in Parliament, Sheridan gets more
speaking time than the average MSP – as do Canavan and Harper –
but he would have made his presence felt anyway. His most spectacular
success has been his Bill to abolish warrant sales, which attracted
enough backbench support in all parts of the Chamber to get through
its first stage against the advice of the Executive. An alternative method
of collecting bad debt is yet to be found and – in one of their many
jousts – Frank McAveety accused him of always bringing simplistic
answers to complex problems. He didn't initially sit on any committees – they do essential work but don't bring much publicity – but

now he's joined Equal Opportunities. Like many a good Liberal, he is in favour of legalising cannabis, which caused the *Daily Record* to blackguard him. Bishop Richard Holloway, on the other hand, called him 'Christ-like'. Indeed he has achieved the amalgamation of the SSP with the SWP, and that's a miracle on the sectarian left.

**Committees:** Equal Opportunities.

**Contact:**  0131-348-5631 Fax 0131-348-5632 (Parliament)
        0141-221-7714/2520 (Constituency)
        e-mail tommy.sheridan.msp@scottish.parliament.uk

**Dr Richard Simpson** (LABOUR)
**Deputy Minister for Justice**
**MSP Ochil**

**Born:** Edinburgh, 1942

**Education:** Perth Academy; Trinity College,
Glenalmond; Edinburgh University.

**Career: 1970– :** GP; **1987– :** Senior Partner in General Practice;
**1976– :** Psychiatrist; **1999:** elected MSP.

**Profile:** Dr Simpson is married with two sons. He has published widely, researched into general practice and prostate cancer, and holds an honorary Chair at Stirling University. He was a founding member of Strathcarron Hospice. He has been a medical adviser in adoption and fostering and medical adviser to the Samaritans and the Scottish Prison Service Suicide Risk group. Throughout his busy and varied career, he was active in his local constituency Labour Party, serving as Vice-Chairman and Chairman. Bearded like the pard, he looks every inch the senior partner and trusty GP.

He cuts an odd but impressive figure on the Labour benches, not given to the free exchange of political abuse or ritual denial that sometimes passes for debate. He specialises in reasoned argument, supported by hard fact. He does not have much clout in internal party machinations, but he is admired for his honesty and intellect. It was to general surprise therefore that the SNP's Lloyd Quinan accused him of being in the pay of the drug manufacturers when Simpson defended the MMR vaccine, jointly developed by a company which gave him a (declared) £5,000 retainer for advice on an unrelated subject. The Standards Committee dismissed the complaint unanimously. As a member of the Health Committee, he reported on the consultation procedures of Greater Glasgow Health Board in the planning of a secure unit proposed for Stobhill Hospital. His report led to a reconsideration. He is undoubtedly ministerial material and his appointment is one of the few in Jack McConnell's reshuffle to have met with absolutely universal approval.

**Contact:** 0131-348-5740 (Parliament)
        01259-212518 (Constituency)
        e-mail richard.simpson.msp@scottish.parliament.uk

# Elaine Smith (LABOUR)
## MSP Coatbridge and Chryston

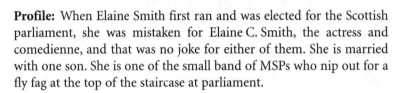

**Born:** Coatbridge, 1963

**Education:** St Patrick's School, Coatbridge; Glasgow College; St Andrew's College.

**Career: 1986–8:** Teacher; **1988–90:** Local Government Officer, Monklands District; **1990–7:** Highland Region; **1997–8:** Volunteer Development Scotland; **1999:** elected MSP.

**Profile:** When Elaine Smith first ran and was elected for the Scottish parliament, she was mistaken for Elaine C. Smith, the actress and comedienne, and that was no joke for either of them. She is married with one son. She is one of the small band of MSPs who nip out for a fly fag at the top of the staircase at parliament.

She is one of the quieter MSPs, but she is a member of two committees and seven cross-party groups. She did get her moment of glory in May 2001 when she secured a members' debate on the decline of breast-feeding by Scotland's young mothers. Apparently, Scottish figures are among the lowest in Europe, and her own constituency of Coatbridge and Chryston has the lowest level in Scotland. The debate was well attended by women MSPs, and many young mothers – with their babies – looked on from the gallery. Ms Smith called on the Executive to help encourage breastfeeding and bring about a change in social attitudes to make the sight of breasts more publicly acceptable than brazen displays on page three. In general, she has failed to shine, and there are suggestions that she might be deselected.

**Committees:** Equal Opportunities; Rural Development.

**Contact:** 0131-348-5824 Fax 0131-348-5834 (Parliament)
01236-449122 (Constituency)
e-mail elaine.smith.msp@scottish.parliament.uk

**Iain Smith** (LIBERAL DEMOCRAT)
**MSP Fife North-East**

**Born:** Gateside, 1960

**Education:** Bell Baxter High School, Cupar;
Newcastle University.

**Career: 1981:** Administrative Assistant,
Northumberland County Council; **1982–99:** Councillor, Fife Region
then Fife Council; **1982:** Advice Worker, Dundee; **1983–5:** Advice
Centre Manager; **1985–7:** Voluntary Agent, NE Fife Liberal
Association; **1987–98:** Constituency Researcher to Menzies Campbell
MP; **1998–9:** Constituency Organiser NE Fife; **1999:** elected MSP;
**1999–2000:** Deputy Minister for Parliament.

**Profile:** Smith is a local boy made good. He was born and brought up
in north-east Fife, schooled locally and – after university in Newcastle
and work in Dundee – returned to represent the area as a councillor
and work for the local MP, Menzies Campbell. Despite his youth (only
twenty-two when first elected), he was leader of the opposition on Fife
Council for fourteen years. Before immersing himself in politics, he
was an advice worker and then manager of the Bonnethill Advice
Centre in Dundee. He is openly gay.

He made a good start to his parliamentary career, being appointed
Deputy Minister for Parliament in the Executive, which also meant
fulfilling the role of Business Manager – and Whip – to the Liberal
Democrat group. After a year, however, he was removed partly because
of dissatisfaction on his own benches, most particularly over his performance in the reorganisation of the committee structure. Moreover,
his relationship with the lead minister, Tom McCabe, was uneasy to say
the least, and they fell out badly over the repeal of Section 28, when
McCabe was suspected of being a trimmer and Smith warned against
'compromise'. The task of whipping the Liberals is masochistic, so he
may now be happier as their spokesperson on Local Government. He
does have a reputation for hard graft and organisation and was a key
figure in the 2001 Westminster campaign.

**Committees:** Local Government.

**Contact:** 0131-348-5817 (Parliament)
    01334-656361 Fax 01334-654045 (Constituency)
    e-mail iain.smith.msp@scottish.parliament.uk

## Margaret Smith (LIBERAL DEMOCRAT)
## MSP Edinburgh West

**Born:** Edinburgh, 1961

**Education:** Broughton High School; Edinburgh University.

**Career: 1983–4:** Pensions Documentation, Guardian Royal Exchange; **1984–7:** Executive Officer, Registers of Scotland; **1990–6:** Scottish Officer, UN Association; **1995–9:** Councillor, Edinburgh City; **1996–7:** Constituency Organiser, Edinburgh West Lib Dems; **1999:** elected MSP.

**Profile:** Margaret Smith is separated and has two children, a son and a daughter. She worked as Constituency Organiser in the Edinburgh West constituency at the 1997 general election and brought home the victory for which the candidate Donald Gorrie and the Liberals had been struggling for thirty years. In the subsequent selection conference for the Liberal Democrat candidate to stand for the same seat in the Scottish elections, she beat Gorrie to the nomination, which may say something nice about the Lib Dems.

She is Convener of the Committee on Health and Community Care and, as such, eloquently explained the Committee's approval of free care for the elderly when the Executive were trying to stall such an expensive commitment. It was a deeply felt and well-delivered plea for compassionate treatment, and the Executive lost the vote. As a rule, she is not one of the Lib Dem awkward squad. Oddly enough, they are all men – or is it odd? She is also the party's spokesperson on Health and Community Care.

**Committees:** Health and Community Care (Convener).

**Contact:** 0131-348-5786 (Parliament)
0131-339-0339 (Constituency)
e-mail margaret.smith.msp@scottish.parliament.uk

## Sir David Steel (LIBERAL DEMOCRAT)
### Presiding Officer
### MSP (List) Lothian

**Born:** Kirkcaldy, 1938

**Education:** Prince of Wales School, Nairobi;
George Watson's College, Edinburgh;
Edinburgh University.

**Career: 1964–5:** Presenter/Interviewer BBC Scotland;
**1965–83:** MP for Roxburgh, Selkirk and Peebles; **1976–88:** Leader,
Liberal Party; **1983–97:** MP for Tweeddale, Ettrick and Lauderdale;
**1988:** Co-founder, Social and Liberal Democrats; **1999:** elected MSP.

**Profile:** Sir David – or, to give him his proper name, the Rt Hon Lord Steel of Aikwood – is married to the redoubtable Judy, a public figure in her own right. They live in a sixteenth-century Peel Tower, restored thanks to a successful action for damages against the *Star* newspaper. They have two sons and a daughter. David Steel has been with us for so long and has contributed so much to British and Scottish politics that it's hard to recapture the surprise and excitement of that by-election in 1965 when a young man of twenty-six swept aside a scion of the Borders Tory gentry. Even the ranks of Labour could not forbear to cheer. Some say he's now a little pompous and self-satisfied, but others say he has the right to be, having led the Liberals out of the wilderness and contrived to let David Owen hang himself. No puppet this.

After a career that included the historic Abortion Act (1967), the Lib–Lab pact with Callaghan, the absorption of the SDP into the Liberal Democrats, and the joint chairmanship of the Scottish Constitutional Convention, he topped the Liberal list for Lothian in the 1999 Scottish elections. He was the natural, indeed inescapable, choice for Presiding Officer and was installed by the new Parliament's first collective vote, enjoying the fruition of a piece of Liberal policy as old as Gladstone. He has kept the show on the road by a mixture of experience, wisdom and invention. The Executive have taken against him because he chastised ministers for leaking policy to the press before announcing it in Parliament; and because he used his casting vote in favour of Parliament and against ministers during the debate on compensation for the fishing industry. In turn, he has criticised sections of the press for unfair reporting, so they're not too keen on him either. They kent his faither. He has been diagnosed with prostate cancer, though it is not thought to be alarming. He retires in 2003 to let his achievements speak for themselves.

**Contact:** 0131-348-5302 Fax 0131-348-5301(Parliament)
e-mail presiding.officer.@scottish.parliament.uk

**Nicol Stephen** (LIBERAL DEMOCRAT)
**Deputy Minister for Education and**
**Young People**
**MSP Aberdeen South**

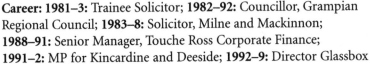

**Born:** Aberdeen, 1963

**Education:** Robert Gordon's College, Aberdeen;
Aberdeen and Edinburgh Universities.

**Career: 1981–3:** Trainee Solicitor; **1982–92:** Councillor, Grampian
Regional Council; **1983–8:** Solicitor, Milne and Mackinnon;
**1988–91:** Senior Manager, Touche Ross Corporate Finance;
**1991–2:** MP for Kincardine and Deeside; **1992–9:** Director Glassbox
Ltd; **1999:** elected MSP and appointed Deputy Minister for
Enterprise and Lifelong Learning.

**Profile:** He looks like the boy next door but, married with one son and
one daughter, he's a big boy now. His legal and management career ran
in parallel with membership of Grampian Regional Council, where he
was chairman of the Economic Development and Planning Committee
and a founder/director of Grampian Enterprise. In 1991 he took the
Kincardine and Deeside seat from the Conservatives at a by-election
and he must have thought his boatie had come in, but – like many
marginal winners before him – he lost in the general election the very
next year. He took his current seat with some comfort.

As one of the Lib Dem ministers in the administration, he was first
Henry McLeish's Deputy in Enterprise and Lifelong Learning and –
after the reshuffle of October 2000 – he became Deputy to Jack
McConnell in Education, Europe and External Relations. So unless
Henry was being exceptionally sleekit and machiavellian towards Jack,
he must consider Stephen a safe pair of hands. His new boss, Cathy
Jamieson, seems to agree, and she has given him the day-to-day run-
ning of Scotland's schools. He performs reasonably well in the
Chamber in his quiet way but is probably at his most effective in smaller meetings and external contacts.

**Contact:** 0131-348-5347 (Parliament)
          01224-252728 Fax 01224-455678 (Constituency)
          e-mail nicol.stephen.msp@scottish.parliament.uk

**Stewart Stevenson (SNP)**
**MSP Banff and Buchan**

**Born:** Edinburgh, 1946

**Education:** Bell Baxter School, Cupar;
Aberdeen University.

**Career: 1969–98:** Bank of Scotland employee in various positions
from trainee computer programmer to Director of Technology
Innovation; **1998–2001:** full-time political activist; Director,
Business for Scotland and Independence Merchandise;
**2001:** elected MSP (by-election).

**Profile:** Stevenson is a Bank of Scotland Executive who spent much of
the 1992 election driving Alex Salmond around the constituency, so
he knows the road to success. He also has a pilot's licence. He was a
leading campaigner against the carpetbaggers who pursued Standard
Life in 2000 and headed the Standard Life Independent Members'
Organisation.

He took 50 per cent of the vote on election night 2001 though – until
Alex Salmond's sudden decision to quit Edinburgh rather than London
– he had expected to be heading for Westminster himself. They
swopped places – no greater love. He arrived at Parliament with a confident air and an obviously good conceit of himself, but it won't be
long before someone has knocked that out of him.

**Committees:** Justice 2; Rural Development.

**Contact:** 0131-348-5894 (Parliament)
01779-470444 Fax 01779-474460 (Constituency)
e-mail stewart.stevenson.msp@scottish.parliament.uk

## Jamie Stone (LIBERAL DEMOCRAT)
## MSP Caithness, Sutherland and Easter Ross

**Born:** Edinburgh, 1954

**Education:** Tain Royal Academy; Gordonstoun School; St Andrews University.

**Career: 1977:** Cleaner/Kitchen Porter, GrandMet; **1977–8:** English Teacher, Sicily; **1978:** Fish gutting, Faroes; **1979–81:** Stores Clerk, Wimpey; **1981–4:** Site Administrator, Bechtel GB Ltd; **1984–6:** Admin Manager, Odfjell Drilling UK Ltd.; **1986–94:** Director, Highland Fine Cheeses Ltd; **1986–96:** Councillor, Ross and Cromarty District Council; **1998–9:** Councillor, Highland Council; **1999:** elected MSP.

**Profile:** He has been around has Jamie and has never been afraid of getting his hands dirty. Fortunately, there was an eight-year gap between the fish-gutting and the fine cheeses. He was also Director at the Highland Festival, a freelance newspaper columnist and served in the 2/51 Highland Volunteers. He is member of the Tain Museum Trust, the Cromarty Port Authority and the Highland Buildings Trust. In Edinburgh he's a member of the New Club, so he has somewhere to go of an evening after his exertions on the Mound. He is married, with one son and two daughters, and has a bit of land.

Until recently, Labour thought Jamie Stone was one of the good guys, a Liberal who could be relied on. You might even say he was popular with his coalition partners. Then came the debate on compensation for the fishing industry when Jamie, the Lib Dems' spokesperson for fisheries, made a speech that gave no indication that he might vote against the Executive proposals. He did, together with other Liberals, the Executive lost the vote and Jamie resigned his position. To underline the point, he and Tavish Scott were the only two Liberal Democrats to vote against when the package was debated a second time. He now speaks on Equal Opportunities and – yes – Fisheries again.

**Committees:** Equal Opportunities.

**Contact:** 0131-348-5789 (Parliament)
0862-892726 (Constituency)
e-mail jamie.stone.msp@scottish.parliament.uk

# Nicola Sturgeon (SNP)
# MSP (List) Glasgow

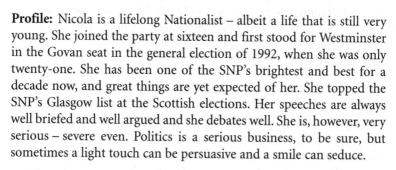

**Born:** Irvine, 1970

**Education:** Greenwood Academy, Irvine;
Glasgow University.

**Career: 1993–5:** Trainee Solicitor; **1995–7:** Solicitor, Stirling;
**1997–9:** Solicitor, Drumchapel Law Centre; **1999:** elected MSP.

**Profile:** Nicola is a lifelong Nationalist – albeit a life that is still very
young. She joined the party at sixteen and first stood for Westminster
in the Govan seat in the general election of 1992, when she was only
twenty-one. She has been one of the SNP's brightest and best for a
decade now, and great things are yet expected of her. She topped the
SNP's Glasgow list at the Scottish elections. Her speeches are always
well briefed and well argued and she debates well. She is, however, very
serious – severe even. Politics is a serious business, to be sure, but
sometimes a light touch can be persuasive and a smile can seduce.

She has been on the SNP Executive since 1992 and was Vice-Convener
for Publicity at the last two elections. In the contest for Alex Salmond's
successor, she was campaign manager for the successful candidate and
new Leader John Swinney. She is the party's spokesperson on Health
and Community Care, and her duels with the minister Susan Deacon
were among the most enthralling episodes in the parliamentary agenda.
She may find that for the present Minister, Malcolm Chisholm, she
needs to develop a new act. If Swinney does not create a larger public
profile for himself soon, she will certainly be one of those in the running
for the leadership. Either way, she is one of the party's truly effective
spokespeople, if sometimes the nippiest of nippy sweeties.

**Committees:** Health and Community Care.

**Contact:** 0131-348-5694 Fax 0131-348-5949 (Parliament)
0141-204-1775 Fax 0141-204-1776 (Constituency)
e-mail nicola.sturgeon.msp@scottish.parliament.uk

**John Swinney** (SNP)
**Leader, SNP**
**MSP North Tayside**

**Born:** Edinburgh, 1964

**Education:** Forrester High School, Edinburgh;
Edinburgh University.

**Career: 1987–8:** Research Officer, Scottish Coal Project;
**1986–92:** National Secretary SNP; **1988–92:** Managing Consultant,
Development Options Ltd; **1992–7:** Strategic Planning Principal,
Scottish Amicable; **1997–2001:** MP for North Tayside;
**1999:** elected MSP; **2000:** elected SNP Leader.

**Profile:** John Swinney has two young children, but – one of the perils
of politics – is divorced. Like Nicola Sturgeon and a few others, he
came up through the youth wing of the party, first joining at the age of
fifteen. His progress had been steady but unspectacular until Alex
Salmond decided to resign the leadership. He was National Secretary for
six years, Publicity Vice-Convener for five, then Treasury Spokesperson
and Senior Vice-Convener. The trusty lieutenant is now commanding
offcer, having soundly beaten Alex Neil. The new challenge is not to his
intellect but to his personality. Salmond was and is a class act. Swinney
has already been unkindly compared to the man from the Bradford
and Bingley, who has a nice line in savings products but no grand
design for life. The SNP, in the person of Linda Fabiani, has been
advising him to get out of the bank manager suits when he can and
have a go at casual chic. He has recently and publicly announced a new
relationship with BBC journalist Elizabeth Quigley, so something's
working.

As Convener of the Enterprise and Lifelong Learning Committee for the
first year of Parliament, John Swinney formed a constructive relationship with the then minister Henry McLeish. Between them, much was
done to forge links with the business community and to encourage an
exchange of ideas on economic development. Then they had the
daunting task of replacing Dewar and Salmond, both masters of the
art of parliamentary politics. They failed to impress and Swinney, who
was outshone by David McLetchie during 'Officegate', now faces a
resurgent Jack McConnell. His poor performance in the Chamber is
matched by his lack of impact outside it. His policies, too, require a

makeover but the trouble is that he was involved in drafting most of them – and was personally responsible for the failed 'Penny for Scotland' wheeze. In his mid-thirties, he has time, but not that much. He has declined to accept the additional salary that goes with being Leader of the Opposition. Honest self-assessment or political opportunism?

**Contact:** 0131-348-5717 Fax 0131-348-5946 (Parliament)
01250-876576 (Constituency)
e-mail john.swinney.msp@scottish.parliament.uk

**Elaine Thomson** (LABOUR)
**MSP Aberdeen North**

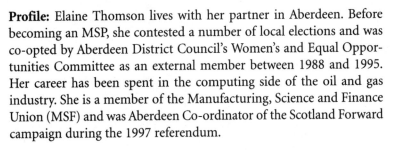

**Born:** Inverness, 1957

**Education:** Aberdeen High School for Girls;
Aberdeen University.

**Career: 1982–95:** Analyst/Programmer/Senior Systems
Administrator, Abb Vetco Gray Ltd; **1995–9:** IT Consultant,
Absoft Ltd; **1999:** elected MSP.

**Profile:** Elaine Thomson lives with her partner in Aberdeen. Before
becoming an MSP, she contested a number of local elections and was
co-opted by Aberdeen District Council's Women's and Equal Opportunities Committee as an external member between 1988 and 1995.
Her career has been spent in the computing side of the oil and gas
industry. She is a member of the Manufacturing, Science and Finance
Union (MSF) and was Aberdeen Co-ordinator of the Scotland Forward
campaign during the 1997 referendum.

She is Deputy Convenor of the Finance Committee, where her
numeracy and IT skills must make her invaluable. She is also on the
Enterprise and Lifelong Learning Committee, for which she is no less
amply qualified. She campaigned successfully to get the Scottish
branch of the Food Standards Agency sited in Aberdeen. Otherwise,
she is a solid, well-behaved backbencher.

**Committees:** Finance (Deputy Convener); Enterprise and Lifelong
          Learning.

**Contact:** 0131-348-5917 Fax 0131-348-5979 (Parliament)
          01224-699666 Fax 01224-685137 (Constituency)
          e-mail elaine.thomson.msp@scottish.parliament.uk

**Murray Tosh** (CONSERVATIVE)
**Deputy Presiding Officer**
**MSP (List) South of Scotland**

**Born:** Ayr, 1950

**Education:** Kilmarnock Academy; Glasgow
University; Jordanhill College.

**Career: 1975:** History Teacher, Ravenspark Academy, Irvine;
**1977–84:** Principal History Teacher, Kilwinning Academy; **1984–99:**
Principal History, Belmont Academy, Ayr; **1987–96:** Councillor, Kyle
and Carrick District Council; **1999:** elected MSP.

**Profile:** Murray Tosh was a Liberal in his youth, even standing as a
parliamentary Liberal candidate for Ayr in 1974. He decided shortly
afterwards that the Conservatives were the better bet in Scotland. You
have to sympathise, don't you? He is married with two sons and a
daughter.

He is one of the jollier MSPs. Scarcely hidebound by dogma, he just
gets on with the job. He is on the liberal wing of the party and
favoured devolution during the years when the Conservatives opposed
it. He is popular across all benches, well liked and respected. All the
more surprising, therefore, that he has decided not to stand again in
2003, but to return to local government – though it may be more of a
comment on his party's fortunes than an expression of his feelings
about the Parliament. Nevertheless, he allowed his name to go forward
for the vacancy of Deputy Presiding Officer, and won – but it is fair to
say that the First Minister's public support for Cathy Peattie helped
him no end. He'll enjoy it and, who knows, he might even stay.

**Committees:** Procedures (Convener).

**Contact:** 0131-348-5637 Fax 0131-348-5932 (Parliament)
01292-470264 Fax 01292-470264(Constituency)
e-mail murray.tosh.msp@scottish.parliament.uk

## Kay Ullrich (SNP)
## MSP (List) West of Scotland

**Born:** Prestwick, 1943

**Education:** Ayr Academy; Queen's College,
Glasgow.

**Career: 1973–81:** Schools Swimming Instructor, North Ayrshire;
**1984–6:** School Social Worker, Westwood Secondary;
**1986–8:** Hospital Social Worker, Crosshouse, **1988–92:** Childcare
Social Worker; **1992–7:** Senior Social Worker, Criminal Justice
Services, Kilmarnock; **1999:** elected MSP.

**Profile:** Kay Ullrich is married with one son and one daughter. She
has spent much of her life in social work. Early in her career, she was a
swimming instructor and a Butlins Redcoat. Even this experience could
not have prepared her for her co-starring role, with Helen Liddell, in
the 1994 Monklands East by-election, brought about by the tragically
early death of John Smith. This bitter battle, following on accusations
of corruption and malpractice by the local Labour Council, featured a
duel of invective between the main candidates, much of it on television.
Mrs Ullrich's voice is even more penetrating than Mrs Liddell's, but
she lost an election that the SNP seemed likely to win. She may have
miscalculated, but it is more likely that Helen Liddell summoned all
her skill and steel.

Kay Ullrich started off in 1999 as the SNP's principal spokesperson on
Health and Community Care, a role she had already fulfilled outside
Parliament, drawing on her experience in social work. However, it was
felt that she was not making much headway against the minister Susan
Deacon, so – in 2000 – she gave way to the less fiery but more penetrating Nicola Sturgeon. She has now assumed the role of SNP Chief
Whip so – if there is any sorting out to be done – Kay will do it. She
could unkindly be called a veteran, whose reward was to get elected
and whose time on the front bench is limited.

**Committees:** Equal Opportunities (Deputy Convener); Standards.

**Contact:**  0131-348-5667 (Parliament)
            01475-806020 Fax 01475-806021(Constituency)
            e-mail kay.ullrich.msp@scottish.parliament.uk

**Ben Wallace** (CONSERVATIVE)
**MSP (List) North-East Scotland**

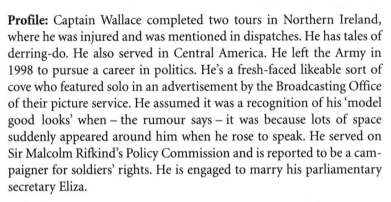

**Born:** Farnborough, 1970

**Education:** Millfield School; Royal Military
Academy, Sandhurst.

**Career: 1987:** Barman, Oxford; **1987–8:** Ski instructor, Austria;
**1991–8:** Commissioned, Scots Guards; **1999:** elected MSP.

**Profile:** Captain Wallace completed two tours in Northern Ireland,
where he was injured and was mentioned in dispatches. He has tales of
derring-do. He also served in Central America. He left the Army in
1998 to pursue a career in politics. He's a fresh-faced likeable sort of
cove who featured solo in an advertisement by the Broadcasting Office
of their picture service. He assumed it was a recognition of his 'model
good looks' when – the rumour says – it was because lots of space
suddenly appeared around him when he rose to speak. He served on
Sir Malcolm Rifkind's Policy Commission and is reported to be a campaigner for soldiers' rights. He is engaged to marry his parliamentary
secretary Eliza.

Captain Ben is Conservative Deputy Spokesperson on Health and
Social Work. He is often heard boasting of his Harley Street GP, which
may not be the image the new Scottish Tories are trying to project,
though in other respects he fits the bill – young, talented and dashing.
Since his election, he has still been actively pursuing nomination for a
Westminster seat. Is this the behaviour of an officer and a gentleman
or is he using Phil Gallie as a role model? Like Gallie, he does not
intend to run again in 2003 but – in the meantime – he has been
hounding the Executive through the Court over its help for the Private
Members Bill on fox-hunting. Yoicks!

**Committees:** European.

**Contact:** 0131-348-5651 (Parliament)
01569-767177 (Constituency)
e-mail ben.wallace.msp@scottish.parliament.uk

**Jim Wallace** (LIBERAL DEMOCRAT)
**Deputy First Minister and Minister for Justice,**
**Europe and External Affairs**
**Leader, Scottish Liberal Democrats**
**MSP Orkney**

**Born:** Annan, 1954

**Education:** Annan Academy; Cambridge and
Edinburgh Universities.

**Career: 1979– :** Advocate; **1997:** Became QC; **1983–2001:** MP for
Orkney and Shetland; **1992:** elected Leader, Scottish Liberal
Democrats; **1999:** elected MSP and appointed Deputy First Minister.

**Profile:** Jim Wallace joined the Liberals at university. He was Chairman
of the Edinburgh University Liberal Club (note that university affectation: not Association or Party but Club). He began his career as a
solicitor before being called to the Bar. He is married, with two daughters, and lives in Orkney when his responsibilities allow. He contested
European and Westminster elections in his home area before being
selected for the plum Liberal seat of Orkney and Shetland in succession
to the great and much loved Jo Grimond. He is something of a contrast,
with a reputation for being dull but competent. Perhaps we should be
grateful for that. He is not interested in stardom but in getting the job
done.

His campaign before the Scottish elections made some bold promises
– like the abolition of student tuition fees – and therefore made the
formation of the coalition more difficult. He must have known that
coalition government was well nigh inevitable – everyone else did
and Donald Dewar is known to have warned him not to be too expan-
sive. Nevertheless, the gamble paid off, though not all his party were
happy with the outcome. When Dewar was ill Wallace took over as
First Minister, despite the misgivings of hardline Labourites. 'That's
what Deputy means,' said Dewar, 'he deputises.' He deputised well, to
the surprise of many, did so again when Dewar died and again when
Henry McLeish resigned. As Justice Minister, he has a key role in
translating liberal values into reform and the Executive is the better
for it. He is no Jack Straw. His party is not always entirely happy with
Executive policies but he fights his corner hard before accepting collec-

tive responsibility. He doesn't have the attributes of The Wallace but – like The Bruce – he's rather more effective.

**Contact:** 0131-348-5815 Fax 0131-348-5807 (Parliament)
01856-876541 Fax 01856-876162 (Constituency)
e-mail jim.wallace.msp@scottish.parliament.uk

# Mike Watson (LABOUR)
## Minister for Tourism, Culture and Sport
## MSP Glasgow Cathcart

**Born:** Cambuslang, 1949

**Education:** Dundee High School; Heriot Watt
University.

**Career: 1974–7:** Development Officer WEA;
**1977–89:** full-time MSF offficial, including Industrial Officer,
Regional Officer; **1989–97:** MP for Glasgow Central; **1993– :** Visiting
Research Fellow, Strathclyde University; **1997–9:** Director PS
Communications; **1999:** elected MSP.

**Profile:** Mike Watson has impeccable Labour credentials but became
involved in the most bitter selection conference in Labour's Scottish
history. After serving Glasgow Central for eight years, he was opposed
by Mohammed Sarwar in the selection conference to become the
candidate for the redistributed seat of Glasgow Govan. He won the
first conference but lost the re-run in an unpleasant contest (confused
by accusations of racial prejudice), which Labour would wish to forget
and which brought credit to neither camp. It was the people's party at
its worst, although there is no evidence that either side broke the rules
– no evidence but lingering suspicion that one of them might have
done. He is a dedicated supporter of Dundee United and, suitably,
takes a pro-Arab position in Middle East Affairs.

Lord Watson of Invergowrie – as he has been since 1997 – was
Convener of the all-important Finance Committee, and is a man of
independent mind. He believes – despite Labour's protestations – that
the Tartan Tax will be invoked after 2003. He was against the Gulf
War and the Maastricht Treaty, though both of these were during
Labour's long years of opposition. He has attracted most publicity for
his 'Protection of Wild Mammals' Bill, or – in more common par-
lance – the Bill to ban fox-hunting in Scotland. After long deliberation
the Bill was deemed unworkable in its present form by the Rural
Development Committee but nevertheless passed its first vote in
Parliament. The race is on between Holyrood and Westminster to see
who can get a workable Bill on the statute book first. Watson is one of
three 'Lords' in the Scottish Parliament and might reasonably have
expected a government post at an earlier stage. He should make a good

job of his new ministry, with Tourism in particular needing inventive and dynamic leadership.

**Contact:** 0131-348-5840 (Parliament)
0141-636-6121 (Constituency)
e-mail mike.watson.msp@scottish.parliament.uk

**Andrew Welsh** (SNP)
**Member Scottish Parliament Corporate Body**
**MSP Angus**

**Born:** Glasgow, 1944

**Education:** Govan High School; Glasgow
University.

**Career: 1964–74:** Teacher; **1974:** Councillor, Stirling District;
**1974–9:** MP for South Angus; **1984–7:** Provost of Angus;
**1987–2001:** MP for Angus East, then Angus; **1999:** elected MSP.

**Profile:** Andrew Welsh is married with one daughter. He has come
along way since he first stood for Westminster in Dunbartonshire
Central in February 1974, when he asked a television interviewer what
he should say in reply to a question. Six months later he was MP for
South Angus and the Angus love affair has continued ever since, with
one interruption by the able and urbane Peter (now Lord) Fraser.
During that interruption, Welsh made a reputation for assiduous work
in local government and was Provost of Thrums – no, Angus – but
remained a character of whom Barrie would have approved: honest,
upright, well meaning. He is still, however, quite shy and rather dull.

He is a member of the Scottish Parliamentary Corporate Body, which
oversees the administration of the Parliament but is sometimes
assumed to be a dumping ground for hard-working but uninspired
journeymen. He is also Convenor of the Audit Committee.

**Committees:** Audit (Convener).

**Contact:**  0131-348-5690 Fax 0131-348-5954 (Parliament)
01241-439369 Fax 01241-871561 (Constituency)
e-mail andrew.welsh.msp@scottish.parliament.uk

# Sandra White (SNP)
## MSP (List) Glasgow

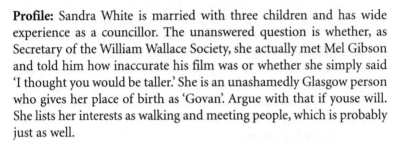

**Born:** Glasgow, 1951

**Education:** Garthamlock Secondary; Glasgow and Cardonald Colleges.

**Career: 1989–99:** Councillor, Renfrewshire Council; Press Officer, William Wallace Society; **1999:** elected MSP.

**Profile:** Sandra White is married with three children and has wide experience as a councillor. The unanswered question is whether, as Secretary of the William Wallace Society, she actually met Mel Gibson and told him how inaccurate his film was or whether she simply said 'I thought you would be taller.' She is an unashamedly Glasgow person who gives her place of birth as 'Govan'. Argue with that if youse will. She lists her interests as walking and meeting people, which is probably just as well.

She is Deputy Convenor of the Social Justice Committee. She sometimes seems to be obsessed by local issues like bus routes, which would be fine for Renfrew Council but may just be a little trivial for Holyrood. She reacted with understandable shock and anger to the news that Glasgow University is considering the closure of a course on Scottish politics. Her pressure has forced a reconsideration.

**Committees:** Local Government.

**Contact:** 0131-348-5688 Fax 0131-348-5945 (Parliament)
0141-204-1767 Fax 0141-204-1781 (Constituency)
e-mail sandra.white.msp@scottish.parliament.uk

## Karen Whitefield (LABOUR)
**MSP Airdrie and Shotts**

**Born:** Bellshill, 1970

**Education:** Calderhead High School, Shotts; Glasgow Caledonian University.

**Career: 1992:** Civil Servant, Benefits Agency; **1992–9:** Personal Assistant to Rachel Squire MP; **1999:** elected MSP.

**Profile:** Karen Whitefield is a member of the Manufacturing, Science and Finance Union and is involved with the Girls' Brigade. She enjoys cake decorating, which must be very relaxing after a hard day on the Mound. She has always been a pillar of her local party, which paid dividends at the selection conference, and was a constituency representative to the National Policy Forum in 1998. She is the grand-daughter of the sainted Peggy Herbison, but does not seem to have inherited either her fire or her vision.

She has been one of those criticised in the early days of Parliament for the poor standard of speaking from some of the backbench Labour women MSPs. The media dismissively referred to a 'shoal of Karens' after she spoke in the debate on members' allowances, and in return there were accusations of male chauvinism. There is little doubt that women are among the hardest workers in Parliament, but Karen has made her reputation dwelling on local Lanarkshire matters, from which we should be spared. She is one of the sweetie-sooking sorority and may not be reselected.

**Committees:** Social Justice.

**Contact:** 0131-348-5832 (Parliament)
            01501-822200 Fax 01501-823650 (Constituency)
            e-mail karen.whitefield.msp@scottish.parliament.uk

**Allan Wilson** (LABOUR)
**Deputy Minister for the Environment and**
**Rural Development**
**MSP Cunninghame North**

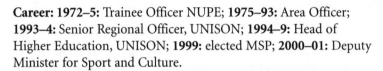

**Born:** Glasgow, 1954

**Education:** Spiers School, Beith.

**Career: 1972–5:** Trainee Officer NUPE; **1975–93:** Area Officer;
**1993–4:** Senior Regional Officer, UNISON; **1994–9:** Head of
Higher Education, UNISON; **1999:** elected MSP; **2000–01:** Deputy
Minister for Sport and Culture.

**Profile:** Allan Wilson is married with two sons. He has served as agent
to Brian Wilson MP and is a member of Labour's Scottish Executive.
When with NUPE, he edited their Scottish journal and with UNISON,
he joined the review body which oversees Pay and Conditions in the
Higher Education sector. At home, however, he is probably better
know for his prowess as a footballer and his membership of that
rugged and ruthless fraternity, Ayrshire junior football.

His appointment to the junior post in Sport and Culture was greeted
with a delight and despair in equal measure. By appointing a traditionalist and a trade unionist, McLeish was seen to be covering another
political base, but there were grave doubts about Wilson's suitability
for the cultural aspect of the job. After a few ill-chosen remarks about
karaoke, he took a vow of silence on artistic matters and declined to be
interviewed. The First Minister said his man could distinguish between
Porrini and Puccini and defended him against 'art snobs'. To everyone's
surprise, Wilson made an unusually thoughtful speech to Parliament
on 'Architecture and the Built Environment'. So thoughtful that his
opposition shadow Mike Russell asked who had written it for him.
Jack McConnell has moved him away from prima donnas and fiddle
bands to the wide open spaces of Environment and Rural Development, where he is less likely to bump into the scenery.

**Contact:** 0131-348-5772 (Parliament)
0131-682847 (Constituency)
e-mail allan.wilson.msp@scottish.parliament.uk

**Andrew Wilson** (SNP)
**MSP (List) Central Scotland**

**Born:** Lanark, 1970

**Education:** Coltness High School, Wishaw;
St Andrews and Strathclyde Universities.

**Career: 1993–5:** Economist, Government Economic Service;
**1995–6:** Scottish Office; **1996–7:** Economist/Senior Researcher SNP;
**1997–9:** Economist, Royal Bank of Scotland; **1999:** elected MSP.

**Profile:** Wilson is one of the SNP's brightest young prospects. His career path is strikingly similar to Alex Salmond's – St Andrews University followed by jobs as an economist in the government service and with the Royal Bank of Scotland. He also shares some of Salmond's other attributes – a friendly manner and a well-developed sense of humour. The only blot on his copybook thus far is that he was Kay Ullrich's agent in the Monklands by-election. Still in his twenties, he needs to build some political muscle. He writes a caustic column in the *Sunday Mail*. He was reported by Cathie Craigie for calling himself a 'local MSP' when he is in fact a 'list' member, and he apologised to the Standards Committee for this breach of etiquette.

He was the SNP's spokesperson on Finance and gave a good account of himself in his verbal battles with Angus Mackay. He now commands the wider portfolio of Economy, Enterprise and Lifelong Learning, passing on the more mundane finance matters to old hand Alasdair Morgan. He has done valuable work for the SNP in developing the economic case for independence. There is, however, some suspicion of him in the ranks of the fundamentalists, who fear his commitment stops short of separation. In a speech at the Party Conference of 1999 he managed to upset the fundies by admitting the reality of British identity, and scandalise Unionists by describing the Union flag as a symbolic of repression. If John Swinney fails to bring electoral success to the SNP, Wilson is an attractive option in the future.

**Contact:**   0131-348-5673 (Parliament)
           01236-736644 (Constituency)
           e-mail andrew.wilson.msp@scottish.parliament.uk

**John Young** (CONSERVATIVE)
**Member, Scottish Parliament Corporate Body**
**MSP (List) West of Scotland**

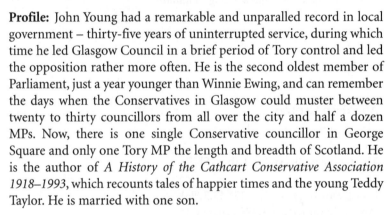

**Born:** Glasgow, 1930

**Education:** Hillhead High School, Glasgow;
Scottish College of Commerce.

**Career: 1949–51:** RAF; Export Manager, PR Consultant, Contracts
Manager, Shipping Manager; **1964–99:** Councillor, Glasgow
Corporation, then Glasgow District then Glasgow City Council;
**1977–9:** Leader, Glasgow District Council; **1999:** elected MSP.

**Profile:** John Young had a remarkable and unparalled record in local
government – thirty-five years of uninterrupted service, during which
time he led Glasgow Council in a brief period of Tory control and led
the opposition rather more often. He is the second oldest member of
Parliament, just a year younger than Winnie Ewing, and can remember
the days when the Conservatives in Glasgow could muster between
twenty to thirty councillors from all over the city and half a dozen
MPs. Now, there is one single Conservative councillor in George
Square and only one Tory MP the length and breadth of Scotland. He
is the author of *A History of the Cathcart Conservative Association
1918–1993*, which recounts tales of happier times and the young Teddy
Taylor. He is married with one son.

He was Conservative spokesperson on Transport and the Environment,
but he lost that post in McLetchie's summer reshuffle (2001). He sits
on the Scottish Parliament Corporate Body, which oversees the house-
keeping. He must be coming to the end of a political career for which
the Conservative Party should be grateful, though he didn't always
see eye to eye with them on devolution. If there were such a thing as
testimonial matches for politicians, he would deserve one. He shames
his younger colleagues by speaking without notes.

**Committees:** Audit; Justice 2.

**Contact:** 0131-348-5640 (Parliament)
0141-887-6161 Fax 0141-889-0223 (Constituency)
e-mail john.young.msp@scottish.parliament.uk

CHAPTER 13

# Scottish Results from the General Election 2001

*Note: asterisk denotes the winning candidate.*

**Aberdeen Central**
Elect 50,098. Turnout 52.75%
**Lab hold**
**Maj 6,646 4.24% swing Lab to SNP**

**Frank Doran (Lab) 12,025 (45.50%)**
Wayne Gault (SNP) 5,379 (20.35%)
Eleanor Anderson (LD) 4,547 (17.20%)
Stewart Whyte (C) 3,761 (14.23%)
Andy Cumbers (SSP) 717 (2.71%)

1997: Lab maj 10,801. *Doran Lab: 17,745 (49.82%) Wisely C: 6,944 (19.50%) Topping SNP: 5,767 (16.19%) Brown LD: 4,714 (13.24%)

**Aberdeen North**
Elect 52,746. Turnout 57.55%
**Lab hold**
**Maj 4,449 5.70% swing Lab to SNP**

**Malcolm Savidge (Lab) 13,157 (43.34%)**
Alasdair Allan (SNP) 8,708 (28.69%)

Jim Donaldson (LD) 4,991 (16.44%)
Richard Cowling (C) 3,047 (10.04%)
Shona Forman (SSP) 454 (1.50%)

1997: Lab maj 10,010. *Savidge Lab: 18,389 (47.87%) Adam SNP: 8,379 (21.81%) Gifford C: 5,763 (15.00%) Rumbles LD: 5,421 (14.11%)

### Aberdeen South
Elect 58,907. Turnout 62.62%
**Lab hold**
**Maj 4,388 2.13% swing LD to Lab**

**Anne Begg (Lab) 14,696 (39.84%)**
Ian Yuill (LD) 10,308 (27.94%)
Moray Macdonald (C) 7,098 (19.24%)
Ian Angus (SNP) 4,293 (11.64%)
David Watt (SSP) 495 (1.34%)

1997: Lab maj 3,365. *Begg Lab: 15,541 (35.27%) Stephen LD: 12,176 (27.63%) Robertson C: 11,621 (26.37%) Towers SNP: 4,299 (9.76%)

### Aberdeenshire West & Kincardine
Elect 61,180. Turnout 61.97%
**LD hold**
**Maj 4,821 3.28% swing C to LD**

**Robert Smith (LD) 16,507 (43.54%)**
Tom Kerr (C) 11,686 (30.82%)
Kevin Hutchens (Lab) 4,669 (12.31%)
John Green (SNP) 4,634 (12.22%)
Alan Manley (SSP) 418 (1.10%)

1997: LD maj 2,662. *Smith LD: 17,742 (41.08%) Kynoch C: 15,080 (34.92%) Mowatt SNP: 5,639 (13.06%) Khan Lab: 3,923 (9.08%)

### Airdrie & Shotts
Elect 58,349. Turnout 54.39%
**Lab hold**
**Maj 12,340 0.73% swing SNP to Lab**

**Helen Liddell (Lab) 18,478 (58.22%)**
Alison Lindsay (SNP) 6,138 (19.34%)
John Love (LD) 2,376 (7.49%)
Gordon McIntosh (C) 1,960 (6.18%)
Mary Dempsey (Scot U) 1,439 (4.53%)
Kenny McGuigan (SSP) 1,171 (3.69%)
Chris Herriot (Soc Lab) 174 (0.55%)

1997: Lab maj 15,412. *Liddell Lab: 25,460 (61.82%) Robertson SNP: 10,048 (24.40%) Brook C: 3,660 (8.89%) Wolseley LD: 1,719 (4.17%)

**Angus**
Elect 59,004. Turnout 59.34%
**SNP hold**
**Maj 3,611 6.67% swing SNP to C**

**Michael Weir (SNP) 12,347 (35.26%)**
Marcus Booth (C) 8,736 (24.95%)
Ian McFatridge (Lab) 8,183 (23.37%)
Peter Nield (LD) 5,015 (14.32%)
Bruce Wallace (SSP) 732 (2.09%)

1997: SNP maj 10,189. *Welsh SNP: 20,792 (48.27%) Leslie C: 10,603 (24.61%) Taylor Lab: 6,733 (15.63%) Speirs LD: 4,065 (9.44%)

**Argyll & Bute**
Elect 49,175. Turnout 62.95%
**LD hold**
**Maj 1,653 9.6% swing LD to Lab**

**Alan Reid (LD) 9,245 (29.86%)**
Hugh Raven (Lab) 7,592 (24.52%)
David Petrie (Con) 6,436 (20.79%)
Agnes Samuel (SNP) 6,433 (20.78%)

1997: LD maj 6,081 (17.03%) *Michie LD: 14,359 (40.2%) MacCormick SNP: 8,278 (23.17%) Leishman C: 6,774 (18.96%) Syed Lab: 5,596 (15.67%) Stewart Ref: 713 (2%)

## Ayr
Elect 55,630. Turnout 69.32%
**Lab hold**
**Maj 2,545 4.01% swing Lab to Con**

**Sandra Osborne (Lab) 16,801 (43.57%)**
Phil Gallie (C) 14,256 (36.97%)
Jim Mather (SNP) 4,621 (11.98%)
Stuart Ritchie (LD) 2,089 (5.42%)
James Stewart (SSP) 692 (1.79%)
Joseph Smith (UK Ind) 101 (0.26%)

1997: Lab maj 6,543. *Osborne Lab: 21,679 (48.44%) Gallie C: 15,136 (33.82%) Blackford SNP: 5,625 (12.57%) Hamblen LD: 2,116 (4.73%)

---

**Banff & Buchan**
Elect 56,496. Turnout 54.53%
**SNP hold**
**Maj 10,503 1.06% swing C to SNP**

**Alex Salmond (SNP) 16,710 (54.24%)**
Alexander Wallace (C) 6,207 (20.15%)
Edward Harris (Lab) 4,363 (14.16%)
Douglas Herbison (LD) 2,769 (8.99%)
Alice Rowan (SSP) 447 (1.45%)
Eric Davidson (UK Ind) 310 (1.01%)

1997: SNP maj 12,845. *Salmond SNP: 22,409 (55.77%) Frain-Bell C: 9,564 (23.80%) Harris Lab: 4,747 (11.81%) Fletcher LD: 2,398 (5.97%)

---

**Caithness, Sutherland & Easter Ross**
Elect 41,225. Turnout 60.32%
**LD hold**
**Maj 2,744 1.64% swing Lab to LD**

**John Thurso (LD) 9,041 (36.36%)**
Michael Meighan (Lab) 6,297 (25.32%)
John Macadam (SNP) 5,273 (21.20%)

Robert Rowantree (C) 3,513 (14.13%)
Karn Mabon (SSP) 544 (2.19%)
Gordon Campbell (Ind) 199 (0.80%)

1997: LD maj 2,259. *Maclennan LD: 10,381 (35.59%) Hendry Lab: 8,122 (27.84%) Harper SNP: 6,710 (23.00%) Miers C: 3,148 (10.79%) Ryder Ref: 369 (1.26%) Martin Green: 230 (0.79%)

---

**Carrick, Cumnock & Doon Valley**
Elect 64,919. Turnout 61.78%
**Lab Co-op hold**
**Maj 14,856 2.90% swing Lab Co-op to C**

**George Foulkes (Lab Co-op) 22,174 (55.29%)**
Gordon Miller (C) 7,318 (18.25%)
Tom Wilson (SNP) 6,258 (15.60%)
Amy Rogers (LD) 2,932 (7.31%)
Amanda McFarlane (SSP) 1,058 (2.64%)
James McDaid (Soc Lab) 367 (0.92%)

1997: Lab maj 21,062. *Foulkes Lab: 29,398 (59.79%) Marshall C: 8,336 (16.95%) Hutchison SNP: 8,190 (16.66%) Young LD: 2,613 (5.31%)

---

**Clydebank & Milngavie**
Elect 52,534. Turnout 61.85%
**Lab hold**
**Maj 10,724 0.54% swing Lab to SNP**

**Tony Worthington (Lab) 17,249 (53.09%)**
Jim Yuill (SNP) 6,525 (20.08%)
Rod Ackland (LD) 3,909 (12.03%)
Catherine Pickering (C) 3,514 (10.82%)
Dawn Brennan (SSP) 1,294 (3.98%)

1997: Lab maj 13,320. *Worthington Lab: 21,583 (55.22%) Yuill SNP: 8,263 (21.14%) Morgan C: 4,885 (12.50%) Moody LD: 4,086 (10.45%)

## Clydesdale
Elect 64,423. Turnout 59.33%
**Lab hold**
**Maj 7,794 5.01% swing Lab to SNP**

**Jimmy Hood (Lab) 17,822 (46.63%)**
Jim Wright (SNP) 10,028 (26.24%)
Kevin Newton (C) 5,034 (13.17%)
Moira Craig (LD) 4,111 (10.76%)
Paul Cockshott (SSP) 974 (2.55%)
Donald MacKay (UK Ind) 253 (0.66%)

1997: Lab maj 13,809. *Hood Lab: 23,859 (52.54%) Doig SNP:
10,050 (22.13%) Izatt C: 7,396 (16.29%) Grieve LD: 3,796 (8.36%)

## Coatbridge & Chryston
Elect 30,311. Turnout 58.1%
**Lab hold**
**Maj 15,314 0.4% from Labour to SNP**

**Tom Clarke (Lab) 19,807 (65.3%)**
Peter Kearney (SNP) 4,493 ( 14.8 %)
Alistair Tough (LD) 2,293 (7.6 %)
Patrick Ross-Taylor (C) 2,171 (7.2 %)
Lynne Sheridan (SSP) 1,547 (5.1%)

1997: Lab maj 19,295 (51.3%) *Clarke Lab: 25,697 (68.32%) Nugent
SNP: 6,402 (17.02%) Wauchope C: 3,216 (8.55%) Daly LD: 2,048
(5.45%) Bowsley REF: 249 (0.66%)

## Cumbernauld & Kilsyth
Elect 49,739. Turnout 59.71%
**Lab hold**
**Maj 7,520 2.78% swing Lab to SNP**

**Rosemary McKenna (Lab) 16,144 (54.36%)**
David McGlashan (SNP) 8,624 (29.04%)
John O'Donnell (LD) 1,934 (6.51%)
Alison Ross (C) 1,460 (4.92%)
Kenny McEwan (SSP) 1,287 (4.33%)

1997: Lab maj 11,128. *McKenna Lab: 21,141 (58.69%) Barrie SNP: 10,013 (27.80%) Sewell C: 2,441 (6.78%) Biggam LD: 1,368 (3.80%) Kara ProLife: 609 (1.69%) McEwan SSA: 345 (0.96%)

## Cunninghame North
Elect 54,993. Turnout 61.49%
**Lab hold**
**Maj 8,398 3.51% swing Lab to SNP**

**Brian Wilson (Lab) 15,571 (46.05%)**
Campbell Martin (SNP) 7,173 (21.21%)
Richard Wilkinson (C) 6,666 (19.71%)
Ross Chmiel (LD) 3,060 (9.05%)
Sean Scott (SSP) 964 (2.85%)
Louise McDaid (Soc Lab) 382 (1.13%)

1997: Lab maj 11,039. *Wilson Lab: 20,686 (50.30%) Mitchell C: 9,647 (23.46%) Nicoll SNP: 7,584 (18.44%) Freel LD: 2,271 (5.52%) McDaid Soc Lab: 501 (1.22%)

## Cunninghame South
Elect 49,982. Turnout 56.04%
**Lab hold**
**Maj 11,230 0.93% swing Lab to SNP**

**Brian Donohoe (Lab) 16,424 (58.64%)**
Bill Kidd (SNP) 5,194 (18.54%)
Pam Paterson (C) 2,682 (9.58%)
John Boyd (LD) 2,094 (7.48%)
Rosemary Byrne (SSP) 1,233 (4.40%)
Bobby Cochrane (Soc Lab) 382 (1.36%)

1997: Lab maj 14,869. *Donohoe Lab: 22,233 (62.73%) Burgess SNP: 7,364 (20.78%) Paterson C: 3,571 (10.08%) Watson LD: 1,604 (4.53%) Edwin Soc Lab: 494 (1.39%)

## Dumbarton
Elect 56,267. Turnout 60.42%
**Lab Co-op hold**
**Maj 9,575 0.89% swing SNP to Lab Co-op**

**John McFall (Lab Co-op) 16,151 (47.51%)**
Iain Robertson (SNP) 6,576 (19.34%)
Eric Thompson (LD) 5,265 (15.49%)
Peter Ramsay (C) 4,648 (13.67%)
Les Robertson (SSP) 1,354 (3.98%)

1997: Lab maj 10,883. *McFall Lab: 20,470 (49.61%) Mackechnie
SNP: 9,587 (23.23%) Ramsay C: 7,283 (17.65%) Reid LD: 3,144
(7.62%) Robertson SSA: 283 (0.69%) Dempster Ref: 255 (0.62%)

## Dumfries
Elect 62,931. Turnout 67.67%
**Lab hold**
**Maj 8,834 0.64% swing C to Lab**

**Russell Brown (Lab) 20,830 (48.91%)**
John Charteris (C) 11,996 (28.17%)
John Ross Scott (LD) 4,955 (11.64%)
Gerry Fisher (SNP) 4,103 (9.63%)
John Dennis (SSP) 702 (1.65%)

1997: Lab maj 9,643. *Brown Lab: 23,528 (47.51%) Stevenson C:
13,885 (28.04%) Higgins SNP: 5,977 (12.07%) Wallace LD: 5,487
(11.08%) Parker Ref: 533 (1.08%)

## Dundee East
Elect 56,535. Turnout 57.24%
**Lab hold**
**Maj 4,475 5.38% swing Lab to SNP**

**Iain Luke (Lab) 14,635 (45.23%)**
Stewart Hosie (SNP) 10,160 (31.40%)
Alan Donnelly (C) 3,900 (12.05%)
Raymond Lawrie (LD) 2,784 (8.60%)
Harvey Duke (SSP) 879 (2.72%)

1997: Lab maj 9,961. *McAllion Lab: 20,718 (51.12%) Robison SNP:
10,757 (26.54%) Mackie C: 6,397 (15.78%) Saluja LD: 1,677 (4.14%)
Galloway Ref: 601 (1.48%) Duke SSA: 232 (0.57%)

**Dundee West**
Elect 53,760. Turnout 54.39%
**Lab hold**
**Maj 6,800 3.65% swing Lab to SNP**

**Ernie Ross (Lab) 14,787 (50.57%)**
Gordon Archer (SNP) 7,987 (27.31%)
Ian Hail (C) 2,656 (9.08%)
Elizabeth Dick (LD) 2,620 (8.96%)
Jim McFarlane (SSP) 1,192 (4.08%)

1997: Lab maj 11,859. *Ross Lab: 20,875 (53.79%) Dorward SNP:
9,016 (23.23%) Powrie C: 5,105 (13.15%) Dick LD: 2,972 (7.66%)
Ward SSA: 428 (1.10%)

---

**Dunfermline East**
Elect 52,811. Turnout 56.97%
**Lab hold**
**Maj 15,063 0.60% swing Lab to SNP**

**Gordon Brown (Lab) 19,487 (64.77%)**
John Mellon (SNP) 4,424 (14.70%)
Stuart Randall (C) 2,838 (9.43%)
John Mainland (LD) 2,281 (7.58%)
Andy Jackson (SSP) 770 (2.56%)
Tom Dunsmore (UK Ind) 286 (0.95%)

1997: Lab maj 18,751. *Brown Lab: 24,441 (66.81%) Ramage SNP:
5,690 (15.55%) Mitchell C: 3,656 (9.99%) Tolson LD: 2,164 (5.92%)

---

**Dunfermline West**
Elect 54,293. Turnout 57.05%
**Lab hold**
**Maj 10,980 0.77% swing SNP to Lab**

**Rachel Squire (Lab) 16,370 (52.85%)**
Brian Goodall (SNP) 5,390 (17.40%)
Russell McPhate (LD) 4,832 (15.60%)
James Mackie (C) 3,166 (10.22%)

Kate Stewart (SSP) 746 (2.41%)
Alastair Harper (UK Ind) 471 (1.52%)

1997: Lab maj 12,354. *Squire Lab: 19,338 (53.08%) Lloyd SNP: 6,984 (19.17%) Harris LD: 4,963 (13.62%) Newton C: 4,606 (12.64%)

## East Kilbride
Elect 66,572. Turnout 62.62%
**Lab hold**
**Maj 12,755 2.52% swing Lab to SNP**

**Adam Ingram (Lab) 22,205 (53.26%)**
Archie Buchanan (SNP) 9,450 (22.67%)
Ewan Hawthorn (LD) 4,278 (10.26%)
Margaret McCulloch (C) 4,238 (10.17%)
David Stevenson (SSP) 1,519 (3.64%)

1997: Lab maj 17,384. *Ingram Lab: 27,584 (56.53%) Gebbie SNP: 10,200 (20.90%) Herbertson C: 5,863 (12.02%) Philbrick LD: 3,527 (7.23%) Deighan ProLife: 1,170 (2.40%) Gray Ref: 306 (0.63%)

## East Lothian
Elect 58,987. Turnout 62.51%
**Lab hold**
**Maj 10,830 1.68% swing Lab to C**

**Anne Picking (Lab) 17,407 (47.21%)**
Hamish Mair (C) 6,577 (17.84%)
Judy Hayman (LD) 6,506 (17.65%)
Hilary Brown (SNP) 5,381 (14.59%)
Jake Herriot (Soc Lab) 624 (1.69%)
Derrick White (SSP) 376 (1.02%)

1997: Lab maj 14,221. *Home Robertson Lab: 22,881 (52.68%) Fraser C: 8,660 (19.94%) McCarthy SNP: 6,825 (15.71%) MacAskill LD: 4,575 (10.53%)

**Eastwood**
Elect 68,378. Turnout 70.74%
**Lab hold**
**Maj 9,141 6.35% swing C to Lab**

**Jim Murphy (Lab) 23,036 (47.63%)**
Raymond Robertson (C) 13,895 (28.73%)
Allan Steele (LD) 6,239 (12.90%)
Stewart Maxwell (SNP) 4,137 (8.55%)
Peter Murray (SSP) 814 (1.68%)
Manar Tayan (Ind) 247 (0.51%)

1997: Lab maj 3,236. *Murphy Lab: 20,766 (39.75%) Cullen C:
17,530 (33.56%) Yates SNP: 6,826 (13.07%) Mason LD: 6,110
(11.70%) Miller Ref: 497 (0.95%) Tayan ProLife: 393 (0.75%)

---

**Edinburgh Central**
Elect 66,089. Turnout 52.04%
**Lab hold**
**Maj 8,142 5.15% swing Lab to LD**

**Alistair Darling (Lab) 14,495 (42.15%)**
Andrew Myles (LD) 6,353 (18.47%)
Alastair Orr (C) 5,643 (16.41%)
Ian McKee (SNP) 4,832 (14.05%)
Graeme Farmer (Green) 1,809 (5.26%)
Kevin Williamson (SSP) 1,258 (3.66%)

1997: Lab maj 11,070. *Darling Lab: 20,125 (47.09%) Scott-Hayward
C: 9,055 (21.19%) Hyslop SNP: 6,750 (15.80%) Utting LD: 5,605
(13.12%) Hendry Green: 607 (1.42%) Skinner Ref: 495 (1.16%)

---

**Edinburgh East & Musselburgh**
Elect 59,241. Turnout 58.16%
**Lab hold**
**Maj 12,168 0.41% swing SNP to Lab**

**Gavin Strang (Lab) 18,124 (52.60%)**
Rob Munn (SNP) 5,956 (17.29%)

Gary Peacock (LD) 4,981 (14.46%)
Peter Finnie (C) 3,906 (11.34%)
Derek Durkin (SSP) 1,487 (4.32%)

1997: Lab maj 14,530. *Strang Lab: 22,564 (53.57%) White SNP: 8,034 (19.07%) Ward C: 6,483 (15.39%) MacKellar LD: 4,511 (10.71%)

### Edinburgh North & Leith
Elect 62,475. Turnout 53.20%
**Lab hold**
**Maj 8,817 3.67% swing Lab to LD**

**Mark Lazarowicz (Lab) 15,271 (45.95%)**
Sebastian Tombs (LD) 6,454 (19.42%)
Kaukab Stewart (SNP) 5,290 (15.92%)
Iain Mitchell (C) 4,626 (13.92%)
Catriona Grant (SSP) 1,334 (4.01%)
Don Jacobsen (Soc Lab) 259 (0.78%)

1997: Lab maj 10,978. *Chisholm Lab: 19,209 (46.91%) Dana SNP: 8,231 (20.10%) Stewart C: 7,312 (17.86%) Campbell LD: 5,335 (13.03%) Graham Ref: 441 (1.08%) Brown SSA: 320 (0.78%)

### Edinburgh Pentlands
Elect 59,841. Turnout 65.06%
**Lab hold**
**Maj 1,742 3.08% swing Lab to C**

**Lynda Clark (Lab) 15,797 (40.58%)**
Malcolm Rifkind (C) 14,055 (36.10%)
David Walker (LD) 4,210 (10.81%)
Stewart Gibb (SNP) 4,210 (10.81%)
James Mearns (SSP) 555 (1.43%)
William McMurdo (UK Ind) 105 (0.27%)

1997: Lab maj 4,862. *Clark Lab: 19,675 (43.01%) Rifkind C: 14,813 (32.38%) Gibb SNP: 5,952 (13.01%) Dawe LD: 4,575 (10.00%) McDonald Ref: 422 (0.92%) Harper Green: 224 (0.49%)

## Edinburgh South
Elect 64,012. Turnout 58.06%
**Lab hold**
**Maj 5,499 7.19% swing Lab to LD**

**Nigel Griffiths (Lab) 15,671 (42.16%)**
Marilyne MacLaren (LD) 10,172 (27.37%)
Geoffrey Buchan (C) 6,172 (16.61%)
Heather Williams (SNP) 3,683 (9.91%)
Colin Fox (SSP) 933 (2.51%)
Linda Hendry (LCA) 535 (1.44%)

1997: Lab maj 11,452. *Griffiths Lab: 20,993 (46.82%) Smith C:
9,541 (21.28%) Pringle LD: 7,911 (17.64%) Hargreaves SNP: 5,791
(12.92%) McLean Ref: 504 (1.12%)

---

## Edinburgh West
Elect 61,895. Turnout 63.78%
**LD hold**
**Maj 7,589 2.59% swing LD to Lab**

**John Barrett (LD) 16,719 (42.35%)**
Elspeth Alexandra (Lab) 9,130 (23.13%)
Iain Whyte (C) 8,894 (22.53%)
Alyn Smith (SNP) 4,047 (10.25%)
Bill Scott (SSP) 688 (1.74%)

1997: LD maj 7,253. *Gorrie LD: 20,578 (43.20%) Douglas-Hamilton
C: 13,325 (27.98%) Hinds Lab: 8,948 (18.79%) Sutherland SNP:
4,210 (8.84%) Elphick Ref: 277 (0.58%) Coombes Lib: 263 (0.55%)

---

## Falkirk East
Elect 57,633. Turnout 58.48%
**Lab hold**
**Maj 10,712 0.20% swing Lab to SNP**

**Michael Connarty (Lab) 18,536 (55.00%)**
Isabel Hutton (SNP) 7,824 (23.22%)
Bill Stevenson (C) 3,252 (9.65%)

Karen Utting (LD) 2,992 (8.88%)
Tony Weir (SSP) 725 (2.15%)


1997: Lab maj 13,385. *Connarty Lab: 23,344 (56.12%) Brown SNP: 9,959 (23.94%) Nicol C: 5,813 (13.98%) Spillane LD: 2,153 (5.18%)

---

**Falkirk West**
Elect 53,583. Turnout 57.65%
**Lab hold**
**Maj 8,532 4.15% swing Lab to SNP**

**Eric Joyce (Lab) 16,022 (51.87%)**
David Kerr (SNP) 7,490 (24.25%)
Simon Murray (C) 2,321 (7.51%)
Hugh O'Donnell (LD) 2,203 (7.13%)
William Buchanan (Ind B) 1,464 (4.74%)
Mhairi McAlpine (SSP) 707 (2.29%)
Hugh Lynch (Ind) 490 (1.59%)
Ronnie Forbes (Soc Lab) 194 (0.63%)


1997: Lab maj 13,783. *Canavan Lab: 22,772 (59.35%) Alexander SNP: 8,989 (23.43%) Buchanan C: 4,639 (12.09%) Houston LD: 1,970 (5.13%)

---

**Fife Central**
Elect 59,597. Turnout 54.55%
**Lab hold**
**Maj 10,075 1.33% swing Lab to SNP**

**John MacDougall (Lab) 18,310 (56.32%)**
David Alexander (SNP) 8,235 (25.33%)
Elizabeth Riches (LD) 2,775 (8.54%)
Jeremy Balfour (C) 2,351 (7.23%)
Morag Balfour (SSP) 841 (2.59%)


1997: Lab maj 13,713. *McLeish Lab: 23,912 (58.66%) Marwick SNP: 10,199 (25.02%) Rees-Mogg C: 3,669 (9.00%) Laird LD: 2,610 (6.40%)

---

**Fife North-East**
Elect 61,900. Turnout 56.05%
**LD hold**
**Maj 9,736 1.66% swing C to LD**

**Menzies Campbell (LD) 17,926 (51.67%)**
Mike Scott-Hayward (C) 8,190 (23.61%)
Claire Brennan (Lab) 3,950 (11.39%)
Kris Murray-Browne (SNP) 3,596 (10.37%)
Keith White (SSP) 610 (1.76%)
Leslie Von Goetz (LCA) 420 (1.21%)

1997: LD maj 10,356. *Campbell LD: 21,432 (51.22%) Bruce C: 11,076 (26.47%) Welsh SNP: 4,545 (10.86%) Milne Lab: 4,301 (10.28%)

---

**Galloway & Upper Nithsdale**
Elect 52,756. Turnout 68.08%
**C gain**
**Maj 74 6.80% swing SNP to C**

**Peter Duncan (C) 12,222 (34.03%)**
Malcolm Fleming (SNP) 12,148 (33.83%)
Thomas Sloan (Lab) 7,258 (20.21%)
Neil Wallace (LD) 3,698 (10.30%)
Andy Harvey (SSP) 588 (1.64%)

1997: SNP maj 5,624. *Morgan SNP: 18,449 (43.91%) Lang C: 12,825 (30.52%) Clark Lab: 6,861 (16.33%) McKerchar LD: 2,700 (6.43%) Wood Ind: 566 (1.35%) Kennedy Ref: 428 (1.02%)

---

**Glasgow Anniesland**
Elect 53,290. Turnout 50.14%
**Lab hold**
**Maj 11,054 1.68% swing Lab to SNP**

**John Robertson (Lab) 15,102 (56.52%)**
Grant Thoms (SNP) 4,048 (15.15%)
Christopher McGinty (LD) 3,244 (12.14%)

Stewart Connell (C) 2,651 (9.92%)
Charlie McCarthy (SSP) 1,486 (5.56%)
Katherine McGavigan (Soc Lab) 191 (0.71%)

1997: Lab maj 15,154. *Dewar Lab: 20,951 (61.84%) Wilson SNP: 5,797 (17.11%) Brocklehurst C: 3,881 (11.46%) McGinty LD: 2,453 (7.24%) Majid ProLife: 374 (1.10%) Bonnar SSA: 229 (0.68%) Milligan UK Ind: 86 (0.25%) McKay Ref: 84 (0.25%) Pringle NLP: 24 (0.07%)

## Glasgow Baillieston
Elect 49,268. Turnout 47.21%
**Lab hold**
**Maj 9,839 2.15% swing Lab to SNP**

**Jimmy Wray (Lab) 14,200 (61.05%)**
Lachlan McNeill (SNP) 4,361 (18.75%)
David Comrie (C) 1,580 (6.79%)
Jim McVicar (SSP) 1,569 (6.75%)
Charles Dundas (LD) 1,551 (6.67%)

1997: Lab maj 14,840. *Wray Lab: 20,925 (65.69%) Thomson SNP: 6,085 (19.10%) Kelly C: 2,468 (7.75%) Rainger LD: 1,217 (3.82%) McVicar SSA: 970 (3.05%)

## Glasgow Cathcart
Elect 52,094. Turnout 52.57%
**Lab hold**
**Maj 10,816 1.80% swing SNP to Lab**

**Tom Harris (Lab) 14,902 (54.41%)**
Josephine Docherty (SNP) 4,086 (14.92%)
Richard Cook (C) 3,662 (13.37%)
Tom Henery (LD) 3,006 (10.98%)
Ronnie Stevenson (SSP) 1,730 (6.32%)

1997: Lab maj 12,245. *Maxton Lab: 19,158 (56.17%) Whitehead SNP: 6,913 (20.27%) Muir C: 4,248 (12.45%) Dick LD: 2,302 (6.75%) Indyk ProLife: 687 (2.01%) Stevenson SSA: 458 (1.34%)

**Glasgow Govan**
Elect 54,068. Turnout 46.76%
**Lab hold**
**Maj 6,400 8.14% swing SNP to Lab**

**Mohammad Sarwar (Lab) 12,464 (49.30%)**
Karen Neary (SNP) 6,064 (23.98%)
Bob Stewart (LD) 2,815 (11.13%)
Mark Menzies (C) 2,167 (8.57%)
Willie McGartland (SSP) 1,531 (6.06%)
John Foster (Comm) 174 (0.69%)
Badar Mirza (Ind) 69 (0.27%)

1997: Lab maj 2,914. *Sarwar Lab: 14,216 (44.09%) Sturgeon SNP: 11,302 (35.05%) Thomas C: 2,839 (8.81%) Stewart LD: 1,915 (5.94%) McCombes SSA: 755 (2.34%) Paton SLU: 325 (1.01%) Badar SLI: 319 (0.99%) Abbasi SCU: 221 (0.69%) MacDonald Ref: 201 (0.62%)

---

**Glasgow Kelvin**
Elect 61,534. Turnout 43.56%
**Lab hold**
**Maj 7,260 4.85% swing Lab to LD**

**George Galloway (Lab) 12,014 (44.83%)**
Tamsin Mayberry (LD) 4,754 (17.74%)
Frank Rankin (SNP) 4,513 (16.84%)
Davina Rankin (C) 2,388 (8.91%)
Heather Ritchie (SSP) 1,847 (6.89%)
Tim Shand (Green) 1,286 (4.80%)

1997: Lab maj 9,665. *Galloway Lab: 16,643 (50.97%) White SNP: 6,978 (21.37%) Buchanan LD: 4,629 (14.18%) McPhie C: 3,539 (10.84%) Green SSA: 386 (1.18%) Grigor Ref: 282 (0.86%) Vanni SPGB: 102 (0.31%)

---

**Glasgow Maryhill**
Elect 55,431. Turnout 40.11%
**Lab hold**
**Maj 9,888 1.76% swing Lab to SNP**

**Ann McKechin (Lab) 13,420 (60.37%)**
Alex Dingwall (SNP) 3,532 (15.89%)
Stuart Callison (LD) 2,372 (10.67%)
Gordon Scott (SSP) 1,745 (7.85%)
Gawain Towler (C) 1,162 (5.23%)

1997: Lab maj 14,264. *Fyfe Lab: 19,301 (64.94%) Wailes SNP: 5,037 (16.95%) Attwooll LD: 2,119 (7.13%) Baldwin C: 1,747 (5.88%) Blair NLP: 651 (2.19%) Baker SSA: 409 (1.38%) Hanif ProLife: 344 (1.16%) Paterson Ref: 77 (0.26%)

## Glasgow Pollok
Elect 49,201. Turnout 51.37%
**Lab Co-op hold**
**Maj 11,268 1.27% swing SNP to Lab Co-op**

**Ian Davidson (Lab Co-op) 15,497 (61.31%)**
David Ritchie (SNP) 4,229 (16.73%)
Keith Baldassara (SSP) 2,522 (9.98%)
Isabel Nelson (LD) 1,612 (6.38%)
Rory O'Brien (C) 1,417 (5.61%)

1997: Lab maj 13,791. *Davidson Lab: 19,653 (59.91%) Logan SNP: 5,862 (17.87%) Sheridan SSA: 3,639 (11.09%) Hamilton C: 1,979 (6.03%) Jago LD: 1,137 (3.47%) Gott ProLife: 380 (1.16%)

## Glasgow Rutherglen
Elect 51,855. Turnout 56.34%
**Lab Co-op hold**
**Maj 12,625 0.48% swing SNP to Lab Co-op**

**Tommy McAvoy (Lab Co-op) 16,760 (57.37%)**
Anne McLaughlin (SNP) 4,135 (14.15%)
David Jackson (LD) 3,689 (12.63%)
Malcolm Macaskill (C) 3,301 (11.30%)
Bill Bonnar (SSP) 1,328 (4.55%)

1997: Lab maj 15,007. *McAvoy Lab: 20,430 (57.52%) Gray SNP: 5,423 (15.27%) Brown LD: 5,167 (14.55%) Campbell Bannerman C: 3,288 (9.26%) Easton Ind Lab: 812 (2.29%) Kane SSA: 251 (0.71%)

## Glasgow Shettleston

Elect 51,557. Turnout 39.69%
**Lab hold**
**Maj 9,818 5.60% swing Lab to SNP**

**David Marshall (Lab) 13,235 (64.67%)**
Jim Byrne (SNP) 3,417 (16.70%)
Rosie Kane (SSP) 1,396 (6.82%)
Lewis Hutton (LD) 1,105 (5.40%)
Campbell Murdoch (C) 1,082 (5.29%)
Murdo Ritchie (Soc Lab) 230 (1.12%)

1997: Lab maj 15,868. *Marshall Lab: 19,616 (73.16%) Hanif SNP: 3,748 (13.98%) Simpson C: 1,484 (5.53%) Hiles LD: 1,061 (3.96%) McVicar SSA: 482 (1.80%) Currie BNP: 191 (0.71%) Montguire Ref: 151 (0.56%)

---

## Glasgow Springburn

Elect 55,192. Turnout 43.67%
**Speaker hold**
**Maj 11,378**

**Michael Martin (Speaker) 16,053 (66.60%)**
Sandy Bain (SNP) 4,675 (19.40%)
Carolyn Leckie (SSP) 1,879 (7.80%)
Daniel Houston (Scot U) 1,289 (5.35%)
Richard Silvester (Ind) 208 (0.86%)

1997: Lab maj 17,326. *Martin Lab: 22,534 (71.36%) Brady SNP: 5,208 (16.49%) Holdsworth C: 1,893 (5.99%) Alexander LD: 1,349 (4.27%) Lawson SSA: 407 (1.29%)

---

## Gordon

Elect 59,996. Turnout 58.34%
**LD hold**
**Maj 7,879 2.97% swing C to LD**

**Malcolm Bruce (LD) 15,928 (45.51%)**
Nanette Milne (C) 8,049 (23.00%)
Rhona Kemp (SNP) 5,760 (16.46%)

Ellis Thorpe (Lab) 4,730 (13.51%)
John Sangster (SSP) 534 (1.53%)

1997: LD maj 6,997. *Bruce LD: 17,999 (42.61%) Porter C: 11,002
(26.04%) Lochhead SNP: 8,435 (19.97%) Kirkhill Lab: 4,350
(10.30%)

**Greenock & Inverclyde**
Elect 47,884 Turnout 59.35%
**Lab hold**
**Maj 8,890 3.77% swing Lab to LD**

**David Cairns (Lab) 14,929 (52.5%)**
Chick Brodie (LD) 5,039 (17.7%)
Andrew Murie (SNP) 4,248 (14.9%)
Alistair Haw (C) 3,000 (10.6%)
David Landels (SSP) 1,203 (4.2%)

1997: Lab maj 13,040 (37.59%) *Godman Lab: 19,480 (56.16%)
Goodall SNP: 6,440 (18.57%) Ackland LD: 4,791 (13.81) Swire C:
3,976 (11.46%)

**Hamilton North & Bellshill**
Elect 53,539. Turnout 56.79%
**Lab hold**
**Maj 13,561 0.16% swing Lab to SNP**

**John Reid (Lab) 18,786 (61.79%)**
Chris Stephens (SNP) 5,225 (17.19%)
Bill Frain Bell (C) 2,649 (8.71%)
Keith Legg (LD) 2,360 (7.76%)
Shareen Blackall (SSP) 1,189 (3.91%)
Steve Mayes (Soc Lab) 195 (0.64%)

1997: Lab maj 17,067. *Reid Lab: 24,322 (64.01%) Matheson SNP:
7,255 (19.09%) McIntosh C: 3,944 (10.38%) Legg LD: 1,924 (5.06%)

**Hamilton South**
Elect 46,665. Turnout 57.32%
**Lab hold**

**Maj 10,775 3.85% swing Lab to SNP**

**Bill Tynan (Lab) 15,965 (59.68%)**
John Wilson (SNP) 5,190 (19.40%)
John Oswald (LD) 2,381 (8.90%)
Neil Richardson (C) 1,876 (7.01%)
Gena Mitchell (SSP) 1,187 (4.44%)
Janice Murdoch (UK Ind) 151 (0.56%)

1997: Lab maj 15,878. *Robertson Lab: 21,709 (65.60%) Black SNP: 5,831 (17.62%) Kilgour C: 2,858 (8.64%) Pitts LD: 1,693 (5.12%) Gunn ProLife: 684 (2.07%) Brown Ref: 316 (0.95%)

---

**Inverness East, Nairn & Lochaber**
Elect 67,139. Turnout 63.24%
**Lab hold**
**Maj 4,716 3.10% swing SNP to Lab**

**David Stewart (Lab) 15,605 (36.75%)**
Angus MacNeil (SNP) 10,889 (25.64%)
Patsy Kenton (LD) 9,420 (22.19%)
Richard Jenkins (C) 5,653 (13.31%)
Steve Arnott (SSP) 894 (2.11%)

1997: Lab maj 2,339. *Stewart Lab: 16,187 (33.89%) Ewing SNP: 13,848 (28.99%) Gallagher LD: 8,364 (17.51%) Scanlon C: 8,355 (17.49%) Wall Ref: 436 (0.91%) Falconer Green: 354 (0.74%)

---

**Kilmarnock & Loudoun**
Elect 61,049. Turnout 61.70%
**Lab hold**
**Maj 10,334 6.07% swing SNP to Lab**

**Des Browne (Lab) 19,926 (52.90%)**
John Brady (SNP) 9,592 (25.47%)
Donald Reece (C) 3,943 (10.47%)
John Stewart (LD) 3,177 (8.43%)
Jason Muir (SSP) 1,027 (2.73%)

1997: Lab maj 7,256. *Browne Lab: 23,621 (49.82%) Neil SNP:

16,365 (34.52%) Taylor C: 5,125 (10.81%) Stewart LD: 1,891 (3.99%) Sneddon Ref: 284 (0.60%)

## Kirkcaldy
Elect 51,559. Turnout 54.61%
**Lab Co-op hold**
**Maj 8,963 0.60% swing SNP to Lab Co-op**

**Lewis Moonie (Lab Co-op) 15,227 (54.08%)**
Shirley-Anne Somerville (SNP) 6,264 (22.25%)
Scott Campbell (C) 3,013 (10.70%)
Andrew Weston (LD) 2,849 (10.12%)
Dougie Kinnear (SSP) 804 (2.86%)

1997: Lab maj 10,710. *Moonie Lab: 18,730 (53.56%) Hosie SNP: 8,020 (22.93%) Black C: 4,779 (13.66%) Mainland LD: 3,031 (8.67%)

## Linlithgow
Elect 54,599. Turnout 57.98%
**Lab hold**
**Maj 9,129 0.75% swing SNP to Lab**

**Tam Dalyell (Lab) 17,207 (54.36%)**
Jim Sibbald (SNP) 8,078 (25.52%)
Gordon Lindhurst (C) 2,836 (8.96%)
Martin Oliver (LD) 2,628 (8.30%)
Eddie Cornoch (SSP) 695 (2.20%)
Helen Cronin (R & R Loony) 211 (0.67%)

1997: Lab maj 10,838. *Dalyell Lab: 21,469 (54.14%) MacAskill SNP: 10,631 (26.81%) Kerr C: 4,964 (12.52%) Duncan LD: 2,331 (5.88%)

## Livingston
Elect 64,850. Turnout 55.56%
**Lab hold**
**Maj 10,616 1.02% swing SNP to Lab**

**Robin Cook (Lab) 19,108 (53.03%)**
Graham Sutherland (SNP) 8,492 (23.57%)

Gordon Mackenzie (LD) 3,969 (11.01%)
Ian Mowat (C) 2,995 (8.31%)
Wendy Milne (SSP) 1,110 (3.08%)
Robert Kingdon (UK Ind) 359 (1.00%)

1997: Lab maj 11,747. *Cook Lab: 23,510 (54.89%) Johnston SNP:
11,763 (27.46%) Craigie Halkett C: 4,028 (9.40%) Hawthorn LD:
2,876 (6.71%) Campbell Ref: 444 (1.04%)

**Midlothian**
Elect 48,625. Turnout 59.07%
**Lab hold**
**Maj 9,014 1.69% swing SNP to Lab**

**David Hamilton (Lab) 15,145 (52.73%)**
Ian Goldie (SNP) 6,131 (21.34%)
Jacqueline Bell (LD) 3,686 (12.83%)
Robin Traquair (C) 2,748 (9.57%)
Bob Goupillot (SSP) 837 (2.91%)
Terence Holden (ProLife) 177 (0.62%)

1997: Lab maj 9,870. *Clarke Lab: 18,861 (53.51%) Millar SNP: 8,991
(25.51%) Harper C: 3,842 (10.90%) Pinnock LD: 3,235 (9.18%)

**Moray**
Elect 58,008. Turnout 57.27%
**SNP hold**
**Maj 1,744 8.25% swing SNP to Lab**

**Angus Robertson (SNP) 10,076 (30.33%)**
Catriona Munro (Lab) 8,332 (25.08%)
Frank Spencer-Nairn (C) 7,677 (23.11%)
Linda Gorn (LD) 5,224 (15.72%)
Norma Anderson (SSP) 821 (2.47%)
Bill Jappy (Ind) 802 (2.41%)
Nigel Kenyon (UK Ind) 291 (0.88%)

1997: SNP maj 5,566. *Ewing SNP: 16,529 (41.57%) Findlay C:
10,963 (27.57%) Macdonald Lab: 7,886 (19.83%) Storr LD: 3,548
(8.92%)

**Motherwell & Wishaw**
Elect 52,418. Turnout 56.61%
**Lab hold**
**Maj 10,956 1.00% swing SNP to Lab**

**Frank Roy (Lab) 16,681 (56.22%)**
Jim McGuigan (SNP) 5,725 (19.29%)
Mark Nolan (C) 3,155 (10.63%)
Iain Brown (LD) 2,791 (9.41%)
Stephen Smellie (SSP) 1,260 (4.25%)
Claire Watt (Soc Lab) 61 (0.21%)

1997: Lab maj 12,791. *Roy Lab: 21,020 (57.40%) McGuigan SNP: 8,229 (22.47%) Dickson C: 4,024 (10.99%) Mackie LD: 2,331 (6.37%) Herriot Soc Lab: 797 (2.18%)

---

**Ochil**
Elect 57,554. Turnout 61.34%
**Lab hold**
**Maj 5,349 2.26% swing SNP to Lab**

**Martin O'Neill (Lab) 16,004 (45.33%)**
Keith Brown (SNP) 10,655 (30.18%)
Alasdair Campbell (C) 4,235 (12.00%)
Paul Edie (LD) 3,253 (9.21%)
Pauline Thompson (SSP) 751 (2.13%)
Flash Gordon Approaching (Loony) 405 (1.15%)

1997: Lab maj 4,652. *O'Neill Lab: 19,707 (45.01%) Reid SNP: 15,055 (34.38%) Hogarth C: 6,383 (14.58%) Watters LD: 2,262 (5.17%) White Ref: 210 (0.48%) McDonald D Nat: 104 (0.24%)

---

**Orkney & Shetland**
Elect 31,909. Turnout 52.44%
**LD hold**
**Maj 3,475 6.48 swing LD to Lab**

**Alistair Carmichael (LD) 6,919 (41.35%)**
Robert Mochrie (Lab) 3,444 (20.58%)
John Firth (C ) 3,121 (18.65%)

John Mowat (SNP) 2,473 (14.78%)
Peter Andrews (SSP) 776 (4.64%)

1997: LD maj 6,968 *Wallace LD: 10,743 (51.99%) Paton Lab: 3,775
(18.27%) Ross SNP: 2,624 (12.70%) Anderson C: 2,527 (12.23%)
Adamson Ref: 820 (3.97%) Wharton NLP: 116 (0.56%) Robertson
Ind: 60 (0.29%)

**Paisley North**
Elect 47,994. Turnout 56.58%
**Lab hold**
**Maj 9,321 1.61% swing Lab to SNP**

**Irene Adams (Lab) 15,058 (55.46%)**
George Adam (SNP) 5,737 (21.13%)
Jane Hook (LD) 2,709 (9.98%)
Craig Stevenson (C) 2,404 (8.85%)
Jim Halfpenny (SSP) 982 (3.62%)
Robert Graham (ProLife) 263 (0.97%)

1997: Lab maj 12,814. *Adams Lab: 20,295 (59.46%) Mackay SNP:
7,481 (21.92%) Brookes C: 3,267 (9.57%) Jelfs LD: 2,365 (6.93%)
Graham ProLife: 531 (1.56%)

**Paisley South**
Elect 53,351. Turnout 57.24%
**Lab hold**
**Maj 11,910 2.44% swing SNP to Lab**

**Douglas Alexander (Lab) 17,830 (58.39%)**
Brian Lawson (SNP) 5,920 (19.39%)
Brian O'Malley (LD) 3,178 (10.41%)
Andrew Cossar (C) 2,301 (7.54%)
Frances Curran (SSP) 835 (2.73%)
Patricia Graham (ProLife) 346 (1.13%)
Terence O'Donnell (Ind) 126 (0.41%)

1997: Lab maj 2,731. *Alexander Lab: 10,346 (44.15%) Blackford
SNP: 7,615 (32.49%) McCartin LD: 2,582 (11.02%) Laidlaw C: 1,643
(7.01%) Deighan ProLife: 578 (2.47%) Curran SSA: 306 (1.31%)
McLauchlan Sc Ind Lab: 155 (0.66%) Herriot Soc Lab: 153 (0.65%)

## Perth
Elect 61,497. Turnout 61.49%
**SNP hold**
**Maj 48 3.46% swing SNP to C**

**Annabelle Ewing (SNP) 11,237 (29.71%)**
Elizabeth Smith (C) 11,189 (29.59%)
Marion Dingwall (Lab) 9,638 (25.49%)
Vicki Harris (LD) 4,853 (12.83%)
Frank Byrne (SSP) 899 (2.38%)

1997: SNP maj 3,141. *Cunningham SNP: 16,209 (36.38%) Godfrey C: 13,068 (29.33%) Alexander Lab: 11,036 (24.77%) Brodie LD: 3,583 (8.04%) MacAuley Ref: 366 (0.82%)

---

## Renfrewshire West
Elect 52,889. Turnout 63.33%
**Lab (notional) gain**
**Maj 8,575 2.77% swing SNP to Lab**

**James Sheridan (Lab) 15,720 (46.93%)**
Carol Puthucheary (SNP) 7,145 (21.33%)
David Sharpe (C) 5,522 (16.49%)
Clare Hamblen (LD) 4,185 (12.49%)
Arlene Nunnery (SSP) 925 (2.76%)

1997: Lab maj 7,979. *Graham Lab: 18,525 (46.56%) Campbell SNP: 10,546 (26.51%) Cormack C: 7,387 (18.57%) MacPherson LD: 3,045 (7.65%)

---

## Ross, Skye & Inverness West
Elect 56,522. Turnout 61.59%
**LD hold**
**Maj 12,952 13.57% swing Lab to LD**

**Charles Kennedy (LD) 18,832 (54.10%)**
Donald Crichton (Lab) 5,880 (16.89%)
Jean Urquhart (SNP) 4,901 (14.08%)
Angus Laing (C) 3,096 (8.89%)
Eleanor Scott (Green) 699 (2.01%)

Stuart Topp (SSP) 683 (1.96%)
Philip Anderson (UK Ind) 456 (1.31%)
James Crawford (Country) 265 (0.76%)

1997: LD maj 4,019. *Kennedy LD: 15,472 (38.72%) Munro Lab: 11,453 (28.66%) Paterson SNP: 7,821 (19.57%) Macleod C: 4,368 (10.93%) Durance Ref: 535 (1.34%)

## Roxburgh & Berwickshire
Elect 47,059. Turnout 61.19%
**LD hold**
**Maj 7,511 1.73% swing C to LD**

**Archy Kirkwood (LD) 14,044 (48.77%)**
George Turnbull (C) 6,533 (22.69%)
Catherine Maxwell-Stuart (Lab) 4,498 (15.62%)
Roderick Campbell (SNP) 2,806 (9.74%)
Amanda Millar (SSP) 463 (1.61%)
Peter Neilson (UK Ind) 453 (1.57%)

1997: LD maj 7,906. *Kirkwood LD: 16,243 (46.50%) Younger C: 8,337 (23.87%) Eadie Lab: 5,226 (14.96%) Balfour SNP: 3,959 (11.33%) Curtis Ref: 922 (2.64%) Neilson UK Ind: 202 (0.58%)

## Stirling
Elect 53,097. Turnout 67.67%
**Lab hold**
**Maj 6,274 1.27% swing C to Lab**

**Anne McGuire (Lab) 15,175 (42.23%)**
Geoff Mawdsley (C) 8,901 (24.77%)
Fiona Macaulay (SNP) 5,877 (16.36%)
Clive Freeman (LD) 4,208 (11.71%)
Clarke Mullen (SSP) 1,012 (2.82%)
Mark Ruskell (Green) 757 (2.11%)

1997: Lab maj 6,411. *McGuire Lab: 20,382 (47.45%) Forsyth C: 13,971 (32.52%) Dow SNP: 5,752 (13.39%) Tough LD: 2,675 (6.23%) McMurdo UK Ind: 154 (0.36%)

## Strathkelvin & Bearsden
Elect 62,729. Turnout 66.14%
**Lab hold**
**Maj 11,717 7.44% swing Lab to LD**

**John Lyons (Lab) 19,250 (46.40%)**
Gordon Macdonald (LD) 7,533 (18.16%)
Calum Smith (SNP) 6,675 (16.09%)
Murray Roxburgh (C) 6,635 (15.99%)
Willie Telfer (SSP) 1,393 (3.36%)

1997: Lab maj 16,292. *Galbraith Lab: 26,278 (52.86%) Sharpe C: 9,986 (20.09%) McCormick SNP: 8,111 (16.32%) Morrison LD: 4,843 (9.74%) Wilson Ref: 339 (0.68%)

---

## Tayside North
Elect 61,645. Turnout 62.48%
**SNP hold**
**Maj 3,283 0.30% swing SNP to C**

**Peter Wishart (SNP) 15,441 (40.09%)**
Murdo Fraser (C) 12,158 (31.57%)
Thomas Docherty (Lab) 5,715 (14.84%)
Julia Robertson (LD) 4,363 (11.33%)
Rosie Adams (SSP) 620 (1.61%)
Tina MacDonald (Ind) 220 (0.57%)

1997: SNP maj 4,160. *Swinney SNP: 20,447 (44.85%) Walker C: 16,287 (35.72%) McFatridge Lab: 5,141 (11.28%)

---

## Tweeddale, Ettrick & Lauderdale
Elect 51,966. Turnout 63.92%
**LD hold**
**Maj 5,157 5.86% swing Lab to LD**

**Michael Moore (LD) 14,035 (42.25%)**
Keith Geddes (Lab) 8,878 (26.73%)
Andrew Brocklehurst (C) 5,118 (15.41%)
Richard Thomson (SNP) 4,108 (12.37%)
Norman Lockhart (SSP) 695 (2.09%)
John Hein (Lib) 383 (1.15%)

1997: LD maj 1,489. *Moore LD: 12,178 (31.22%) Geddes Lab:
10,689 (27.41%) Jack C: 8,623 (22.11%) Goldie SNP: 6,671 (17.10%)
Mowbray Ref: 406 (1.04%) Hein Lib: 387 (0.99%)

---

## Western Isles
Elect 21,807. Turnout 60.34%
**Lab hold**
**Maj 1,074 7.02% swing Lab to SNP**

**Calum MacDonald (Lab) 5,924 (45.02%)**
Alasdair Nicholson (SNP) 4,850 (36.86%)
Douglas Taylor (C) 1,250 (9.50%)
John Horne (LD) 849 (6.45%)
Joanne Telfer (SSP) 286 (2.17%)

1997: Lab maj 3,576. *MacDonald Lab: 8,955 (55.60%) Gillies SNP:
5,379 (33.40%) McGrigor C: 1,071 (6.65%) Mitchison LD: 495
(3.07%)

---

# CHAPTER 14

# Profiles of Scottish Members of Parliament (MPs)

# Irene Adams (LABOUR)
## MP Paisley North

**Born:** Paisley, 1947

**Education:** Stanely Green High School, Paisley.

**Career: 1970–4:** Councillor, Paisley Town Council; **1974–8:** Councillor, Renfrew District Council; **1979–84:** Councillor, Strathclyde Region; **1984–90:** Secretary/Researcher to sitting MP and husband Allen Adams; **1990:** first elected MP.

**Profile:** Irene Adams was widowed in 1990 when her husband Allen, sitting MP for Paisley North, died suddenly of a viral infection. She has one son and two daughters. Allen was her first boyfriend when she was sweet seventeen and she followed him into local government, then into Parliament in the by-election after his death. Her courage at that time, and often since, has been much admired. She stood out against drug-dealing in her constituency in the 1990s, and again against the neighbouring Labour MP Tommy Graham, whom she accused of trying to undermine her and her close colleague Gordon McMaster, MP for Paisley South, who committed suicide. Graham was expelled from the Labour Party after an internal inquiry.

Mrs Adams is a left-wing pro-home ruler who, with four others, tried to prevent the removal of the mace in a protest again the Conservative government's intransigent opposition to devolution. Officials were warned by Gordon McMaster, then a Whip, to tackle the others but not her: 'her son is six foot five'. She opposed the Gulf War and is anti-EC. She hates London but is a very effective MP, with a sharp, sardonic wit. She has, according to no less an authority than Teresa Gorman, 'subtle glamour' – but she has never lied about her age.

**Contact:** 020-7219-3564 (Parliament)
0141-887-5949 Fax 0141-887-8025 (Constituency)
e-mail contact@ireneadams-mp.new.labour.org.uk

## Douglas Alexander (LABOUR)
**Minister of State, Trade and Industry**
**MP Paisley South**

**Born:** Glasgow, 1967

**Education:** Park Mains High School, Erskine;
Lester B. Pearson College, Vancouver, Canada;
Edinburgh and Pennsylvania Universities.

**Career: 1990–1:** Parliamentary Researcher to Gordon Brown MP;
**1994–6:** Solicitor, Brodies WS; **1996–7:** Solicitor, Digby Brown;
**1997:** first elected MP (by-election ); **2001– :** Parliamentary
Secretary, Trade and Industry.

**Profile:** Douglas Alexander is younger brother of the Scottish Executive
minister Wendy Alexander and the son of the Rev. Douglas Alexander,
the minister who conducted Donald Dewar's funeral service in Glasgow
Cathedral. He is recently married. He is a close political colleague and
confidant of the Chancellor Gordon Brown (also a son of the manse).
They share an acute political intelligence, a passion for social justice
and a burning ambition. Both have an interest in American politics,
from which come many of their shared ideas on why people vote the
way they do. Together they wrote the pamphlet *New Scotland, New
Britain*. Alexander is more outgoing than his mentor, but they both
present a greater commitment to social justice than some of their New
Labour colleagues – though perhaps it's just the accent.

Alexander ran Labour's Scottish Parliament election campaign, under
Brown's watchful eye, where he added a Unionist rinse to the devolution
message. He was given the role of UK election co-ordinator in 2001
– while his big sister ran the Scottish end – and got his reward after the
election when he was made minister for e-commerce and competitiveness, a new post. He is a gifted politician and – though he has been
'Gordon's boy' so far – now is his chance to show what he can do on
his own.

**Contact:** 020-7219-1345 (Parliament)
           0141-561-0333 Fax 0141-561-0334 (Constituency)

**John Barrett** (LIBERAL DEMOCRAT)
**MP Edinburgh West**

**Born:** Hobart, Australia, 1954

**Education:** Forrester High School, Edinburgh; Telford College; Napier Polytechnic.

**Career: 1985– :** Director ABC Productions; **1995– :** Board member Edinburgh Film Festival; **1997–9:** Director, EDI Group; **1995–2001:** Edinburgh City Councillor; **2001– :** first elected MP for Edinburgh West.

**Profile:** John Barrett is a freelance video producer, making corporate and training videos, and an Edinburgh councillor. His wife Carol is a wildlife artist. They have one daughter. He was Donald Gorrie's election agent in the 1997 election, and David Steel's in 1999.

It is a comment on the collapse of the Tory Party in Scotland that – without diminishing Barrett's achievement – he won this seat at the first attempt after it had taken Donald Gorrie thirty years to make the breakthrough. Seven of the ten wards in the constituency are now Liberal held. He was the Lib Dem's Transport Spokesperson on the Council before going on to lead the group. His predecessor in the Transport brief was Margaret Smith, now an MSP, so speaking out on this issue seems to guarantee electoral success in Edinburgh. He will maintain his interest in transport in the Commons, particularly air and rail safety matters. He is also strong on green energy issues and can be expected to oppose any extension of nuclear power – something the government seems likely to consider.

**Contact:** 020-7219-8224 Fax 020-7219-1762 (Parliament)
         0131-339-0339 (Constituency)
         e-mail johnbarrettmp@parliament.uk

## Anne Begg (LABOUR)
## MP Aberdeen South

**Born:** Forfar, 1955

**Education:** Brechin High School; Aberdeen University and College of Education.

**Career: 1978–88:** English and History Teacher, Webster High School, Kirriemuir; **1988–97:** Assistant Principal then Principal Teacher of English, Arbroath Academy; **1999:** first elected MP.

**Profile:** Anne Begg has used a wheelchair for some years now. She has a progressive, degenerative disease, which is now ameliorated by enzyme replacement treatment. She was Disabled Scot of the Year in 1988 and her disability has lent an added prominence to her activities. Despite the obvious problems of getting around, she has never allowed her condition to hold her back. She was a member of the EIS National Council, the GTC, and of Labour's National Executive Committee.

Her seat has been the classic marginal in Scottish politics over the decades – taken by the young Donald Dewar from Lady Tweedsmuir, recovered from Dewar by Iain Sproat, held by Gerry Malone when Sproat deserted unsuccessfully to the Borders, lost by him to Frank Doran, who in turn was defeated by Raymond Robertson, who was beaten in 1997 by Anne Begg. All these bewildering changes were between Conservative and Labour, but the Liberal Democrats are now Ms Begg's main opponents. Her high profile and her sterling work as a constituency MP saw her through comfortably in 2001. Although she has resisted the role of 'spokesperson for the disabled', she can be expected to be in the forefront of the scrutiny of Alistair Darlings's proposed reforms of incapacity allowances for the disabled.

**Contact:**  020-7219-2140 Fax 020-7219-1264 (Parliament)
             01224-252704 Fax 01224-252705 (Constituency)
             e-mail begga@parliament.uk

## Gordon Brown (LABOUR)
## Chancellor of the Exchequer
## MP Dunfermline East

**Born:** Glasgow, 1951

**Education:** Kirkcaldy High School;
Edinburgh University.

**Career: 1972–5:** Student Rector Edinburgh University;
**1975–6:** Lecturer, Edinburgh University; **1976–80:** Lecturer in
Politics, Glasgow College of Technology; **1980–3:** Journalist, then
Editor, Current Affairs, STV; **1983:** first elected MP;
**1997– :** appointed Chancellor of the Exchequer.

**Profile:** Gordon Brown is one of three sons of the manse, his two
brothers being respected journalists. He is without doubt the most
intelligent man in British politics, the keeper of the party conscience,
whose sound stewardship is the main reason for Labour being returned
so handsomely at the 2001 election. Since his days as a Student Rector
at Edinburgh, he has shown every sign of knowing where he was
going, though Labour's unelectability in the 1980s meant he took
longer to get there. He is now married, finally silencing the laughable
metropolitan rumours about his sexuality. His wife may have difficulty
in ameliorating two of his famous characteristics: he is a workaholic and
he's never on time. His other alleged trait – a humourless dourness
– is completely at odds with the private personality.

Brown keeps an almost paternal interest in Scottish affairs. He was a
close ally of Donald Dewar, but his relationship with Henry McLeish
is less intimate and less trusting. In Dewar's absence, he now regards
himself as the guardian of the constitutional settlement and the guar-
antor of Labour votes in Scotland. His other relationship, with Tony
Blair, is often characterised as intense rivalry, and certainly supporters
in both camps have done little to dispel that impression. In fact – as
Dewar once privately said – they are 'like Siamese twins'. They need each
other and the Labour Party needs both if 'the project' is to be completed
successfully. The new PM's department is meant to counterbalance
Brown's influence as well as to ensure delivery of policy commitments.
Brown undoubtedly wants to be Prime Minister but we must wait to
see if Blair will serve him as well as he has served Blair.

**Contact:**  020-7219-3000 (Parliament)
            01383-611702 Fax 01383-611703 (Constituency)

## Russell Brown (LABOUR)
## MP Dumfries

**Born:** Annan, 1951

**Education:** Annan Academy.

**Career: 1974–97:** Production Supervisor;
**1986–96:** Councillor, Dumfries and Galloway Region;
**1988–96:** Councillor, Annandale and Eskdale District;
**1995–7:** Councillor, Dumfries and Galloway Council;
**1997:** first elected MP.

**Profile:** Russell Brown achieved one of the most surprising results on the 1997 election in Scotland. Labour had tried unsuccessfully to make a showing in Dumfries for decades, but then – in the second safest Tory seat in Scotland (Eastwood was safest but it, too, went to Labour) – Brown won with a swing of 16.5%, roughly twice the Scottish average. The collapse of the Tory vote was partly the result of the retirement of the veteran MP Sir Hector Munro – local, respected and almost non-political – as well as the general swing to Labour. Brown had the advantage of being another local man – albeit a representative of the working class – whereas the new Tory candidate Struan Stevenson came from – whisper it – the next county, Ayrshire. In 2001 Brown increased his majority, not something many Labour MPs could claim, and Dumfries is a marginal no more.

Russell Brown, married with two daughters, was born and brought up in the area and has spent all his working life there. He held office in the TGWU. He was a councillor for over ten years before and after local government reorganisation, and served on the Dumfries and Galloway Tourist Board before being elected to Parliament. He is not a great performer, but he spoke with authority when he drew attention, at a very early stage, to the catastrophic impact of foot and mouth on the local economy. He shares a constituency office with the local MSP and voluntarily presented his office accounts to the Commons authorities after erroneous allegations that he might have overclaimed expenses.

**Contact:** 020-7219-4429 Fax 020-7219-0922 (Parliament)
01387-247902 Fax 01387-247903 (Constituency)
e-mail russell@brownmp.new.labour.org.uk

# Des Browne (LABOUR)
## Parliamentary Secretary, Northern Ireland Office
## MP Kilmarnock and Loudoun

**Born:** Stevenson, 1952

**Education:** St Michael's Academy, Kilwinning; Glasgow University.

**Career: 1976:** Qualified as Solicitor; **1993:** called to the Scottish Bar; **1997:** first elected MP; **2001– :** Parliamentary Secretary, Northern Ireland Office.

**Profile:** Des Browne is married with two sons and practised as a solicitor for sixteen years before going to the Bar under the new solicitor/advocate provisions. He has always been heavily involved in civil liberties and children's rights. He has made the drugs issue one of his main areas of interest and has recently promoted the idea of a drugs register for traffickers.

He took the nomination for Kilmarnock and Loudoun only shortly before the 1997 election, when the incumbent Willie McKelvey decided not to stand again. Mr McKelvey did not end up in the Lords as expected, but his sudden departure did create the opportunity for Donald Dewar to get one of his favourite candidates into a reasonably safe seat. Browne became PPS to Dewar briefly from 1998 to 1999 before the Scottish elections removed Dewar to Edinburgh. He was then appointed PPS to Adam Ingram at the Northern Ireland Office, and has now succeeded him as a minister there. In pre-devolution days, he was precisely the kind of bright and loyal MP who could have expected earlier promotion. Not only have opportunities for Scots shrunk with devolution, there is also a general feeling that too many ministers from north of the border simply inflames opinion in England. He will be glad to have a grip on the ladder.

**Contact:** 020-7219-4501 Fax 020-7219-2423 (Parliament)
020 1563-520267 Fax 01563-539439 (Constituency)
e-mail browned@parliament.uk

## Malcolm Bruce (LIBERAL DEMOCRAT)
## MP Gordon

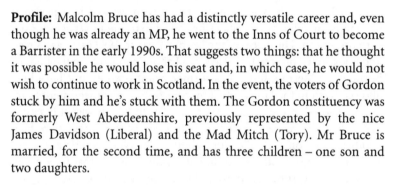

**Born:** Birkenhead, 1944

**Education:** Wrekin College; St Andrews and Strathclyde Universities.

**Career: 1966–7:** Trainee journalist, *Liverpool Post*; **1968–9:** Boots section buyer; **1971–5:** Research and Info Officer, NE Scotland Development Authority; **1975–81:** Director Noroil Publishing House; **1981–4:** Joint Editor/Publisher, Aberdeen Petroleum Publishing; **1983:** first elected MP.

**Profile:** Malcolm Bruce has had a distinctly versatile career and, even though he was already an MP, he went to the Inns of Court to become a Barrister in the early 1990s. That suggests two things: that he thought it was possible he would lose his seat and, in which case, he would not wish to continue to work in Scotland. In the event, the voters of Gordon stuck by him and he's stuck with them. The Gordon constituency was formerly West Aberdeenshire, previously represented by the nice James Davidson (Liberal) and the Mad Mitch (Tory). Mr Bruce is married, for the second time, and has three children – one son and two daughters.

In Parliament, he has been equally versatile, covering almost all the main portfolios, though mostly those with an industrial or economic bias. He is affable and approachable, energetic and knowledgeable, though sometimes he knows too much for the clarity of his argument. He was Leader of the Scottish Liberals and Lib Dems for five years, worked harder than his predecessor Russell Johnston but lacked his stature and oratory. He stood, optimistically, for the UK party leadership but was defeated by his friend Charles Kennedy. He had a good campaign in 2001 as the President of the Liberal Democrats.

**Contact:** 020-7219-6233 Fax 020-7219-2334 (Parliament)
01467-623413  Fax 01467-624994 (Constituency)
e-mail gordonlibdems@cix.co.uk

## David Cairns (LABOUR)
## MP Greenock and Inverclyde

**Born:** Greenock, 1966

**Education:** Notre Dame High School, Greenock; Gregorian University, Rome; Franciscan Study Centre, Canterbury.

**Career: 1991–4:** Catholic priest; **1994–7:** Co-ordinator, Christian Socialist Movement; **1997–2001:** Research Assistant to Siobhain McDonagh MP; **1998–2001:** Councillor, Merton Borough; **2001– :** first elected MP for Greenock and Inverclyde.

**Profile:** David Cairns is a former priest who worked in a parish in Clapham for three years, where he found extreme poverty alongside extreme wealth. The defeat of the Labour Party in 1992 came as a severe and unexpected blow to him. He was a Labour councillor in the London borough of Merton, but – as a former priest – would not have been allowed to sit in the House of Commons but for an amendment to the law sponsored in the Lords earlier in 2001. In fact, it was only passed just before the recess on 10 May – otherwise there might have been another name on the ballot for Labour. Ann Widdecombe and other zealots were against the amendment on the grounds that holy orders should not be superseded by political considerations. Some cynics suggested that the government was keen to repeal the disqualification to distract attention from its failure to change the Act of Succession.

He thinks he won the nomination because Greenock is his home town, not because of his religious affiliation. In the campaign, the Liberal candidate Chic Brodie was shot and wounded by an airgun-toting constituent. (All other parties denied complicity.) Cairns wants to see the regeneration of the constituency after decades of unemployment and deprivation. Politics was a natural step for him after the priesthood. He cites communist grandfathers and the destruction of Greenock's ship-yards as the major influences in his political development. Siobhain McDonagh, for whom he worked before his election, is the sister of Margaret, former General Secretary of the Labour Party, and respect-ably new Labour.

**Contact:** 020-7219-8242 (Parliament)

# Menzies Campbell (LIBERAL DEMOCRAT)
## MP Fife North-East

**Born:** Glasgow, 1941

**Education:** Hillhead High School, Glasgow; Universities of Glasgow and Stanford, California.

**Career: 1965–6:** Captain, British Athletics Team; **1968:** called to the Scottish Bar; **1982:** appointed QC; **1987:** first elected MP.

**Profile:** Ming Campbell – the Rt Hon Menzies – is married to Elspeth and has one stepson. He ran in the Tokyo Olympics and the Jamaica Commonwealth Games, captained the British Athletics Team and held the British 100 metres record for seven years. It is said that Elspeth still refers to him as the fastest white man in the world, though Margo Wells would undoubtedly have something to say about that. At university, when he wasn't running, he was debating, and the friendships formed then – with John Smith, Donald Dewar, Derry Irvine and John Mackay among others – remained strong across the years. He came from a working-class family – hard to guess now from his accent, refined in the Courts and the House – and he is a perfect example of the Scots lad o' pairts.

He was once asked on *Any Questions* what class he was and he replied, 'I am no class, I am Scottish.' That may be a rather over-sanguine view of Scottish society, but 'class' is something he brings to the Liberal front bench as Foreign and Defence spokesperson. If the relationship between the Blair's New Labour and the Liberal Democrats had developed differently, he would certainly have progressed to the Cabinet post his talent merits. That didn't happen, nor did he compete for the Lib Dem leadership against the much younger Charles Kennedy. He was a candidate for the Speaker's chair but dropped out early in the bizarre voting procedure. He would have done it well – elegant, urbane, witty and wise – but he probably didn't campaign hard for it. Politically, he lacks that selfish determination over the last stretch which made him such a winner on the track. Just too decent.

**Contact:** 020-7219-4446 Fax 020-7219-0559 (Parliament)
        01334-656361 Fax 01334-654045 (Constituency)
        e-mail nefifelibdem@cix.co.uk

**Alistair Carmichael** (LIBERAL DEMOCRAT)
**MP Orkney and Shetland**

**Born:** Islay, 1965

**Education:** Islay High School; Aberdeen University.

**Career: 1984–9:** Hotel Manager;
**1993–6:** Procurator Fiscal Depute; **1996– :** Solicitor;
**2001– :** first elected MP for Orkney and Shetland.

**Profile:** Alistair Carmichael is married, with two sons, and is highly rated by his party leadership as a sensible, moderate and articulate voice. He is a Church of Scotland elder, a qualification which shone through a reasoned and compassionate speech he made on Section 28 to the 2001 LibDem Conference, supporting its repeal. His work as a solicitor brought him cases involving domestic violence, and he became Director of Aberdeenshire Women's Aid.

His count in Orkney and Shetland was delayed for several hours when a plane carrying the ballot boxes had to be diverted to the mainland with an expectant mother – just as it should be in an island community. In the event, Carmichael won with less than the normal Lib Dem majority, possibly because he is not a local man. He previously lived in Aberdeenshire and was prominent in the Gordon constituency. He is now established in Orkney, so his new domicile should bring him a higher local profile and a more comfortable majority next time in this safe Liberal seat. He is interested in transport and energy policy, and expects to take a campaigning role on the operation of the Crown Estates Office, a particularly strong issue in his constituency. He speaks for the party on Tourism.

**Contact:**   020-7219-8307 (Parliament)
          01856-761317 (Constituency)
          e-mail carmichaela@parliament.uk

## Lynda Clark (LABOUR)
### Advocate General for Scotland
### MP Edinburgh Pentlands

**Born:** Dundee, 1949

**Education:** Lawside Academy, Dundee; St Andrews and Edinburgh Universities.

**Career: 1971–3:** Part-time tutor, Dundee University; **1973–6:** Lecturer in Jurisprudence; **1977–89:** Scottish Bar; **1989:** appointed QC; **1990:** called to the English Bar; **1997:** first elected MP; **1999– :** Advocate-General for Scotland.

**Profile:** Dr Clark is well qualified – a member of the Bar on both sides of the Border, a PhD, a governing member of the Inner Temple, and now the first woman Law Officer in Scotland, the Advocate-General, a post created after devolution. It is said that her ambitions do not end there. She would like to be on the bench – a Dundonian on the bench, michty me! Since she reportedly lacks the common touch, perhaps we are oversubscribed in that direction.

After standing unsuccessfully in 1992 for North-East Fife, she took the scalp of Malcolm Rifkind, then Foreign Secretary and the Tory MP least likely to lose. But lose he did, which is a measure of the Conservative collapse in Scotland. Dr Clark has failed to make much of an impact either in the House or in her constituency and she must consider herself fortunate to have won again in 2001. She concentrated her campaigning on how little the Tories and Rifkind did to improve the social divisions in Pentlands when they had the chance for over twenty years. It has been rumoured that she is not entirely happy at Westminster and any measurable Tory recovery would surely have solved her problem.

**Contact:** 020-7219-4492 (Parliament)
0131-556-4834 (Constituency)
e-mail scottishsecretary@scotland.gov.uk

## Tom Clarke (LABOUR)
## MP Coatbridge and Chryston

**Born:** Coatbridge, 1941

**Education:** Columba High School, Coatbridge;
Glasgow College of Commerce.

**Career: 1956–66:** Clerical worker;
**1966–82:** Assistant Director, Scottish Council for Educational
Technology; **1964–74:** Councillor, Coatbridge Town Council;
**1975–82:** Provost of Monklands; **1982:** first elected MP for Airdrie and
Coatbridge (then Monklands West), now Coatbridge and Chryston;
**1997–8:** Minister of State, Department of Culture and Sport.

**Profile:** Tom Clarke is the answer to the question 'Which Provost of
Monklands won an award as a film director?' He is a Lanarkshire Catholic on the loyalist right of the party who, in his youth, acted as agent
for his predecessor James Dempsey. He is very sensitive to charges that
Monklands Council favoured the Catholic side of its constituency and
was openly annoyed when Helen Liddell admitted as much in the
Monklands by-election. He is, himself, a man of personal kindness and
sensitivity. In pre-New Labour days he always did well in Shadow
Cabinet elections in the Parliamentary Labour Party, though that may
have had as much to do with assiduous canvassing as outstanding
ability. His great passion in life, apart from politics, is the cinema. He
worked for six years with the Scottish Film Council, became an unpaid
director of the British Film Institute, and his short film *Give Us A Goal*
won an amateur prize in 1972.

He held shadow responsibilities in Scottish Affairs, Overseas Development, Social Services and Disability in the 1990s, though his spell as
Shadow Scottish Secretary, after Donald Dewar and under John Smith,
was not a success. His local government 'fixing' skills were not enough
to bring together a Scottish party divided over its direction on devolution after the morale-sapping defeat of 1992. After the 1997 victory, he
was briefly Minister of State in the Department of Culture, mainly
responsible for the film industry. His dreams of red boxes must now
be over, but he has one lasting monument – he piloted through the
Disabled Persons Act (1986), a landmark advance in the rights of the
disabled.

**Contact:** 020-7219-6997 Fax 020-7219-6094 (Parliament)
          01236-600800  Fax 01236-600808 (Constituency)

# Michael Connarty (LABOUR)
## MP Falkirk East

**Born:** Coatbridge, 1947

**Education:** St Patrick's High School, Coatbridge; Stirling and Glasgow Universities; Jordanhill College of Education.

**Career: 1970–1:** President, Student Association, Stirling University; **1976–92:** Teacher, Special Needs; **1977–90:** Councillor, Stirling District Council; **1980–90:** Council Leader; **1999:** first elected MP.

**Profile:** Michael Connarty is married, with one son and one daughter, and looks younger than he actually is. He is always fashionably dressed – smart suits and good haircuts. His style of politics is, however, very much out of fashion in the new Labour Party. He was a highly active and visible Leader of Stirling District Council, pursuing the economic development of the area as well as espousing innovative policies on equal opportunities and women's rights. He was a founding member of the Labour Co-ordinating Committee in Scotland and stood twice in the Stirling Constituency, only to be defeated twice by Michael Forsyth.

In Parliament he was PPS to Tom Clarke when Clarke was briefly a Minister of State, but no further preference has followed. He has been Chairman of the Scottish Labour Parliamentary Group and does good committee work which – since devolution – passes almost unnoticed. He has been prominent, as the local MP, in pursuing BP for their safety shortcomings at Grangemouth. In keeping with his well-established home rule sentiments, he put himself forward for Labour's Scottish Parliament list but – avoiding the fate of the other awkward customers Dennis Canavan and Ian Davidson – withdrew before he could be turned down. He was not in favour of the Scottish Executive's approach to the abolition of Section 28, an attitude which did not seem to fit with his liberal credentials.

**Contact:** 020-7219-5071 Fax 020-7219-2541 (Parliament)
01324-474832  Fax 01324-666811 (Constituency)
e-mail mc003@post.almac.co.uk

**Robin Cook** (LABOUR)
**Leader of the House of Commons**
**MP Livingston**

**Born:** Bellshill, 1946

**Education:** Aberdeen Grammar School; Royal
High School, Edinburgh; Edinburgh University.

**Career: 1969–70:** Teacher, Bo'ness Academy; **1970–4:** Tutor WEA;
**1971–4:** Councillor, Edinburgh Corporation; **1974:** first elected MP
for Edinburgh North; **1983:** MP for Livingston; **1997–2001:** Foreign
and Commonwealth Secretary; **2001– :** Leader of the House.

**Profile:** Robin Cook is married, for the second time, and has two sons
by his first marriage. Politicians' personal lives, unless they are corrupt
or depraved, should not affect their political standing. In Robin Cook's
case, his reputation has undoubtedly suffered from the circumstances
surrounding his very public divorce and remarriage. This darling of
the left, much respected though not exactly loved, was acknowledged
in opposition as the most brilliant tactician and debater on the Labour
front bench. In the last years of the Conservative government, his
witheringly witty but devastatingly accurate attacks did more than
most to destroy its morale and credibility. Now, his unusual looks and
speech patterns – the same as they always were – are satirised.

Cook might have escaped such treatment if his period as Foreign
Secretary had been studded with diplomatic successes. In fact, his early
months were gaffe-strewn – like the royal tour of the Far East – and
his more grandiose ambitions for an ethical foreign policy remained
unfulfilled. He admittedly steadied in later months, but he seemed
isolated in Cabinet and – always a loner – he lacked the popular base to
advance on the summit or even to consolidate his position. Blair moved
him to Leader of the House, a post that will suit his parliamentary
skills but not his ambition, and where his pro-Europe and single-
currency sympathies will be less obvious. After an early backbench
rebellion on the composition of Select Committees, he has espoused
the cause of parliamentary reform – an approach which might just
restore him to the position of backbench hero.

**Contact:**   020-7219-1500 (Parliament)
             0131-346-0266 (Constituency)

# Tam Dalyell (LABOUR)
## MP Linlithgow

**Born:** Edinburgh, 1932

**Education:** Edinburgh Academy; Eton College; Cambridge University; Moray House College of Education.

**Career: 1950–2:** National Service Royal Scots Greys; **1956–60:** Teacher, Bo'ness Academy; **1961–2:** Deputy Director of Studies, schoolship 'Dunera'; **1962:** first elected MP for West Lothian; **1983– :** MP for Linlithgow.

**Profile:** Not everyone loves Tam but most people do, and those who dislike politicians think he should be their role model: he always tells the truth as he sees it, even if it is invariably uncomfortable and sometimes wrong. He is married to Kathleen, daughter of the late Lord Wheatley, and has one son and one daughter. He did his national service in the Royal Scots Greys, the regiment raised by his ancestor and namesake General Tam, though it is difficult to see the gangling Tam as a soldier and nearly impossible to see him marching in step with anyone for long. He showed early promise as ministerial material when he was PPS to Richard Crossman but – apart from a brief stint as Labour Shadow Spokesperson on Science – he took to non-conformist ways.

Tam's campaigns are legion and some legendary – devolution, the *Belgrano*, Westland, sanctions against Libya and Iraq – involving trenchant criticism of his own party, though mostly of Mrs Thatcher and the Conservatives. His main weapon is sheer persistence. He may sometimes draw a controversial conclusion from his extensive research of the facts but he will repeat and repeat where weaker souls retire. There was a rumour he would retire himself at the 1997 election, but he has remained to become Father of the House. As such, he was called on to organise the re-election of the Speaker, having already and controversially endorsed the incumbent Michael Martin. He was incapacitated during the 2001 election, but managed – from a sedentary position – to criticise the lack of principle in all the party campaigns, especially his own. Bad leg, but still functioning as normal.

**Contact:**  020-7219-3427 (Parliament)
01506-834255 (Constituency)

## Alistair Darling (LABOUR)
### Secretary of State for Work and Pensions
### MP Edinburgh Central

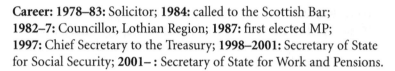

**Born:** London, 1953

**Education:** Loretto School, Edinburgh;
Aberdeen University.

**Career: 1978–83:** Solicitor; **1984:** called to the Scottish Bar;
**1982–7:** Councillor, Lothian Region; **1987:** first elected MP;
**1997:** Chief Secretary to the Treasury; **1998–2001:** Secretary of State
for Social Security; **2001– :** Secretary of State for Work and Pensions.

**Profile:** With his close-cut grey hair, back beard and eyebrows, Alistair
Darling looked like a medieval Italian prince or prelate. He has lost
the beard now, but at whose behest? Style-conscious New Labour is
reported not to favour beards much, though perhaps he simply got
tired of it, or his wife did. She is the journalist Margaret Vaughan,
and they have one son and one daughter. Beardless, he still a very
'contained' performer, a master of his brief not given to rushes of
blood to the head, or any obvious emotion. He is the great-nephew of
Will Y. Darling, a prominent Edinburgh character and the Conservative
MP for Edinburgh South for twelve years after the war. Young Darling
was born in England and brought up there till he was twelve. He was
not initially in favour of devolution, though he did vote 'Yes' in 1979.

His ministerial career began as Gordon Brown's Chief Secretary to the
Treasury, and his work on the spending review showed how politically
able and administratively assiduous he is. He describes himself as a
reformer not a radical, and his reforming zeal was put to the test when,
in the first major reshuffle, he was made Secretary of State for Social
Security – a department which has claimed several reputations, those
of Harriet Harman and Frank Field among them. The social security
system is one in dire need of change, but where improvement is not
always immediately obvious. Nevertheless, Darling seems to be making
a difference and he was amply rewarded in the post-election reshuffle
with a much enlarged department.

**Contact:** 020-7219-4584 (Parliament)
  0131-476-2552 Fax 0131-476-3574 (Constituency)

# Ian Davidson (LABOUR)
## MP Glasgow Pollok

**Born:** Jedburgh, 1950

**Education:** Jedburgh Grammar School; Galashiels Academy; Edinburgh University; Jordanhill College of Education.

**Career: 1973–4:** Chair, National Organisation of Labour Students; **1975–6:** President, Jordanhill Student Association; **1978–85:** Researcher to Janey Buchan MEP; **1985–92:** Community Service Volunteers; **1978–92:** Councillor, Strathclyde Region; **1986–92:** Chairman, Strathclyde Education Committee; **1992:** first elected MP for Glasgow Govan; **1997:** MP for Glasgow Pollok.

**Profile:** Ian Davidson made his name as an anti-Trotskyite in the National Organisation of Labour Students. He attended Jordanhill College of Education after university but was not destined for the classroom. In fact as Chairman of Education in Strathclyde Region, he was unpopular in schools for his tough line with teachers, and failed to make much headway with school closures. He was also a Euro-sceptic researcher to the Euro-sceptic MEP, the Glasgow treasure Janey Buchan. He is married with one son and one daughter. As a Borderer by background, he still plays rugby – for the House of Commons.

He was able to draw blood in debate in Scotland but he has not made much impact at Westminster. Nevertheless, his criticisms of the lack of socialism in New Labour's programme displeased the hierarchy and, together with Dennis Canavan, he was one of the MPs not selected for the Scottish Parliament list. Both appealed unsuccessfully. Unlike Canavan, he has stayed within the party, resigned if not content to be a Westminster foot soldier. He has concentrated recently on law-and-order issues and spent a summer secondment with Strathclyde at Chief Superintendent level.

**Contact:** 020-7219-3610 Fax 020-7219-2238 (Parliament)
0141-883-8338 Fax 0141-883-4116 (Constituency)

# Brian Donohoe (LABOUR)
## MP Cunninghame South

**Born:** Kilmarnock, 1948

**Education:** Irvine Royal Academy; Kilmarnock
Technical College.

**Career: 1965–70:** Apprentice Engineer, Ailsa Shipyard;
**1977:** Hunterston Power Station; **1977–81:** Draughtsman ICI;
**1981–92:** NALGO District Officer; **1992:** first elected MP.

**Profile:** Brian Donohoe was a trade union activist before he joined
the Labour Party. He is married with two sons. At Westminster he is
somewhat overshadowed by his Cunninghame neighbour Brian
Wilson, but not in the local Ayrshire press, which he has cultivated
brilliantly. He has made noises about the possible confusion over who
looks after constituents' complaints and queries – the MP or the MSP
– but his main complaint was about list MSPs from the SNP. He has a
workable arrangement with the local Labour MSP, Irene Oldfather,
that he answers whatever comes to him.

He is a hard-working, middle-ground loyalist who greatly admires
Gordon Brown. In 1994 he encouraged Brown not to step aside for
Tony Blair and run for the leadership. One of his finest moments was
asking John Major whom he thought would be his Brutus, though he
did not mean to imply that Major had imperial qualities. His other
great moment (literally) was when Downing Street phoned him after
the 1997 election to offer a job on the assumption he was Lord
(Bernard) Donohue. He is close to British Airways and has been against
the quasi-privatisation of air-traffic control, like most Ayrshire MPs.

**Contact:** 020-7219-6230 Fax 020-7219-5388 (Parliament)
020 01294-276844 Fax 01294-313463 (Constituency)

# Frank Doran (LABOUR)
## MP Aberdeen Central

**Born:** Edinburgh, 1949

**Education:** Ainsley Park Secondary School; Leith Academy, Edinburgh; Dundee University.

**Career: 1977–87:** Solicitor; **1987–92:** MP for Aberdeen South; **1992–7:** Co-ordinator, National Trade Union Political Ballot Fund Campaign; **1997:** elected MP for Aberdeen Central.

**Profile:** Frank Doran was active in Labour local politics in Dundee together with George Galloway and Willie McKelvey, and all three were named in a Channel 4 documentary investigation into the use of funds from Labour drinking clubs. All three advanced to better things. He has two sons. His partner is Joan Ruddock, formerly Chair of CND and now MP for Lewisham. He acted as her secretary after he lost the notoriously volatile seat of Aberdeen South. At the same time, he was also co-ordinator of the National Trade Union Political Ballot Fund Campaign, which is a mouthful though clearly not a handful.

In his first stint in Parliament, he was an opposition spokesperson on Energy for four years, but obviously lost his place in the promotion queue when he was defeated in Aberdeen South. On his return, he was PPS to Ian McCartney for four years – most recently when McCartney held the influential post of Minister of State in the Cabinet Office.

**Contact:** 020-7219-3481 (Parliament)
020 01224-252715 Fax 01224-252716 (Constituency)
e-mail doranf@parliament.uk

## Peter Duncan (CONSERVATIVE)
## MP Galloway and Upper Nithsdale

**Born:** Kilwinning, 1965

**Education:** Ardrossan Academy; Birmingham
University.

**Career: 1985–8:** Project Manager, Mackays Stores;
**1988–2000:** Director, John Duncan & Son; **2001:** first elected MP
for Galloway and Upper Nithsdale.

**Profile:** Peter Duncan is an Ayrshire businessman, not very well
known in the Tory Party let alone in the rest of Scotland. He is, of all
things, a Leicester City supporter (he has a pal there) and admires
Tony Benn because he is a conviction politician. Unfortunately, Benn
has retired from the Commons, so they won't meet for a cuppa in the
members' tearoom. He is married, with one son and one daughter, but
lost his father just before the 2001 campaign and his mother during it.

A first time candidate, he took the seat in 2001 by claiming that
Galloway – always prone to feeling left out on a limb – had been
ignored by Labour and the SNP. It worked – if only by 74 votes – and
he achieved what Sir Malcolm Rifkind, Phil Gallie and Raymond
Robertson failed to do. He was returned to Westminster as the sole
representative of his party from Scotland, one of a kind, king of the hill,
cock of the walk. He puts it down to rediscovering the art of community politics. The foot and mouth outbreak is thought to have helped
him win, so he will need to keep the concentration on community
politics if he hopes to hold on to the seat next time. He has called for
a more tolerant, inclusive Conservative Party, so his survival may
also depend on how the Tories sort themselves out. PS. In what may
be fairly described as mixed fortunes, his dog died too.

**Contact:**   020-7219-8235 (Parliament)
          01556-504265 (Constituency)
          e-mail duncanp@parliament.uk

## Annabelle Ewing (SNP)
## MP Perth

**Born:** Glasgow, 1960

**Education:** Craigholme School, Glasgow; Glasgow and Johns Hopkins (Bologna) Universities; Europa Institute, University of Amsterdam.

**Career: 1987:** Stage, European Commission; **1987–96:** EC law specialist, Brussels; **1996–7:** Solicitor; **1997– :** Solicitor/Partner Ewing & Co., Glasgow; **2001:** first elected MP for Perth.

**Profile:** Another Ewing, but this time the only one in the House of Commons. The hacks will be pleased that she's not the fourth Ewing in the Scottish Parliament where her mother, brother and sister-in-law swell the SNP benches. She must have absorbed politics by osmosis as well as conviction. She prefers to talk about issues rather than the family, but then she doesn't need to – having the name is pedigree enough.

She followed the family path of taking law at Glasgow University (and elsewhere) before working in Brussels as a specialist in EU law for an American company. She previously and unsuccessfully stood for the Scottish Parliament in Stirling and for Westminster at the Hamilton South by-election in 1999. In Hamilton, site of her mother's first famous victory, she came within five hundred votes of defeating the Labour candidate. In Stirling, she doubled the SNP share of the vote and pushed the Tories into third place. (Whaur's yer Michael Forsyth noo? Making a mint in London, actually.) In Perth, she was following Roseanna Cunningham's reign. Roseanna's groundwork and her own vivacious campaign just did the trick, though – with a majority of only 48 votes – it was what her Tory opponents might call a damned close-run thing. The Tories did run a good campaign – and Annabelle has work to do. Her instant appointment as the party's Social Security and Pensions spokesperson should help raise her profile. She has also joined the SNP's Shadow Cabinet.

**Contact:** 020-7219-8309 (Parliament)
          01786-463054 (Constituency)
          email ewinga@parliament.uk

## George Foulkes (LABOUR)
## Minister of State, Scotland Office
## MP Carrick, Cumnock and Doon Valley

**Born:** Oswestry, 1942

**Education:** Keith Grammar School; Haberdashers' Aske's School; Edinburgh University.

**Career: 1964–6:** President, Scottish Union of Students; **1966–8:** Director, European League for Economic Cooperation; **1968–9:** Scottish Organiser, European Movement; **1969–73:** Director, Enterprise Youth; **1973–9:** Director, Age Concern Scotland; **1970–5:** Councillor, Edinburgh Corporation; **1974–9:** Councillor, Lothian Region; **1979:** first elected MP for South Ayrshire; **1983:** MP for Carrick, Cumnock and Doon Valley; **1997–2001:** Under-Secretary for International Development; **2001– :** Minister of State, Scotland Office.

**Profile:** George Foulkes is one of those Labour MPs of a certain age whose chances of a long ministerial career were taken away by Mrs Thatcher and eighteen years of Conservative government. He was a local councillor with Rifkind and Cook. Major office has come late and less conspicuously than he might have hoped. If there is disappointment, he hides it well. He is a great enthusiast, throwing himself into every cause he espouses – and there have been many, as a look at his cv substantiates. He was also a front-bench spokesman on a range of subjects, mostly international, in the long dark years. He had one dark moment personally, when – after a whisky reception – he was involved in a stramash with an old lady, a policeman, was fined and resigned his front-bench post. He is married to the Provost of South Ayrshire, with two grown-up sons and a daughter.

After the 1997 victory, he was appointed Parliamentary Secretary in the new Department for International Development, prised away from the Foreign Office and headed by Clare Short with her own seat in the Cabinet. The profile of Britain's aid effort has increased immeasurably, thanks also to Gordon Brown's lead on debt cancellation, and George was always there to press the flesh when Ms Short went over the top: Monserrat was the most public example. He was much appreciated and well liked abroad and in the Department. Now in the Scotland

Office, he plays a similar but more senior role as emollient minister to Helen Liddell's severe Secretary of State. For someone who has championed devolution all his political life and who chaired the Campaign for a Scottish Assembly for fifteen years, it's modest reward.

**Contact:** 020-7219-3474 Fax 020-7219-6492 (Parliament)
01290-422990 Fax 01290-424973 (Constituency)
e-mail scottishsecretary@scotland.gsi.gov.uk

## George Galloway (LABOUR)
## MP Glasgow Kelvin

**Born:** Dundee, 1954

**Education:** Harris Academy, Dundee.

**Career: 1972:** General labourer, Garden Works, Dundee; **1973:** Production worker, Michelin Tyres; **1977–83:** Labour organiser; **1983–7:** General Secretary, War on Want; **1987:** first elected MP for Glasgow Hillhead; **1997:** MP for Glasgow Kelvin.

**Profile:** He is married, for the second time. 'Gorgeous George' is how he is universally known, and he doesn't mind a bit. He likes to dress well, sport an all-year tan and puff on a Cuban cigar. The nickname could equally well have been 'gifted George' since he is a man of considerable intelligence and talent. On the other hand, as Menzies Campbell has said 'his judgement frequently fails to match his ability'. With more judgement, he could have been a contender. Instead, controversy has followed him, sometimes scandal. There were unproven allegations of misuse of money from the Dundee Labour Clubs and War on Want; there was the bizarre admission – at a press conference – of 'carnal knowledge' with two women at a conference in Greece; there was the televised meeting with Saddam Hussein when he seemed to praise the President for his indefatigability. He earns good money for his weekly column in the *Mail on Sunday*.

He was Organiser of the Dundee Labour Party by the age of twenty-three, Chairman of the Scottish Labour Party at twenty-six, yet he was nearly deselected by his constituency before the 1992 election. His pro-Arab, anti-Zionist sympathies are perfectly respectable standpoints, but many of his constituents would prefer him to exercise a little more energy at home. For all the controversy, he speaks brilliantly and won the *Spectator*/Zurich 2001 parliamentary award for Debater of the Year. Foolish quite often, vain to a fault, he is nevertheless no hypocrite. He has considerable charm when he wishes, but does he ever ask himself why he has become so disliked? To get things done, you need more friends than enemies.

**Contact:** 020-7219-3000 Fax 020-7219-2879 (Parliament)
020141-357-2073 Fax 0141-357-2073 (Constituency)
e-mail gallowayg@parliament.uk

# Nigel Griffiths (LABOUR)
**Parliamentary Secretary, Trade and Industry**
**MP Edinburgh South**

**Born:** Glasgow, 1955

**Education:** Hawick High School; Edinburgh
University; Moray House College of Education.

**Career: 1978:** Secretary Lothian Devolution Campaign;
**1979–87:** Rights Adviser, Mental Handicap Pressure Group;
**1979–87:** Councillor, Edinburgh District Council; **1987:** First elected
MP for Edinburgh South; **1997–8:** Parliamentary Secretary, Trade
and Industry; **2001– :** Under-Secretary, Trade and Industry.

**Profile:** The boyish Nigel Griffiths suffers from an almost juvenile
excess of zeal. In fact he is older than he seems, and joined Edinburgh
Council over twenty years ago while he was an adviser on the rights of
the mentally handicapped. He is the author of *The Welfare Rights
Guide for Mentally Handicapped People and Their Families* (1982). He
also wrote *A Practical Guide to Housing in Edinburgh* (1981) and later
became Chairman of Housing on the Council. His boyhood hero was
Ralph Nader. He is married.

In opposition, Griffiths was first a Whip, then a Consumer Affairs
spokesperson. In the latter role, eventually as part of Gordon Brown's
team, his hyperactive style brought rewards. He highlighted the Hoover
debacle, embarrassed three of the four clearing banks into processing
cheques faster, and generally bombarded the press with proposed
initiatives. His frenetic style did not seem to suit office and he lasted
only fourteen months as a Consumer Affairs minister. He blamed
senior civil servants who didn't like his forthright methods; they even
resented him publicising his mobile phone number to constituents, he
said. A week before he was sacked, he told BBC Radio Scotland that he
feared the axe was about to fall – in an interview on his mobile phone.
He is irrepressible and, after the election, returned to the same department from which he was sacked, a little older and – it is to be hoped
– wiser. But he was another MP whose office expenses caused media
interest and general consternation at the end of 2001.

**Contact:**  020-7219-2424 (Parliament)
0131-662-4520 (Constituency)
e-mail nigelgriffithsmp@parliament.uk

## David Hamilton (LABOUR)
## MP Midlothian

**Born:** Dalkeith, 1954

**Education:** Dalkeith High School.

**Career: 1965–84:** Miner, National Coal Board;
**1987–9:** Employment Training Scheme Superviser;
**1989–92:** Placement/Training Officer, Craigmillar Festival;
**1992–2000:** Chief Executive, Craigmillar Opportunities;
**1993–2001:** Councillor, Midlothian; **2001:** first elected MP for
Midlothian.

**Profile:** He was jailed during the Miners' Strike in 1984 in connection
with an assault. In the event, he was acquitted of the charge when the
case came to court. His wife Jean was a prominent member of the
Women's Support Network during the strike. While a member of
Midlothian Council, he was Convener of Strategic Development and
then a member of the Council Cabinet. As such he played a major role
in the controversial plans to develop the A701 – plans which have now
been shelved. He has championed new industry in the area, especially
biotechnology – like PPL, the company responsible for Dolly the
Sheep, based in Midlothian.

It was a surpise that, as a former communist, he got the Labour endorse-
ment. He has promised to carry on the 'socialist values' followed by his
predecessor in the seat, Eric Clarke, another NUM stalwart. Scotland
is one of the few areas in the UK which still returns 'Old Labour' supporters to bolster the New Labour majority. Hamilton has taken his
old habit of direct action with him to the Commons. He and his
Scottish colleagues John Lyons and John MacDougall refused to vacate
their temporary office – a handsome committee room with a view of
the Thames – even after pressure from the Serjeant at Arms.

**Contact:** 020-7219-8257 (Parliament)
0131-663-5799 (Constituency)
e-mail hamiltonda@parliament.uk

## Tom Harris (LABOUR)
## MP Glasgow Cathcart

**Born:** Irvine, 1964

**Education:** Garnock Academy; Glasgow College; Napier College, Edinburgh.

**Career: 1988–90:** Reporter, *Paisley Daily Express*; **1990–2:** Press Officer, Scottish Labour Party; **1993–6:** Press Officer, Strathclyde Region; **1996–8:** Press Officer/PR Manager, East Ayrshire Council; **1998–2001:** Chief PR and Marketing Officer, Strathclyde Passenger Transport Executive; **2001:** first elected MP for Glasgow Cathcart.

**Profile:** Tom Harris is married, for the second time, and has one son. The most fraught episode of his career so far was occasioned by the decision of SPTE to ask football fans not to use the Glasgow Underground on match days. Since Ibrox Stadium is next door to a station, this was not unnaturally seen as an initiative which victimised Rangers supporters more than others, even though the subway system is colour-blind, planned as it was before the rise of football clubs. At any rate, it was a supreme challenge to his public-relations skills, to which the fanzines were not susceptible.

He is one of two new Glasgow MPs, replacing John Maxton, nephew of the great Jimmy and the man who sent Teddy Taylor scuttling off to Southend, beginning the exodus from Scotland of senior Tories. Harris is interested in transport issues, pensions and work, and welfare reform, but made his maiden speech on the other form of PR – proportional representation – to which he is vehemently opposed: whether it's for the UK Parliament, the Scottish Parliament, local councils or the golf club committee, women's section.

**Contact:** 020-7219-3000 (Parliament)
0141-583-9099 (Constituency)
e-mail harrist@parliament.uk

**Jimmy Hood** (LABOUR)
**MP Clydesdale**

**Born:** Lesmahagow, 1948

**Education:** Lesmahagow Higher Grade School;
Nottingham University.

**Career: 1964–87:** Mining Engineer; **1973–87:** NUM
Official; **1984–5:** Leader, Nottingham Miners during national strike;
**1979–87:** Councillor, Newark and Sherwood District Council;
**1987:** first elected MP for Clydesdale.

**Profile:** Clydesdale constituency, when it was called Lanark, was represented by the sophisticated and sexy left-wing intellectual Dame Judith
Hart. Jimmy Hood is different. He was an NUM stalwart and supporter of Arthur Scargill, leading the militant wing of the Nottingham
miners during the national coal strike. He was also a councillor for
Newark and Sherwood, not the first Hood to get a popular mandate in
those parts. He is quite a toughie and once allegedly struck the Vice-
President of the Nottingham miners, Mick McGinty. Just as well it
wasn't Mick McGahey or they would have been selling tickets. He had
a serious heart attack in 1997, saved only by being near Crosshouse
Hospital. Afterwards he gave good advice on diet, exercise and weight
control, though history does not relate how well he stuck to it himself.
He is married with a son and a daughter.

Jimmy is not a great debater and his accent is sometimes difficult for
southern parliamentarians, but he is a skilled and hard-working chairman of committees – most recently European Scrutiny. He caused a
synthetic uproar when he admitted that a parliamentary clerk had
given an agriculture minister prior notice of questions to be put to him
– a procedure long practised on the quiet. He is a pro-European left-
winger who voted for John Prescott as Leader and Deputy Leader. His
style in cardigans was once rashly criticised by Sir Anthony Beaumont
Dark no less, but the Speaker came to his sartorial defence.

**Contact:**  020-7219-4585 Fax 020-7219-5872 (Parliament)
          01555-673177  Fax 01555-673188 (Constituency)
          e-mail hoodj@parliament.uk

# Adam Ingram (LABOUR)
## Minister of State, Defence
## MP East Kilbride

**Born:** Glasgow, 1947

**Education:** Cranhill Secondary School; Open University.

**Career: 1967–77:** Computer programmer/systems analyst; **1977–87:** full-time union official, NALGO; **1980–7:** Councillor then Leader, East Kilbride Council; **1987:** first elected MP; **1997–2001:** Minister of State, Northern Ireland Office; **2001– :** Minister of State, Defence.

**Profile:** Adam Ingram is one of the quiet men. He slipped out of school without the qualifications for university but took his degree later from the Open University. His union career required a fair measure of backroom fixing. He has never been a compulsive speaker in the House, even when he was a front-bench spokesperson, and was considered a likely future Chief Whip. His Northern Ireland post demanded discretion. He's an angler who likes cooking and reading. He is married.

His organising ability was quickly spotted in the House and he became PPS to Neil Kinnock fifteen months after his election and lasted for four years. John Smith moved him to the front bench to speak on Social Security, then Tony Blair made him Margaret Beckett's Deputy on Trade and Industry. After the Labour victory of 1997, he was made Minister of State for security matters in Northern Ireland under Mo Mowlam. He provided her with sound support and they became friends. When Mowlam and then Mandelson left, he stayed, the continuity of his presence considered too vital to disrupt. It was clear, however, that he was still going places, and – after the election – he was transferred to Defence as Armed Forces Minister. A grafter who keeps out of the limelight.

**Contact:** 020-7219-4093 (Parliament)
01355-235343 Fax 01355-265252 (Constituency)
e-mail adam_ingram@compuserve.com

**Eric Joyce (LABOUR)**
**MP Falkirk West**

**Born:** Perth, 1960

**Education:** Perth High School; Stirling, Keele and Bath Universities.

**Career: 1978–99:** Army Officer, retired with rank of Major; **1999–2000:** Public Affairs Consultant, Commission for Racial Equality; **2000:** first elected MP (by-election).

**Profile:** Eric Joyce first burst onto the scene in 1998 as the rebel army officer who wrote a Fabian pamphlet *Arms and the Man*, in which he accused the Army of every conceivable form of discrimination – racial, sexual, social. He was threatened with a court martial but the Army sensibly surmised that such a case would bring more embarrassment than was advisable. Instead, Joyce was retired/sacked and joined the Executive of the Fabian Society, for whom he edited another pamphlet *Now's the Hour: New Thinking for Holyrood*. He was on the approved list of Labour candidates for the Scottish Parliament, but his big chance came with the decision of Dennis Canavan to resign his Westminster seat.

The Labour Party had thought that Canavan was about to return to the fold and that they could avoid a potentially disastrous by-election. But Dennis is full of surprises; he suddenly changed his mind and an attractive candidate had to be found. In the event, though the result was close, Joyce was an inspired choice – he could present himself as fresh, untouched by the Canavan affair but something of a fearless rebel all the same. He is a moderniser, clearly ambitious, very well organised, a good performer on the box, and a former Scottish Judo champion. In 2001 he had double the votes of the SNP.

**Contact:** 020-7219-6210 (Parliament)
01324-638919 (Constituency)
e-mail ericjoyce@parliament.uk

## Charles Kennedy (LIBERAL DEMOCRAT)
### Leader Liberal Democrat Party
### MP Ross, Skye and Inverness West

**Born:** Inverness, 1959

**Education:** Lochaber High School; Glasgow and Indiana Universities.

**Career: 1980–1:** President Glasgow University Union; **1982:** Winner, Observer Mace Debating Tournament; **1982:** Journalist, BBC Highland; **1983–97:** first elected MP for Ross, Cromarty and Skye; **1997– :** MP for Ross, Skye and Inverness West; **1999:** Leader, Liberal Democratic Party.

**Profile:** He was the youngest member of the House of Commons when first elected – to his surprise – at twenty-three, even younger than the Boy David twenty years before. He was elected then as a Social Democrat, having deserted the Labour Party at university after hearing Roy Jenkins speak, and, he says, because the Labour Club had stopped debating. He won the Observer Mace for debating, researched 'The Political Rhetoric of Roy Jenkins' at Indiana (sic) University, and spent a few months at BBC Radio Highland before starting his great adventure. These months were the only time of his career not spent in politics. He was pro-Alliance, then pro-merger (making the Lib Dems his third political allegiance in a decade) and landed the top prize after Paddy Ashdown.

He has two challenges now if he is to succeed in advancing Liberal fortunes. He needs to live down his reputation as a showbiz Liberal, more at home making (admittedly) good jokes than inspiring the troops with policy and passion. He also needs to encourage cohabitation with Labour in Scotland and Wales without being neutralised by them at Westminster. His stated goal in the 2001 election, perhaps deliberately over-ambitious, was to replace the Conservatives as the opposition. It is worth remembering that Charles is always late, but he always gets there. The other most distinctive thing about him is that – in his affable, downbeat way – he tries to tell the truth, and the electorate seems to like his style. He was perceived to have the best campaign in 2001, even including the call for more spending on public services, and the

Lib Dems added an extra 2 per cent to their popular vote, translating into eight more seats. Now for the difficult bit.

**Contact:** 020-7219-6226 Fax 020-7219-4881 (Parliament)
01463-714377  Fax 01463-714380 (Constituency)
e-mail rossldp@cix.co.uk

## Archy Kirkwood (LIBERAL DEMOCRAT)
**MP Roxburgh and Berwickshire**

**Born:** Glasgow, 1946

**Education:** Cranhill School, Glasgow; Heriot Watt University.

**Career:** Pharmacist; Solicitor and Notary Public; **1971–9:** Personal Assistant to David Steel; **1975:** Youth Campaign Director, Britain in Europe; **1983:** first elected MP.

**Profile:** Archie Kirkwood is married with one son and one daughter. He met his wife at his first Liberal Assembly (Liberals didn't confer, they assembled), in 1971. The year before, he had attended the Labour Party Conference (Labour definitely conferred in those days) as a branch secretary and delegate. He left Labour because it was 'too right wing', and obviously because he found the women members less appealing. He remains more sympathetic to some of Labour's policies than he ever was to the Social Democrats. He opposed merger with the SDP. He is one of the nicest people in politics – but no less effective for that.

He has had a range of posts on the Liberal and Lib Dem front bench, most persuasively on Social Security, latterly chairing the Social Security Select Committee as well. It is behind the scenes that he is most influential where he can bring to bear his considerable charm and 'people skills'. He is one of the best 'fixers' in the business, but his 'fixes' are not based on bullying or blackmail but on compromise and diplomacy. He never talks people down – equally no-one seems to have a bad word to say about him.

**Contact:** 020-7219-6523  Fax 020-7219-6437 (Parliament)
   01750-52256 (Constituency)
   e-mail kirkwooda@parliament.uk

**Mark Lazarowicz** (LABOUR)
**MP Edinburgh North and Leith**

**Born:** Romford, 1953

**Education:** St Benedict's School, London;
St Andrews and Edinburgh Universities.

**Career:** Solicitor; **1980–96 and 1999–2001:** Edinburgh Councillor;
**1989–90:** Chair, Scottish Labour Party; **1996– :** Advocate; **2001:** first
elected MP for Edinburgh North and Leith.

**Profile:** He is married with three sons and one daughter. He is perhaps
best remembered in Edinburgh politics for leading the soft-left coup
which overthrew the hard-left regime of Alex Wood on Edinburgh
Council in the early 1980s. He thereby became Leader of Edinburgh
District Council and subsequently a high-profile Transport Convener,
suggesting several controversial schemes like Greenways for bus pri-
ority, and road and workplace charges. These policies have yet to be
implemented, due to strong opposition. He is a founder member of
the centre-left think-tank, the Centre for Scottish Public Policy.

He was the most significant casualty (*pace* Dennis Canavan) of Labour's
selection procedures for the Scottish Parliament. He described the
process as a 'cock-up with conspiracy round the edges'. His result in
the 2001 general election was the 330th Labour win to be declared and
secured Blair's majority – though that may not be how either of them
see it. He is fiercely ambitious and, with Ann McKechin, one of the
few bright sparks in Labour's new Scottish intake. He supports PR for
local government and has written on this and a range of legal and
political topics. Though not a great speaker, he should make his mark
in the Commons. He drew sixth place in the ballot for private
member's bills, so has an outside chance of initiating legislation in his
maiden parliamentary term.

**Contact:**  020-7219-8222 (Parliament)
             0131-555-0598 (Constituency)
             e-mail lazarowiczm@parliament.uk

# Helen Liddell (LABOUR)
## Secretary of State for Scotland
## MP Airdrie and Shotts

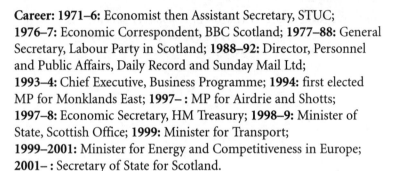

**Born:** Coatbridge, 1950

**Education:** St Patrick's High School, Coatbridge; Strathclyde University.

**Career: 1971–6:** Economist then Assistant Secretary, STUC; **1976–7:** Economic Correspondent, BBC Scotland; **1977–88:** General Secretary, Labour Party in Scotland; **1988–92:** Director, Personnel and Public Affairs, Daily Record and Sunday Mail Ltd; **1993–4:** Chief Executive, Business Programme; **1994:** first elected MP for Monklands East; **1997– :** MP for Airdrie and Shotts; **1997–8:** Economic Secretary, HM Treasury; **1998–9:** Minister of State, Scottish Office; **1999:** Minister for Transport; **1999–2001:** Minister for Energy and Competitiveness in Europe; **2001– :** Secretary of State for Scotland.

**Profile:** Helen Liddell has two children (one of each) with her highly successful husband, but they try – not always successfully – to keep the weekends to themselves. She is a dynamo, who has powered her way through a series of influential jobs and continues to do so. There have been some temporary embarrassments. She was – as Helen Reilly – fired by BBC Scotland because London did not like her accent. (Many are hoping that her career may eventually give her some responsibility for the BBC.) As General Secretary of Labour in Scotland, she cautioned members against consorting with other parties in the 1979 referendum campaign. Later, she was too close for subsequent comfort to Robert Maxwell, and published a racy novel of the kind that Edwina Currie has made a speciality.

She just scraped into Parliament after a bitter by-election battle with the SNP in 1994, dogged by accusations of malpractice on the part of the local Monklands Council. Now, she is the first woman Secretary of State for Scotland, after short but successful spells in four other posts since the 1997 election. She is obviously trusted, and her career movement is still in an upward direction. She is a highly articulate, deeply committed, very tough operator, but considerably gentler in private than her public image of 'Stalin's Granny' would suggest. She has reshaped the Westminster–Holyrood relationship more convincingly than John Reid had managed and has not been afraid to tell Henry and Wendy to bury the hatchet and behave themselves. She continues the habits of a lifetime – extolling the virtues of devolution and Nat-bashing are synonomous. She and Henry were overheard discussing their comrades Reid and Wilson in unflattering tones after the election, but that's likely to damage Henry not her. She's been in bigger jams before.

**Contact:** 020-7219-6507 Fax 020-7219-3390 (Parliament)
01236-748777 Fax 01236-748666 (Constituency)
e-mail scottishsecretary@scotland.gsi.gov.uk

**Iain Luke** (LABOUR)
**MP Dundee East**

**Born:** Dundee, 1951

**Education:** Harris Academy, Dundee; Dundee and
Edinburgh Universities; Jordanhill College.

**Career: 1969–74:** Assistant Tax Collecter;
**1983–2001:** Lecturer, Dundee College; **1984–96:** Dundee District
Councillor, and Leader (1990–2); **1996–2001:** Dundee City
Councillor; **2001:** first elected MP for Dundee East.

**Profile:** Stop the presses, Labour sends another town councillor to
Westminster. But don't hold the front page, he is not expected to make
as much of a stir as his predecessor, John McAllion. Iain Luke is married with three children and supports Dundee. He is a former Social
Work Convener.

There was controversy before his selection conference when the
popular local left-winger Marilyn Glen was omitted from the shortlist,
despite having nominations from every branch in the constituency.
Luke is a member of Labour's Scottish Policy Forum and no Blair clone.
His leadership of the council passed without any notable controversy.

**Contact:** 020-7219-8165 (Parliament)
01382-224628 (Constituency)

**John Lyons** (LABOUR)
**MP Strathkelvin and Bearsden**

**Born:** Glasgow, 1949

**Education:** Woodside Secondary School, Glasgow;
West Middlesex Polytechnic; Stirling University.

**Career: 1966–87:** Mechanical Engineer;
**1987–2001:** Regional Officer, Nupe then Unison;
**1999–2001:** Member, Forth Valley Health Board; **2001:** first elected
MP for Strathkelvin and Bearsden.

**Profile:** John Lyons has a fairly low profile but is well known in trade
union circles. His latest project was negotiating union recognition for
workers in the Archdiocese of Glasgow. He has specialised for UNI-
SON in the local government and health sectors. He will be a good
local MP, but is not expected to cut a dash on any wider level, though
he has strong views on the relief of Third World debt. He went to university as a mature student. He is divorced, with two children, and now
lives in Perthshire with his partner and stepson.

His political career was nearly still born when, at the selection conference to replace Sam Galbraith as Labour candidate, he was defeated by
two votes by a New Labour airline pilot Doug Maughan. Somewhat
controversially, the contest was re-run because of irregularities and
Lyons won handsomely second time around. His UNISON connection
did not harm his chances. He is a member (see David Hamilton) of the
'Squatting Three'.

**Contact:**   020-7219-8325 (Parliament)
              e-mail lyonsj@parliament.uk

## Thomas McAvoy (LABOUR)
### Government Whip
### MP Glasgow Rutherglen

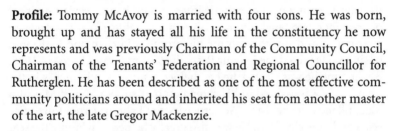

**Born:** Rutherglen, 1943

**Education:** St Columbkills Primary, Junior and Secondary Schools, Glasgow.

**Career:** Engineering Storeman; AEU shop steward; **1982–7:** Councillor, Strathclyde Region; **1987– :** first elected MP for Rutherglen; **1997– :** Government Whip.

**Profile:** Tommy McAvoy is married with four sons. He was born, brought up and has stayed all his life in the constituency he now represents and was previously Chairman of the Community Council, Chairman of the Tenants' Federation and Regional Councillor for Rutherglen. He has been described as one of the most effective community politicians around and inherited his seat from another master of the art, the late Gregor Mackenzie.

Tommy has long defended Rutherglen against Glasgow, battling successfully to have it removed from Glasgow City Council. His other personal causes have been abortion, which – as a Roman Catholic – he opposes, and peace in Northern Ireland. After several years as an opposition whip, he is now third in seniority in the government Whips office and rejoices in the un-Rutherglen title of 'Comptroller of HM Household'.

**Contact:** 020-7219-3000 (Parliament)
020-7219-3000 (Parliament)
0141-634-8083 (Constituency)
e-mail thomas.mcavoy@hm-treasury.gov.uk

## Calum MacDonald (LABOUR)
## MP Western Isles

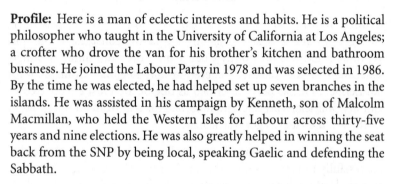

**Born:** Stornoway, 1956

**Education:** Nicolson Institute, Stornoway; Edinburgh University and UCLA.

**Career: 1982–5:** Teaching fellow UCLA; **1986–7:** Worked in brother's retail business; **1987:** first elected MP for Western Isles; **1997:** PPS to Donald Dewar; **1997–9:** Under-Secretary of State for Scotland.

**Profile:** Here is a man of eclectic interests and habits. He is a political philosopher who taught in the University of California at Los Angeles; a crofter who drove the van for his brother's kitchen and bathroom business. He joined the Labour Party in 1978 and was selected in 1986. By the time he was elected, he had helped set up seven branches in the islands. He was assisted in his campaign by Kenneth, son of Malcolm Macmillan, who held the Western Isles for Labour across thirty-five years and nine elections. He was also greatly helped in winning the seat back from the SNP by being local, speaking Gaelic and defending the Sabbath.

MacDonald quickly caught the eye of Donald Dewar, who made him first his PPS, then an Under-Secretary with responsibility for Housing, Transport and European Affairs. He did not survive Dewar's departure to the Scottish Executive and the resulting reduction of the ministerial team at the Scotland Office. He is strongly pro-European, favouring regionalism but also the single currency. Although pro-devolution, he also wants left-leaning Unionists to join the Labour Party in Ulster. Although consensualist, he supported bombing Serbia. Contradictory? No, eclectic. It is the Highlander's privilege. He only just held on to his seat last time round after a 7 per cent swing to the SNP.

**Contact:** 020-7219-3000 (Parliament)
          01851-704684 (Constituency)

# John MacDougall (LABOUR)
## MP Fife Central

**Born:** Dunfermline, 1947

**Education:** Templehall School, Kirkcaldy; Rosyth Dockyard Technical College; Glenrothes College; Fife Technical College.

**Career: 1964–78:** Boilermaker; **1978–83:** full-time Shop Steward; **1982–2001:** Councillor, Fife Council; **1987–2001:** Leader then Convener Fife Council; **2001:** first elected MP for Fife Central.

**Profile:** John MacDougall, married with two children, is from solid working-class stock and boasts of 'a habit of being elected to things'. He was Deputy to Henry McLeish as Leader of Fife Regional Council, then Leader in his own right when Henry went to Parliament, finally Convener of the new Fife Council when the Region was wound up. He got the nomination in a surprise victory over Alex Rowley, former General Secretary of the Scottish Labour Party and confidant of Gordon Brown.

He had a reputation for getting things done in Fife, developing initiatives like Invest in Fife to fasttrack development opportunities and foster co-operation on investment decisions. He also founded the Fife Race Equality Group. From his eight years as a Scottish representative on the Assembly of the European Regions came the East of Scotland European Consortium. He has fought hard for Rosyth dockyard and naval base and will concentrate on local issues in his new role as Westminster representative for Central Fife, the seat formerly held by – yes, that's right – Henry McLeish. He is a member (see David Hamilton) of the 'Squatting Three'.

**Contact:** 020-7219-8233 (Parliament)
  01592-712204 (Constituency)
  e-mail macdougallj@parliament.uk

**John McFall** (LABOUR)
**MP Dumbarton**

**Born:** Glasgow, 1944

**Education:** St Patrick's Secondary, Dumbarton;
Paisley College of Technology; Strathclyde and the
Open Universities.

**Career: 1974–87:** Chemistry Teacher and Assistant Head, Bellarmine
School, Glasgow; **1987:** first elected MP for Dumbarton;
**1998–2001:** Under-Secretary Northern Ireland Office.

**Profile:** He is married to a fellow teacher and has three sons and one
daughter. He was Secretary then Chairman of his local constituency
party over a seven-year period, plus other community involvement, so
he was well placed when Ian Campbell announced his intention to
stand down. He is reputed to be sports-obsessed, plays golf and took
part in the London Marathon in 1988. He benefited from several fact-
finding (i.e. free) trips – to the Middle East, the Far East and Eastern
Europe – which suggests the Labour Party didn't give him enough to do.

He was a whip between 1989 and 1991, but resigned in opposition to
the Gulf War. He was called up as a Shadow Scottish spokesperson and
became Deputy to George Robertson in 1994. He was disappointed in
government not to be made second-in-command at the Scottish Office
by Donald Dewar. Instead he became a government whip until his
translation in 1998 to the Northern Ireland Office. With Tony Blair
looking to introduce new and younger blood, he was dropped after the
2001 general election. He is nevertheless well regarded, now less overtly
left wing, but still highly principled.

**Contact:** 020-7219-3521 (Parliament)
            01389-731437 Fax 01389-761699 (Constituency)

# Anne McGuire (LABOUR)
## MP Stirling

**Born:** Glasgow, 1949

**Education:** Our Lady of St Francis, Glasgow; Glasgow University.

**Career: 1971–4:** Registrar, Glasgow University; **1980–2:** Councillor, Strathclyde Region; **1983–5:** Teacher; **1985–9:** Fieldworker, Community Service Volunteers; **1989–93:** Scottish National Officer, CSV; **1993–7:** Director, Scottish Council for Voluntary Organisations; **1997:** first elected MP for Stirling; **1998– :** Assistant Whip.

**Profile:** Anne McGuire is married to a chartered accountant and they have one son and one daughter. She comes from a political family – her father was Strathclyde Councillor Albert Long, the much- respected Convener of Social Work. She was agent for Norman Hogg MP in three elections but – try as she might – failed to get selected herself until she was chosen for Stirling by courtesy of an all-women shortlist. It must have been fate, apart from male prejudice, but it eventually fell to her to defeat Michael Forsyth in 1997 by a resounding majority.

Hard-working and right-thinking, she was turned down in 1992 for the post of Scottish General Secretary when Jack McConnell was appointed. Ironically, she became Chairman of the party one year later, having served on the Scottish Executive since 1984. In government, Donald Dewar rewarded her by making her his PPS, before she moved on to become an assistant whip. She doesn't seem hard enough to be a whip, but she has organisational skills aplenty. She probably deserves more.

**Contact:** 020-7219-5014 Fax 020-7219-2503 (Parliament)
01786-446515 Fax 01786-446513 (Constituency)
e-mail mcguirea@parliament.uk

**Ann McKechin** (LABOUR)
**MP Glasgow Maryhill**

**Born:** Paisley, 1961

**Education:** Sacred Heart High School; Paisley
Grammar School; Strathclyde University.

**Career: 1983–2001:** Solicitor; **1990–2001:** Partner, Pacitti Jones;
**2001:** first elected MP for Glasgow Maryhill.

**Profile:**  Ann McKechin was selected to succeed the redoubtable Maria
Fyfe from an all-women shortlist, though none of the three candidates
was from the constituency. Ms McKechin is a former secretary and
women's officer of Glasgow Kelvin constituency, not a million miles
from Maryhill, and took the nomination comfortably. At the election,
Maryhill had the second lowest turnout in Scotland at 40.2 per cent.
She is a lawyer, partner in a large practice, and is a senior member of
the Muir Society of Lawyers. She was on Labour's list of candidates for
the Scottish Parliament and lost the nomination for Paisley North to
Wendy Alexander.

One of only two new Scottish Labour women, she has spent fifteen years
in international development campaigning, representing Scotland on
the UK's principal development campaign, the World Development
Organisation. She initiated a Labour Conference on the Arms Trade.
She is very bright, and stands out in one of the dullest intakes of new
Scottish Labour MPs for a long time.

**Contact:**  020-7219-8239 (Parliament)
          0141-946-1300 (Constituency)
          e-mail mckechina@parliament.uk

## Rosemary McKenna (LABOUR)
## MP Cumbernauld and Kilsyth

**Born:** Kilmacolm, 1941

**Education:** St Augustine's Comprehensive, Glasgow; Notre Dame College of Education.

**Career: 1974–93:** Primary Teacher; **1984–96:** Councillor, Cumbernauld and Kilsyth; **1984–8:** Council Leader (Leader again **1992–4**); **1988–92:** Provost; **1997– :** first elected MP for Cumbernauld and Kilsyth.

**Profile:** She is married with three sons and one daughter. Her husband Jim is a North Lanarkshire Councillor. She was herself a major figure in Scottish local government: President of Cosla in 1994, Chair of Scotland Europa, a member of Cumbernauld Development Corporation and the Board of Scottish Enterprise. She was a tireless worker for devolution and is still a campaigner for a more prominent role for women in the party. Her selection for the seat was a fairly last- minute affair when Dewar's friend, the anti-devolutionist Norman Hogg, decided (or was persuaded) to retire. She defeated five men and three other women. She is a close friend of the neighbouring MP, Anne McGuire, and sent volunteers charging over the border into Stirling to help McGuire beat Michael Forsyth in 1997.

She is a moderniser, and founder-member of the Blairite Scottish Labour Forum, despite her family's bitter struggle against poverty when she was growing up. In Parliament, she has been PPS to the Ministers of State at the Foreign Office. The only whiff of controversy, possibly unjustified, came when her daughter was selected as a candidate for Labour's Scottish Parliament list. McKenna was Chair of the overall selection process, though she played no part in the panel that picked her daughter. The final selection, which omitted many left- and nationalist-minded applicants, was described as 'Rosemary's babies'. Rightly or wrongly, McKenna's reputation was damaged.

**Contact:** 020-7219-3145  Fax 020-7219-2544 (Parliament)
01236-457788  Fax 01236-457313 (Constituency)
e-mail mckennar@parliament.uk

## David Marshall (LABOUR)
## MP Glasgow Shettleston

**Born:** Glasgow, 1941

**Education:** High Schools of Larbert, Denny, Falkirk; Woodside Secondary, Glasgow.

**Career: 1956:** Office Junior; **1956–9:** Farm Worker; **1960:** spirit trade; **1960–9:** Tram and Bus Conductor (Shop Steward); **1969–71:** Labour Party Organiser for Glasgow; **1971–9:** Scottish secretary (part-time), Industrial Orthopaedic Society; **1972–5:** Councillor, Glasgow Corporation; **1975–9:** Councillor, Strathclyde Region (Chairman, Manpower Services); **1979– :** First elected MP for Shettleston.

**Profile:** David Marshall is married with two sons and a daughter. After a quiet start to his career, he progressed rapidly in the Labour movement from transport shop steward to the House of Commons in ten years. Not much of the original Shettleston constituency remains except the name, and Marshall himself. In 1997 he had the safest Labour seat in Scotland, and presumably he could continue carry on until he is carried off. He is very Glasgow-focused and has put much time into the various regeneration organisations which have tried to breathe life into the East End, once a workshop now the poorest area of the city.

He is an assiduous committee man: sometime chairman, vice-chairman, secretary or treasurer of groups relating to transport or to international inter-parliamentary relations. His days on the trams have obviously given him a taste for foreign travel. He is, like many of Scotland's Labour MPs, a strange mixture of liberal principles – pro-CND and devolution – and deeply conservative attitudes on abortion and homo-sexuality. He is also one of that generation of Labour MPs doomed to opposition for most of their career, only to find when their party takes power that it is not the party they joined. He has one lasting contribu-tion – the Solvent Abuse (Scotland) Act, which began as his private measure. In 2001, though he won well enough, his constituency had the lowest turnout in Scotland. Perhaps it is time he looked to his organisation.

**Contact:**   020-7219-3000 (Parliament)
            0141-778-8125 (Constituency)

## Michael Martin (THE SPEAKER)
## MP Glasgow Springburn

**Born:** Glasgow, 1945

**Education:** St Patrick's Boys School, Glasgow.

**Career: 1970–4:** Sheet metal worker, RR (AUEW shop steward); **1973–9:** Councillor, Glasgow City then Glasgow District; **1976–9:** NUPE Organiser; **1979– :** first elected MP for Glasgow Springburn; **2000:** elected Speaker of the House of Commons.

**Profile:** Michael Martin is married with one son (a member of the Scottish Parliament, also for Springburn) and one daughter. There is more to him than meets the eye – he plays the pipes and he took his only O grade, in Italian, in 1987 when he became Secretary of the British–Italian parliamentary group. His career followed one of the classic Labour paths – trade union, council, Commons. Like his colleague David Marshall – whose mixture of radical and conservative attitudes he shares – he is one of what Lord (Jim) Callaghan called the 'lost generation' who spent decades in opposition. Only in Martin's case, his membership of the Speaker's panel has brought an unexpected climax: a life from single-end to Speaker's House is a singular achievement.

The sudden decision by Betty Boothroyd to resign created a vacancy in the Speaker's chair. There were twelve candidates, including Sir George Young for the Tories (whose turn it was, strictly speaking) and Martin, who was already a Deputy Speaker. In an arcane process unlikely to be repeated, Martin stayed the course while the others were eliminated by the large Labour majority. He is the first Roman Catholic Speaker since the Reformation and the first Scot since 1835. He has not, however, been an unqualified success – unpopular in some quarters because of his strong accent and his occasional bad temper under pressure, though those who describe him as 'Gorbals Mick' should sweep their vocabulary for prejudice. A further indignity came when some parties – though not the Tories or the Liberals – ignored convention and opposed him in the general election, while his campaign was politically neutral. On his return, he was re-elected unopposed as Speaker. He has an over-sensitive tendency to see all criticism as an insult to his dignity, but his pawky Glaswegian humour should see him through to become an adequate, though not a great, Speaker.

**Contact:** 020-7219-3000 (Parliament)
0141-762-2329 Fax 0141-762-1519 (Constituency)

**Lewis Moonie** (LABOUR)
**Parliamentary Secretary, Defence**
**MP Kirkcaldy**

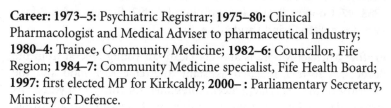

**Born:** Dundee, 1947

**Education:** Grove Academy, Dundee; St Andrews
and Edinburgh Universities.

**Career: 1973–5:** Psychiatric Registrar; **1975–80:** Clinical
Pharmacologist and Medical Adviser to pharmaceutical industry;
**1980–4:** Trainee, Community Medicine; **1982–6:** Councillor, Fife
Region; **1984–7:** Community Medicine specialist, Fife Health Board;
**1997:** first elected MP for Kirkcaldy; **2000– :** Parliamentary Secretary,
Ministry of Defence.

**Profile:** Lewis Moonie is a big man in lots of ways. He trained as a
psychiatrist initially, then switched to pharmacology before settling on
community medicine. He pioneered community care clinics in Fife.
He worked in Switzerland and Holland before resettling in Scotland
and can get by in a number of languages. He plays bridge and chess to
a high standard. When not in office, he was Parliamentary Adviser to
William Hill and – just to cover himself – Scottish Coal. In his youth,
he was both a Conservative and a communist. He is married, with two
sons.

The surprising thing is that he was left on the backbenches till 2000.
He seems almost a reluctant speechmaker, but what he does say exudes
wit and intelligence. He was a friend of John Smith and did well as a
front-bench spokesperson, mostly on science and industry matters,
before the 1997 election. As old-fashioned Labour, he seemed to have
been squeezed out by the Blair revolution, but the resignation of Peter
Kilfoyle – another old Labourite – offered a space for him at the
Ministry of Defence. He could go further.

**Contact:** 020-7219-4097 (Parliament)
          01592-564115 Fax 01592-201873 (Constituency)

## Michael Moore (LIBERAL DEMOCRAT)
## MP Tweeddale, Ettrick and Lauderdale

**Born:** Ulster, 1965

**Education:** Strathallan School; Jedburgh Grammar
School; Edinburgh University.

**Career: 1987–8:** Assistant to Archie Kirkwood MP;
**1988–97:** Coopers & Lybrand, Edinburgh; **1997:** first elected MP for
Tweeddale, Ettrick and Lauderdale.

**Profile:** Michael Moore is another clean-cut young Liberal from the
Borders, a former research assistant to Archie Kirkwood and the
inheritor of the seat David Steel represented for thirty-two years. His
girlfriend is the Liberal Democrats' director of Press and Broadcasting,
Elizabeth Peplow, so his mother was chauffeur during the last campaign.
At university, he read politics and history then – after his spell with
Kirkwood – he became a chartered accountant and manager of corporate finance. Like Steel, he is a son of the manse but – at six foot, five
inches – somewhat taller.

For a relative newcomer, Moore has a high profile. He ran the Liberal
Democrat campaign for the 1999 Scottish election and the Scottish
end of the campaign for the 2001 UK election. He also led the Liberal
Democrat team which drove such a hard bargain in negotiating the
coalition with Labour to form the Scottish Executive and was spokesperson on Scottish affairs in the last Parliament. He is personable,
persuasive and undoubtedly a rising star.

**Contact:** 020-7219-2236 (Parliament)
         01896-831011 Fax 01896-831437 (Constituency)
         e-mail michaelmoore@cix.compulink.co.uk

# Jim Murphy (LABOUR)
# MP Eastwood

**Born:** Glasgow, 1967

**Education:** Bellarmine Secondary School, Glasgow; Milnerton High School, Cape Town, South Africa; Strathclyde University.

**Career: 1992–4:** President, Scottish National Union of Students; **1994–6:** President UK NUS; **1997:** Projects Manager, Scottish Labour Party; **1997:** first elected MP for Eastwood.

**Profile:** Jim Murphy took Eastwood before he was thirty – the first time the constituency, formerly East Renfrewshire, had voted Labour since 1924, when Ramsay Macdonald was a lad. He spent his teenage years in South Africa, where he witnessed the horrors of apartheid, then threw himself into the political process when he returned home to Strathclyde University. He persuaded the NUS, when President, to turn itself into a charity and support post-graduate repayment of fees. He continued his mission to modernise as Projects Manager for 'Partnership into Power' in Scottish Labour HQ in the run-up to the 1997 election and was selected to stand in the truest, bluest Tory seat in Scotland. He is married, with two children. Despite his gauche and gangling Hugh Grant looks, he is a mean midfielder, starring in various House of Commons teams.

Murphy's victory owed much to the decline and fall of the former Conservative Minister Alan Stewart, a genuinely nice man who temporarily lost the place. Then the first Tory replacement candidate, Michael Hirst, had to resign amid scandal. To that was added the nationwide move away from the Tories to Labour to produce a truly sensational swing of 14.34 per cent and give Jim his first proper job. In the House of Commons Murphy has been so loyal, it's almost painful – impaled on message. It took him a little time to get used to House of Commons procedures and Madam Speaker Boothroyd had to remind him that questions were just that, and not ill-concealed attacks on the SNP. In 2001 he became Helen Liddell's PPS and is the only Labour MP who can name all five Spice Girls. He humiliated the heavyweight Tory Chairman Raymond Robertson last time, having worked the constituency well since 1997, playing the local man. 'They were saving the pound,' he said, 'but I was saving the hospital.' He is also a champion of Labour Friends of Israel, which – given the social mix of his constituency – is hardly surprising. Together with Russell Brown, he went cap (and accounts)-in-hand to the Commons authorities after an SNP allegation that he had overclaimed his office expenses. In fact, he had underclaimed by £200.

**Contact:** 020-7219-4615 Fax 020-7219-5650 (Parliament)
　　　　　0141-644-3330 Fax 0141-644-4771 (Constituency)

# Martin O'Neill (LABOUR)
## MP Ochil

**Born:** Edinburgh, 1945

**Education:** Trinity Academy, Edinburgh; Heriot Watt University, Edinburgh; Moray House College of Education.

**Career: 1963–7:** Insurance Clerk, Scottish Widows; **1970–1:** President, Scottish Union of Students; **1971–3:** Assistant, Estates Duty Office of Scotland; **1974–9:** Modern Studies Teacher, Boroughmuir, then Craigmount High Schools; **1976–9:** Tutor, Open University; **1979–83:** first elected MP for East Stirling and Clackmannan; **1983–97:** MP for Clackmannan; **1997– :** MP for Ochil.

**Profile:** Martin O'Neill was an insurance clerk after his schooling, but took evening classes to help him leave insurance for university and a teaching career. He presided over the Scottish Union of Students on the way and then became involved in local Edinburgh politics. He took the East Stirling and Clackmannan seat from George Reid when the SNP was practically wiped out in 1979, but the Nationalists remain a threatening force in the constituency. He is an easy-going but shrewd politician who moved from unilateralism to multilateralism and was probably made to suffer for it by his former Tribune friends. He married a fellow teacher, has two sons, and is a lifelong Hibee.

He was close to the late John Smith, though they came from very different wings of the party, and was chosen by Neil Kinnock to manage Labour's new multilateral defence policy. He did it well, and continued to be given front-bench jobs despite his repeated failure to get elected to the Shadow Cabinet. (He should have taken lessons from Tom Clarke.) He had a reputation for being laid-back and this, together with his comparative maturity, meant that he was sidelined by Tony Blair. Despite that, as Chairman of the Trade and Industry Select Committee he has been in much demand by the media, and has brought sense and gravitas to the task. It's better than being a vulnerable middle-grade minister – at least you are listened to.

**Contact:** 020-7219-5059 (Parliament)
01259-721536 Fax 01259-216716 (Constituency)
e-mail cartere@parliament.uk

## Sandra Osborne (LABOUR)
## MP Ayr

**Born:** Paisley, 1956

**Education:** Camphill Senior Secondary School, Paisley; Anniesland and Jordanhill Colleges, Glasgow; Strathclyde University.

**Career: 1976–80:** Community Worker, Glasgow; **1983–7:** Women Aid Worker, Kilmarnock; **1990–5:** Councillor, Kyle and Carrick; **1994–7:** Councillor, South Ayrshire; **1997– :** first elected MP for Ayr.

**Profile:** Sandra Osborne followed her husband as Labour candidate. He had previously come close – 85 votes close – to winning the seat after the retiral of George Younger, but there was an all-women shortlist for 1997. She had worked with victims of domestic abuse and was also a finalist for 1997 'Scotswoman of the Year'. She handsomely turned the family tables on Phil Gallie, whom she defeated again in 2001. The Conservative victory (John Scott) in the Scottish Parliament by-election had suggested a harder battle second time around, and so it was.

She is the first Labour and first woman MP for Ayr and – with her strong accent and direct manner – is something of a contrast to George Younger, whose urbane and diplomatic skills seemed more in keeping with auld Ayr, and certainly with douce Prestwick and Troon. She has been, successively, PPS to Brian Wilson and George Foulkes, despite the fact that she opposed student loans, tuition fees, and single-parent benefit cuts and was on Peter Mandelson's Millbank list of potential trouble-makers. In other respects, she is a moderniser and would like to see the resumption of women-only shortlists and other gender-equality measures.

**Contact:**   020-7219-6402 (Parliament)
          01292-476650 Fax 01292-478540 (Constituency)

## Anne Picking (LABOUR)
**MP East Lothian**

**Born:** Dunfermline, 1958

**Education:** Woodhills High School.

**Career: 1985–2001:** NHS Nursing Sister; Nurse, Lynebank Hospital; **1996–2000:** Councillor, Ashford, Kent; **1999–2000:** President, Unison; **2001:** first elected MP for East Lothian.

**Profile:** She is married with one son. She is the first woman to have been elected to represent East Lothian but must consider herself a little fortunate to have been selected in the first place. She is not well known in Scotland, having lived in the south of England for many years, and has no specific connection with the area. She does point out, however, that her family background is 'steeped in the tradition of the Scottish miners'. Her grandfather was the legendary leader of the Fife and Scottish Miners, Abe Moffat, predecessor of Mick McGahey. She had the backing of the big union battalions in seeking the nomination.

She is a long-time trade unionist, a past President of the largest union UNISON and still their representative on Labour's National Executive Council. In a speech at the TUC in September 2000, she criticised Labour's flirtation with private initiatives for public services: 'Let's modernise the NHS not privatise it. PFI is mortgaging our future. It's costly and it hands over our NHS to contractors.' That's a message she will no doubt be aiming at Tony Blair from the Labour benches behind him.

**Contact:** 020-7219-8220 (Parliament)
  01875-610320 Fax 01875-610320 (Constituency)
  e-mail annepicking@email.labour.org.uk

## Alan Reid (LIBERAL DEMOCRAT)
## MP Argyll and Bute

**Born:** Ayr, 1954

**Education:** Ayr Academy; Strathclyde University.

**Career: 1977–85:** Computer Programmer, Strathclyde Region; **1985–2000:** Computer Project Manager, Glasgow University; **1988–96:** Councillor, Renfrew District; **2001– :** first elected MP for Argyll and Bute.

**Profile:** Alan Reid was Vice-Convener of the Scottish Liberal Democrats between 1994 and 1998. He was also election agent for George Lyon in his successful campaign for the Scottish Parliament in 1999. He was not the original candidate for this seat in 2001, but the man first selected – the Dumbarton Councillor Paul Coleshill – presented a cv which appeared to claim a PhD he had not attained and was forced to stand down.

Despite being second choice, Reid is expected to prove a steady and dependable MP. He will probably not take Westminster by storm or hammer at the media's gate, but he will have a strong constituency focus. His party portfolio is the Common Agricultural Policy – no soft option.

**Contact:**  020-7219-8127 (Parliament)
             01389-841862 (Constituency)
             e-mail reida@parliament.uk

# John Reid (LABOUR)
**Secretary of State for Northern Ireland**
**MP Hamilton North and Bellshill**

**Born:** Bellshill, 1947

**Education:** St Patrick's Senior Secondary,
Coatbridge; Open and Stirling Universities.

**Career: 1965–72:** Labourer, Clerk, Insurance Rep.; **1972:** President,
Stirling University Student Association; **1979–83:** Research Officer,
Scottish Labour Party; **1983–5:** Political Adviser to Neil Kinnock;
**1986–7:** Scottish Organiser, Trade Unionists for Labour;
**1987–97:** first elected MP for Motherwell North; **1997– :** MP for
Hamilton North and Bellshill; **1997–8:** Armed Forces Minister;
**1998–9:** Minister of Transport; **1999–2000:** Secretary of State for
Scotland; **2000– :** Secretary of State for Northern Ireland

**Profile:** Dr John Reid is a new man. It takes up almost as much space
to say who the old John Reid was as it does to profile the new. He was
a guitar-playing member of rock group The Graduates, who had gone
late to university, and become a hard-drinking, chain-smoking communist. Since those days, he has marched hand in hand with the
modernisers, sometimes leading them. He worked for Kinnock, now
serves Blair in increasingly important roles. In 1998 he suffered a personal tragedy with the sudden death of his wife, aged 49, but showed
great strength in coming back from that through sheer hard work. He
has two sons, and has now publicly announced that he is ready to get
married again, to the film-maker Carine Adler.

In each of his ministerial jobs thus far, Dr Reid has shown great energy
and ability, though he may have been just a little too energetic initially
as Scottish Secretary when, probably to make something of the job and
encourage recalcitrant Scottish Labour MPs, he rather threw his
weight about. A public argument with Donald Dewar at a Conference
'Scots Night' brought them both to the peace table. His son Kevin was
involved in the Lobbygate affair and he himself was investigated by the
Commissioner for Standards, whose criticisms of his use of parliamentary allowances were not upheld by the Standards Committee. His
translation to Northern Ireland owed something to luck and Peter
Mandelson, but there is no doubt he has earned a reputation for

mastering his brief and getting things done without shaking the big tent. IRA moves to disarm began on his watch and – though Ireland tests every reputation – his open, witty manner, tough intellect, and fixer's instinct should give him as good a chance as anyone of making a difference.

**Contact:** 020-7219-4118 (Parliament)
01698-454672 Fax 01698-424732 (Constituency)
e-mail scott.barrie.msp@scottish.parliament.uk

## Angus Robertson (SNP)
**MP Moray**

**Born:** London, 1969

**Education:** Broughton High School; Aberdeen University.

**Career: 1991–9:** BBC reporter in Austria and News Editor, Austrian Broadcasting Corporation; **1999:** SNP International Press Officer; **1999–2001:** SNP European Policy Adviser, Holyrood; **2001:** first elected MP for Moray.

**Profile:** He is one of the new intake of SNP MPs whom Alex Salmond had to lead round Westminster like a (very) small flock of sheep. Angus is one of Salmond's bright young men, alongside his close friends Andrew Wilson and Duncan Hamilton, with whom he shares an easy-going charm and intelligence. The younger school of SNP representatives are not as thrawn and chippy as some of the older brethren.

When he was SNP European spokesperson, he accused Ross Finnie of 'lying or at best misleading' the Scottish Parliament over his attendance at meetings of European agriculture ministers. He can be expected to make an reasonable impact at Westminster, where his media experience will not go wrong. He is Scotland's youngest MP in the current Parliament and has been appointed SNP Spokesperson on Foreign Affairs. And we thought that was Sean Connery.

**Contact:**  020-7219-8259 (Parliament)
01343-352058  Fax 01343-542058 (Constituency)
e-mail angusrobertsonmp@parliament.uk

**John Robertson** (LABOUR)
**MP Glasgow Anniesland**

**Born:** Glasgow, 1952

**Education:** Shawlands Academy; Langside
College; Stow College, Glasgow.

**Career: 1973–2000:** BT Engineer and Manager;
**2000:** first elected MP for Anniesland.

**Profile:** John Robertson was Donald Dewar's election agent and constituency chairperson. He was therefore well known in the local party
and carried the selection conference – which took place before Dewar's
death – with some comfort. He admits that he had no political ambitions beyond his constituency work until Dewar confided that he
intended to leave Westminster and suggested Robertson consider it.
He seems a solid citizen. His by-election victory was convincing, even
on a low turnout, and so, too, was his result in 2001. He is married
with three daughters, one of whom had drug problems on which the
tabloids feasted.

He has scarcely been at Westminster long enough to make an impression. He made his maiden speech in the debate on the Queen's Speech
and has managed two more speeches and interventions in Prime
Minister's and Scottish Questions since then. No shrinking violet. He
has also made a busy start in constituency matters, publishing regular
bulletins, which is just as well since he has had to face the electorate
twice in seven months. It remains to be seen if he will maintain this
level of activity when the heat is off.

**Contact:**   020-7219-6964 (Parliament)
          0141-944-7298 (Constituency)
          e-mail robertsonjo@parliament.uk

# Ernie Ross (LABOUR)
## MP Dundee West

**Born:** Dundee, 1942

**Education:** St John's Secondary School, Dundee.

**Career: 1957–62:** Apprentice Marine Engineer, Caledon Shipyard; **1962–4:** Marine Engineer, Ben Line; **1970–9:** Quality Control Engineer, Timex; **1979:** first elected MP for Dundee West; **1999:** Chairman, Westminster Foundation for Democracy.

**Profile:** Ernie Ross should be preserved. His career, both before Parliament and since, speaks of a bygone age. Consider the now-lost names – Caledon, Ben Line, Timex – and the jobs – Apprentice, Marine Engineer – going back to the days when Scotsmen went to sea in ships that had been built and maintained in Scotland. And (2001), he's not yet sixty. Ernie is married, with two sons and a daughter, and is a Dundonian through and through. He had major abdominal surgery in the 1980s, but rallied after a long convalescence.

His political career also has echoes of a different era. He began as a hard-left Soviet sympathiser ('MP for Moscow West') who welcomed the Russian invasion of Afghanistan ('Afghan Ernie'), who toured the Arab world as the guest of the PLO ('MP for Nablus West'), who supported the militant class politics still favoured by Arthur Scargill. Lately, there has been a change. His uncritical pro-Arab sentiments have become an effort for peace in the Middle East which has brought praise, even from Conservatives. He could not remotely be called a Blairite, but he did help Robin Cook by leaking a delicate report of the Foreign Affairs Committee. He was suspended for his trouble. That is as nothing compared to the punishment he might have received from former comrades Canavan, Davidson and Connarty for helping turn them down for the Scottish Parliament candidates list. Is he going soft? Settling old scores? Changing heart? We should be told.

**Contact:** 020-7219-3480 Fax 020-7219-2359 (Parliament)
01382-207000 Fax 01382-221280 (Constituency)
e-mail rossm@parliament.uk

## Frank Roy (LABOUR)
## MP Motherwell and Wishaw

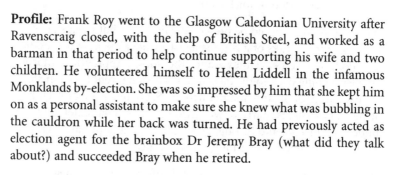

**Born:** Motherwell, 1958

**Education:** St Joseph's and Our Lady's High
Schools, Motherwell; Motherwell College; Glasgow
Caledonian University.

**Career: 1977–91:** Ravenscraig Steelworker; **1997:** first elected MP for
Motherwell and Wishaw.

**Profile:** Frank Roy went to the Glasgow Caledonian University after
Ravenscraig closed, with the help of British Steel, and worked as a
barman in that period to help continue supporting his wife and two
children. He volunteered himself to Helen Liddell in the infamous
Monklands by-election. She was so impressed by him that she kept him
on as a personal assistant to make sure she knew what was bubbling in
the cauldron while her back was turned. He had previously acted as
election agent for the brainbox Dr Jeremy Bray (what did they talk
about?) and succeeded Bray when he retired.

His Commons career began promisingly when he appeared to have
found his niche as PPS to Helen Liddell, then John Reid, then Mrs
Liddell again. Then disaster struck, largely self-inflicted. He took it on
himself to advise the Taoiseach Bertie Aherne not to attend a ceremony
at Carfin Grotto on the day after an old firm match in case of sectarian
demonstrations and violence. In a letter, he associated Dr Reid and
Mrs Liddell with his fears and was promptly sacked. The ceremony was
rescheduled. However well intentioned, the intervention by Mr Roy –
himself a Catholic – made Scotland and the Scots look backward and
intolerant. It was a misjudgement which will dog him for some considerable time. It came after he had been censured for placing a bet on
Michael Martin to win the Speaker's chair, winning himself £3,400. On
both counts, he was unrepentant, and will probably be unrepentant at
leisure.

**Contact:** 020-7219-6467 (Parliament)
01698-303040 Fax 01698-303060 (Constituency)

## Alex Salmond (SNP)
## MP Banff and Buchan

**Born:** Linlithgow, 1954

**Education:** Linlithgow Academy; St Andrews University.

**Career: 1978–80:** Assistant Economist, Scottish Office; **1980–7:** Energy Economist, Royal Bank of Scotland; **1987:** first elected MP for Banff and Buchan; **1999–2001:** MSP for Banff and Buchan (stood down).

**Profile:** Alex Salmond is quite the most impressive politician produced by the Nationalists in their history. He combines considerable intellect and debating skill with a grasp of the issues and a flair for presentation. If he has a flaw, it is that he cannot resist the cheap crack at an opponent and, in media discussions, will shamelessly steal the last word. Hence the nickname 'smart Alex'. It may not be a flaw but rather an excess of the political instincts that took him to the top of the SNP even after his expulsion in 1982 for forming 'a party within a party', the socialist '79 Group. After his readmission he planned and, yes, plotted to take over the leadership and transform the party into a modern social democratic alliance on the European model (sounds familiar). In achieving both, despite the misgivings of the right wing and the fundamentalists, he displayed great strategic vision. He is married to Moira, some years his senior, whose interests may have played a part in his decision to resign the leadership in September 2000. He tips horses, plays golf and supports Hearts.

Salmond's sudden decision to leave the leadership and, later, to resign from the Scottish Parliament and concentrate on Westminster, left observers looking for a reason other than his own explanation that he had served long enough. He certainly had a surprisingly poor election in 1999, as did his long-time adviser Mike Russell, and had not seemed in top form on the Mound. Having resigned, he obviously felt it wise to leave the Edinburgh stage to his successor John Swinney and concentrate on leading the new group of MPs in the Commons, where he has always excelled. The absence of Salmond and Dewar from the Holyrood proceedings has left a huge gap, and it will be hard for him not to be regarded as the King over the Border. Who would bet against his return?

**Contact:** 020-7219-4500 (Parliament)
01779-470444 Fax 01779-474460 (Constituency)
e-mail asmp.peterhead@snp.org

# Mohammed Sarwar (LABOUR)
## MP Glasgow Govan

**Born:** Faisalabad, 1952

**Education:** University of Faisalabad.

**Career:** Owner, United Grocers, United Homestores, United Wholesale Grocers.

**Profile:** Mohammed Sarwar came to Scotland to join his parents and brother at the age of twenty-four. In Pakistan, he had been a member of the Bhutto People's Party and President of its students' organisation. He built up a cash-and-carry business, joined the Labour Party in 1984 and Glasgow Council in 1992 by winning a famous victory in Pollokshields against the Tories. He became a member of Labour's Scottish Executive two years later before being (eventually) selected to contest Govan. He is married with three sons and one daughter.

Mohammed Sarwar is a strange mixture of ambition and naivety. He desperately wanted to be an MP and, after the first selection in Govan in 1995 was allegedly rigged against him, he foolishly lent money to a potential opponent. He won the second selection conference and the election, but was charged with breaches of the Representation of the People Act and suspended from the Labour Party. When he was cleared in the subsequent trial, his suspension was lifted but his judgement was questioned and his reputation damaged. As a rich man, he is victim to sycophants as well as supporters. He regards himself as a protector of the Islamic community and travelled to Pakistan in 1996 to rescue two Glasgow sisters who had been abducted and married off by their father against their own wishes and those of their mother. He has worked hard to restore his good name among traditional Labour voters by campaigning for shipbuilding on the Clyde, and Govan in particular. He has also encouraged the government to help resolve the Kashmir crisis and the tension on the Indo-Pakistan border, thereby appeasing Muslim interests. His work has paid off. Govan is no longer a Labour graveyard.

**Contact:**  020-2719-5024 (Parliament)
 0141-427-5250 Fax 01141-427-5938 (Constituency)
 e-mail msarwar@govanlabour.fsnet.co.uk

# Malcolm Savidge (LABOUR)
## MP Aberdeen North

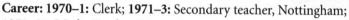

**Born:** Redhill, 1946

**Education:** Wallingham Grammar School;
Aberdeen University and College.

**Career: 1970–1:** Clerk; **1971–3:** Secondary teacher, Nottingham;
**1973–97:** Maths Teacher, Kincorth Academy, Aberdeen;
**1980–96:** Councillor, Aberdeen City; **1994–6:** Finance Convener and
Deputy Leader; **1997:** first elected MP for Aberdeen North.

**Profile:** Malcolm Savidge is a long-serving Maths teacher – a rare
species – and party activist and councillor, who got his reward in
1997 after unsuccessfully contesting Kincardine and Deeside in the
by-election of 1991 and the general election on 1992. He has been a
member of many peace and aid charities and is described locally as
'Savidge by name but not by nature'.

He has made little impact in the House, except to be singled out as a
particularly boring speaker. He is able and knowledgeable, but these
qualities are rather hidden by a diffident and dull delivery. He is an
exponent of world peace and a party loyalist, though he did take
exception to the Wakeham proposals on the House of Lords on the
grounds that they would merely create another talking quango. He
proposed a chamber democratically elected by proportional representation. Fat chance, Malcolm.

**Contact:** 020-7219-3570 Fax 020-7219-2398 (Parliament)
         01224-252708  Fax 01224-252712 (Constituency)
         e-mail mksavidge@aol.com

# James Sheridan (LABOUR)
## MP Renfrewshire West

**Born:** Glasgow, 1952

**Education:** St Sextus Primary; St Pius Secondary, Glasgow.

**Career: 1970–8:** Shipyard Worker;
**1978–84:** Machine Operator; **1984–99:** Barr & Stroud (later Pilkington, then Thales), TGWU Convener; **1999–2000:** full-time official, Transport and General Workers Union;
**1999–2001:** Councillor, Renfrewshire; **2001:** first elected MP for Renfrewshire West.

**Profile:** He is married with two children, and – with David Hamilton – one of two Old Labour manual workers (or ex-manual workers) returned to Westminster from Scotland in 2001. Apart from his TGWU activities (which included the Chairmanship of the Union's National Mechanical and Engineering Committee), he was also a long-serving member of the Glasgow Children's Panel system. He succeeds Tommy Graham, expelled by the Labour Party and now in the wilderness.

He has campaigned vigorously to protect the jobs of workers at the Bishopton's Royal Ordnance Factory. He can be expected to maintain the pressure at Westminster but may not otherwise hit the headlines. That's the challenge, Mr Sheridan, to prove that there's life after big Tommy. West Renfrewshire deserves nothing less.

**Contact:** 020-7219-8314 (Parliament)
        0141-840-3579 Fax 0141-840-3366 (Constituency)

## Robert Smith (LIBERAL DEMOCRAT)
## MP Aberdeenshire West and Kincardine

**Born:** London, 1958

**Education:** Merchant Taylors' School, London;
Aberdeen University.

**Career: 1983–97:** Family Estate Manager;
**1995–7:** Councillor, Aberdeenshire; **1997:** first elected MP for
Aberdeenshire West and Kincardine.

**Profile:** Sir Robert is the grandson of a former Tory MP for the area
and the 'double second cousin' (landed gentry care about these things)
of the late and much lamented Alick Buchanan-Smith, who also represented the Conservatives hereabouts. He is a cerebral but practical
landowner-baronet who has been active in politics since his student
days, joined the SDP in the early 1980s, though he had campaigned for
Lord (then George) Mackie when he stood for the Liberals. He is
married with three daughters.

He first took this seesaw seat from the unconvincing Tory Minister
George Kynoch with a considerable swing. The constituency, though it
has been subject to boundary changes, has switched between the
Liberals and the Tories for thirty years. Sir Robert has shown himself
to be a stout champion of the interests of the local oil industry and
sufficiently Europhile to be a member of the European Movement. He
is affable, easy going and popular. He served as Scotland Spokesperson
for the Liberal Democrats, having completed his apprenticeship on
the Transport team. He has now been promoted to the position of
Deputy Chief Whip. His constituents, many of them affluent, are no
doubt pleased to be able to vote for a Liberal Democrat who is also a
local laird but not a birkie.

**Contact:** 020-7219-6233 Fax 020-7219-4526 (Parliament)
          01330-820330  Fax 01330-820106 (Constituency)
          e-mail bobsmith@cix.co.uk

# Rachel Squire (LABOUR)
## MP Dunfermline West

**Born:** Carshalton, 1954

**Education:** Godolphin and Latymer School; Durham and Birmingham Universities.

**Career: 1972–5:** part-time worker; **1975–81:** Senior Social Worker, Birmingham; **1981–92:** NUPE Education Officer, latterly all-Scotland; **1992:** first elected MP for Dunfermline West.

**Profile:** Rachel Squire was assistant agent for Tam Dalyell in Linlithgow in 1987, then went on to become Chair of the constituency association. She also acted as agent for David Martin MEP in the Euro-elections. She was approached to let her name go forward for the Dunfermline West nomination when the sitting member Dick Douglas defected to the SNP in protest against Labour's approach to the poll tax. Having complained previously about limited opportunities for women, she accepted the challenge and, though a non-Scot, beat off four men with the help of the trade union vote. After election, she survived a brain tumour in 1993. She is married, for the second time, and has two grown-up children.

She has fought a doughty campaign for the Rosyth Dockyard workers, though her neighbouring MP, a Mr Brown, used to get most of the publicity for their protests and petitions to the Conservative government. In government, she has been a PPS to Stephen Byers and, most recently, to the high-flying Estelle Morris. She is a member of the Labour Women's Network, which – among other things – involves a lot of Pavlovian head-nodding when ministers speak.

**Contact:** 020-7219-5144 (Parliament)
         01383-622889 Fax 01383-623500 (Constituency)

# David Stewart (LABOUR)
## MP Inverness East, Nairn and Lochaber

**Born:** Inverness, 1956

**Education:** Inverness High School; Paisley
College; Stirling and Open Universities.

**Career:** Lecturer, Community Care, Esk Valley College;
**1981–7:** Social Worker, Dumfries, Dingwall; **1984–6:** Councillor,
Dumfries District; **1987–97:** Social Work Manager, Highland
Council; **1988–96:** Councillor, Inverness District Council;
**1997:** first elected MP for Inverness East, Nairn and Lochaber.

**Profile:** David Stewart, a well-kent face in Labour circles, contested
this seat three times before capturing it in 1997. He had come within
458 votes of defeating the veteran MP Sir Russell Johnston in 1992.
He is a local man, born and educated here, who returned to the area
fifteen years ago to become a team manager in social work. He also
served as a councillor and has taken an interest in everything local from
the Eden Court to Caley Thistle. He is married to Linda Macdonald, a
college lecturer and European Officer of the University of Highlands
and Islands project.

He made a loyal but assiduous start to his parliamentary career, sensibly
concentrating on the problems of employment and transport in the
Highlands – given the precarious nature of his majority – but also
taking a leading role in debates on diabetes. He is secretary of the all-
party group on diabetes and led a motion on the need for a national
screening programme. With the SNP breathing down his neck, he has
joined them in complaining about the 'extortionate' cost of fuel in the
Highlands. His efforts allowed him to consolidate in 2001, reversing
the trend with a swing from the SNP to Labour. As one elector put it
'a better MP than a candidate'.

**Contact:**  020-7219-3586 Fax 020-7219-5687 (Parliament)
01463-237441  Fax 01463-237661 (Constituency)
e-mail stewartd@parliament.uk

# Gavin Strang (LABOUR)
## MP Edinburgh East and Musselburgh

**Born:** Dundee, 1943

**Education:** Morrison's Academy, Crieff;
Edinburgh and Cambridge Universities.

**Career: 1966–8:** Tayside Economic Planning Consultative Group;
**1968–70:** Research Scientist, Scottish Agricultural Research Council;
**1970:** first elected MP for Edinburgh East; **1974:** Under-Secretary for
Energy; **1974–9:** Under-Secretary for Agriculture; **1997– :** MP for
Edinburgh East and Musselburgh; **1997–8:** Minister for Transport
(Cabinet).

**Profile:** Gavin Strang, married with three children, is one of
Scotland's longest serving MPs. He worked for only three years after
his education before he was elected. That education took him from
Edinburgh University (BSc) to Churchill College, Cambridge
(DipAgriSci), then back again to Edinburgh (PhD). Scientists are rare
in the House, and he was in office for the whole of Labour's tenure
between 1974 and the annus horribilis of 1979. He was a tremendously
hard worker then and remained so in opposition in a number of posts,
though mostly relating to agriculture. He also remained true to his
Tribunite sympathies, supporting CND, the Greenham Common
protests, Labour Action for Peace, and opposing apartheid, Trident,
the Gulf War. He did well in Shadow Cabinet elections on the Tribune
ticket.

He was appointed in 1997 to the Cabinet post of Minister of Transport
in John Prescott's huge department. There had been rumours that
Tony Blair might ignore him, despite his elected place (fourth) in the
Shadow Cabinet. He was dropped in the first reshuffle after a little over a
year in office. Until Lord (Gus) Macdonald, Transport has been a tricky
post, and Strang did no better or worse than anyone else. He is not a
great speaker and John Prescott accused him of being inarticulate at
the Dispatch Box – well, he should know. In fact, Prescott just did not
rate him and he had no left-wing defenders. He has subsequently
conducted an entirely convincing but unsuccessful campaign against
Prescott's semi-privatisation of the air-traffic-control system. He is
still considered a good guy in the rural community, who grasped the

implications of BSE before most. Ochone, ochone, Gavin, it was a sad day you ever left the farming brief.

**Contact:** 020-7219-4032 (Parliament)
0131-669-6002 (Constituency)
e-mail strangg@parliament.uk

# Viscount John Thurso (LIBERAL DEMOCRAT)
## MP Caithness, Sutherland and Easter Ross

**Born:** Thurso, 1953

**Education:** Eton.

**Career: 1971–85:** Trainee Hotelier, Savoy and
Claridges, and General Manager, Savoy Group; **1981:** General
Manager, Hotel Lancaster, Paris; **1985–92:** MD Cliveden House;
**1992–5:** Chief Exec, Granfel Holdings; **1995–2001:** Managing
Director, Champneys; **1995–2000:** Hereditary Peer;
**2001:** first elected MP for Caithness, Sutherland and Easter Ross.

**Profile:** It is, as the cliché goes, just an accident of birth, but if you
were to put 100 random men in a line-up, no-one would have any
difficulty in picking out John Archibald Sinclair, third Viscount
Thurso ('just call me Johnny'), as the aristocrat. It is the bearing, the
Lord Lucan moustache and hairstyle, the classy clothes. There the
stereotype ends. He is a successful businessman and a non-conformist
laird. His family, descended from the Earls of Orkney, have been
parliamentarians since the days of the old Scottish Parliament and
prominent Liberals for over a century. He worked his way through the
(of course) up-market hotel trade and rescued the health and fitness
company Champneys. His appointment was the subject of the BBC
TV documentary *Blood on the Carpet,* in which he was the undoubted
star. He demonstrated the efficacy of Champneys by losing three
stones in its expensive gyms and earning himself the nickname of Lord
Torso. He is married and has three children.

He must be the only person, except those few who have surrendered
their titles as peers, to have moved from the Lords to the Commons and
not the other way around. He spoke for the Liberals on Scottish affairs
in the Lords (and obviously served on the catering committee) before
he was disqualified by the reforms to the upper house. He followed the
long-serving but less colourful Bob Maclennan, claiming that his
family were innocent in the Clearances despite the jibes of his opponents. He likes Westminster, but not London, and his practical views
and plummy tones will add a new dimension to the Liberal benches.

**Contact:** 020-7219-8154 (Parliament)
01847-892600 (Constituency)

## Bill Tynan (LABOUR)
## MP Hamilton South

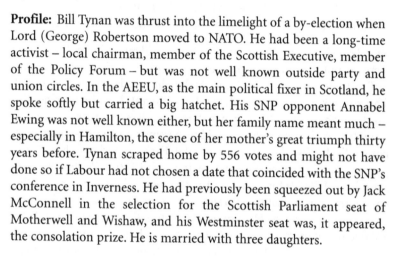

**Born:** Glasgow, 1940

**Education:** St Mungo's Academy, Glasgow;
Stow College, Glasgow.

**Career: 1961–88:** Toolmaker; **1988–99:** Political
Officer, AEEU; **1999:** first elected MP for Hamilton South
(by-election).

**Profile:** Bill Tynan was thrust into the limelight of a by-election when Lord (George) Robertson moved to NATO. He had been a long-time activist – local chairman, member of the Scottish Executive, member of the Policy Forum – but was not well known outside party and union circles. In the AEEU, as the main political fixer in Scotland, he spoke softly but carried a big hatchet. His SNP opponent Annabel Ewing was not well known either, but her family name meant much – especially in Hamilton, the scene of her mother's great triumph thirty years before. Tynan scraped home by 556 votes and might not have done so if Labour had not chosen a date that coincided with the SNP's conference in Inverness. He had previously been squeezed out by Jack McConnell in the selection for the Scottish Parliament seat of Motherwell and Wishaw, and his Westminster seat was, it appeared, the consolation prize. He is married with three daughters.

He is one of those MPs who, after election, disappears from public view until he turns up four or five years later to renew his contract. That does not mean he isn't doing his job; in fact he's quietly competent – just that he is never likely to cause a fuss or make a stir. His constituents seem well pleased with his performance – in 2001 he was returned with the traditional Labour majority of over 10,000 and 60 per cent of the vote.

**Contact:** 020-7219-6285 Fax 020-7219-6285 (Parliament)
01698-454925 Fax 01698-454926 (Constituency)
e-mail tynanb@parliament.uk

## Michael Weir (SNP)
## MP Angus

**Born:** Arbroath, 1957

**Education:** Arbroath High School;
Aberdeen University.

**Career: 1981– :** Solicitor; **1984–8:** Angus District
Councillor; **2001:** first elected MP for Angus.

**Profile:** Michael Weir is a local boy made good, but by remaining local.
He was born and brought up in Arbroath and has always worked there,
save for a spell in Kirkcaldy and his university sojourn in Aberdeen.
He is married with two children. He was the SNP branch organiser
and a former councillor. In the 1980s, he rode shotgun for old Doc
Welsh (now Andrew Welsh MSP), who ran things in them thar parts
as Provost of Angus.

He has a very strong interest in land reform and the abolition of
feudalism, as anyone will know who reads the letters' columns of our
Scottish broadsheets. That came from his legal experience. He is also
interested in disability matters – a more personal cause, since he has
an artificial leg. His maiden speech was on the problems of health-care
funding in rural areas like Angus, which illustrates the problem at
Westminster for the SNP members in particular. Almost all local issues
are handled in Edinburgh. He seems thoughtful and articulate but not
exactly exciting.

**Contact:**  020-7219-8125 (Parliament)
          01241-874522 (Constituency)
          e-mail mikeweirmp@parliament.uk

## Brian Wilson (LABOUR)
## Minister of State, Trade and Industry
## MP Cunninghame North

**Born:** Dunoon; 1948

**Education:** Dunoon Grammar School; Dundee University; University College, Cardiff.

**Career:** Journalist/Author; **1972–97:** Founder/Publisher (and sometime Editor) West Highland Free Press; **1987:** first elected MP for Cunninghame North; **1997–8:** Minister of State, Scottish Office; **1998–9:** Minister for Trade; **1999–2000:** Minister of State, Scotland Office; **2001:** Minister of State, Foreign and Commonwealth Office; **2001– :** Minister of State, Trade and Industry.

**Profile:** From his long-haired (very long-haired) student days, Brian Wilson has been a man of many causes. He was a Nationalist in his youth in Dunoon, demonstrating against American nuclear submariners, but now he hates the Nats with a convert's passion and has had to accept devolution without approving of it. He hates Tories (that hasn't changed) and his pro-Highlander, anti-landlord creation the *West Highland Free Press* has for thirty years now trumpeted the cause of land reform and economic revival, while still surviving as a paying concern. He has also been against apartheid, America, NATO, left-wing rebels, rail privatisation and in favour of Celtic FC, Gaelic, community land-ownership, a revised Clause Four, English devolution within the framework of the Union. He is married to Joni, from Lewis, and they have three children, one of whom has Down's Syndrome. That, too, is a subject on which he is passionate.

As every schoolboy knows, Henry McLeish thinks Wilson is a liability. On the other hand, he is a fearsome performer – fluently witty and biting, frequently used by Labour as a rebuttal weapon. Obviously trusted by Downing Street if not by Henry, he has had five Minister of State posts since 1997. The vital question is whether he can go higher, with so many Scots already in senior positions, or whether he has reached his level. He is now energy minister, against the expansion of nuclear facilities, in favour of wind power – especially in his beloved Western Isles – and the standard bearer against the SNP on the oil issue. Although he has largely controlled his tendency to outburst, it still bursts out now and again.

**Contact:** 020-7219-4033 (Parliament)
01505-682847  Fax 01505-684648 (Constituency)

**Peter Wishart** (SNP)
**MP Tayside North**

**Born:** Dunfermline, 1962

**Education:** Queen Anne High School,
Dunfermline; Moray House College of Education.

**Career: 1981:** Musician, Big Country; **1984–5:** Community Worker,
Central Region; **1985– :** Keyboardist, Runrig; **2001:** first elected MP
for Tayside North.

**Profile:** He was the non-Highland keyboard player with the Gaelic
rock band Runrig and has had better luck in finding a seat than his
former colleague, Labour hopeful Donny Munro. Wishart fell heir to
John Swinney's seat, succeeding a prominent and respected politician,
whereas Munro has struggled to make a political breakthrough after
leaving the group. Wishart has already set a record – the first rock
musician at the Palace of Westminster, unless you count Tony Blair
with his talisman guitar. He is married with one son.

He was Leader of the Youth for Independence campaign in 1997. He
takes a strong and positive interest in the drugs issue and was involved
with Scotland Against Drugs. He is currently SNP Vice-Convener for
Fundraising, and Chief Whip of the group of five MPs at Westminster.
Big Chief, not many Indians.

**Contact:**   020-7219-8303 (Parliament)
               01250-876576 Fax 01250-570125 (Constituency)
               e-mail pw@petewishart.com

# Tony Worthington (LABOUR)
## MP Clydebank and Milngavie

**Born:** Lemsford, Hertfordshire, 1941

**Education:** City of Lincoln; LSE, York, Durham, and Glasgow Universities.

**Career: 1962–6:** Staffer, HM Borstal, Dover;
**1967–71:** Lecturer, Monkwearmouth FE College;
**1971–87:** Lecturer in Sociology, Jordanhill College;
**1974–87:** Councillor, Strathclyde Region (finally Finance Convener);
**1987:** first elected MP for Clydebank and Milngavie.

**Profile:** When Tony Worthington came to Scotland to teach at Jordanhill College, he quickly made his way in a Strathclyde Region Labour Party that was not overburdened with intellectuals. It did, however, have some really crafty politicians like Dick Stewart and Charlie Gray. He could have, should have, learned much from them that might have been useful in his later career. He is extremely able and well informed, but seems to lack the directness and economy of style that is required to make your mark in the big league. He was once considered a likely candidate for high office, but the promise and the moment have passed.

He had a number of shadow posts. He spoke on Scotland, International Development, Foreign and Commonwealth Affairs, and Northern Ireland in the 1990s. For the first year of the 1997 administration, he was a Parliamentary Secretary at Stormont, but fell at the first reshuffle. He knows his stuff, but he tends to be academic and wordy. He's a decent man, an expert on international development and aid, especially in Africa, and can make a contribution in that field.

**Contact:** 020-7219-3507 Fax 020-7219-3507 (Parliament)
        01389-873195  Fax 01389-873195 (Constituency)
        e-mail worthingtont@parliament.uk

## Jimmy Wray (LABOUR)
## MP Glasgow Baillieston

**Born:** Glasgow, 1935

**Education:** St Bonaventure Secondary, Glasgow.

**Career: 1950–80:** Lorry Driver, Plumber,
Chimney Sweep ('when slimmer'), Coalman,
Rag-and-Bone Man; **1980–7:** unemployed; **1972–5:** Councillor,
Glasgow Corporation; **1976–88:** Councillor, Strathclyde Region;
**1987:** first elected MP for Glasgow Provan; **1997– :** MP for Glasgow
Baillieston.

**Profile:** Jimmy Wray is a phenomenon. A Gorbals boy who tried his
hand at everything from lorry driver to chimney sweep to rag-and-
bone man before falling into a long period of unemployment when
clearly his ingenuity failed him. He was, by this time, a Strathclyde
Councillor who had also acted as agent for Frank McElhone MP in the
Gorbals and Robert McTaggart MP in Glasgow Central. He took over
Provan when Hugh Brown retired, beating a militant-backed candidate in the selection conference by one vote on the second ballot. He
is a great supporter of amateur boxing. He married, for the third time,
and became a father again before pursuing a sensational damages case
against the *Mail On Sunday*. It had published allegations of violence by
his second wife, whom he had unfairly dismissed as his secretary some
years earlier. The soap opera ended when he won £60,000.

Tony Blair's project for the Labour Party will never be complete while
Jimmy is around. He is an unreconstructed old Labour community
politician who has led local campaigns against dampness, fluoridation,
evictions and rent increases. He gives the impression, deliberately, of
being a Gorbals hard man, in his double-breasted suits of comfortable
shapelessness, but he is a great deal shrewder than most people think.
He was Michael Heseltine's pair. King of the Jungle and King of the
Gorbals. The BBC TV programme *Watchdog* found him to be one of
Britain's 'laziest MPs' on the basis of his voting and speaking record.
Would they step outside and say that? Jimmy blames it on his membership of the British delegation to the Council of Europe and the
Western European Union, from both of which he has promptly
resigned.

**Contact:**     020-7219-4606 Fax 020-7219-2008 (Parliament)
          0771-421-8138 (Constituency)

# The Scotland Office

## Role

The role of the Scotland Office is to represent Scottish interests within the UK government on matters that are reserved to the UK Parliament in terms of the Scotland Act 1998.

To promote the devolution settlement by encouraging co-operation between Edinburgh and London, or otherwise intervene as required by the Scotland Act.

To pay grants to the Scottish Consolidated Fund and manage other financial transactions.

To exercise certain residual functions in reserved matters (for example, the conduct and funding of elections and the making of private legislation at Westminster).

## Reserved Matters

Reserved matters include the constitution, foreign affairs, defence, international development, the civil service, financial and economic matters, national security, immigration and nationality, the misuse of drugs, trade and industry, aspects of energy regulation and transport, social security, employment, broadcasting, equal opportunities, medicines, and ethical matters such as abortion, surrogacy and genetics.

## The Ministers

Secretary of State for Scotland: Helen Liddell.

Minister of State at the Scotland Office: George Foulkes.

Advocate General: Dr Lynda Clark QC.

Spokesperson in the House of Lords: Baroness Ramsay of Cartvale.

## Contact

Scotland Office, Dover House, Whitehall, London SW1A 2AU
020-7270-6754 Fax 020-7270-6812
e-mail scottishsecretary@scotland.gsi.gov.uk
website www.scottishsecretary.gov.uk

# The Scottish Executive

### First Minister
### Jack McConnell MSP
Development, implementation and presentation of the policy of the Executive.

### Deputy First Minister and Minister for Justice, Europe and External Affairs
### Jim Wallace QC MSP
Assists the First Minister with policy, and is responsible for Home Affairs, including civil law, criminal justice, social work services, police, fire, prisons and courts, law and land reform, freedom of information; also responsible for external affairs, including Europe.

*Deputy Minister for Justice*
### Dr Richard Simpson MSP
Assists the Minister for Justice and has special responsibility for co-ordination of the Executive's drugs policy.

### Minister for Education and Young People
### Cathy Jamieson MSP
Responsible for pre-school and school education, children and young people.

*Deputy Minister for Education and Young People*
### Nicol Stephen MSP
Deputy to the Minister for Education and Young People.

### Minister for Enterprise, Transport and Lifelong Learning
### Wendy Alexander MSP
Responsible for the economy, business and industry, including the enterprise network, transport, trade and inward investment, further and higher education, the science base and e-commerce, Digital Scotland, lifelong learning, training and delivery of the New Deal.

*Deputy Minister for Enterprise, Transport and Lifelong Learning*

## Dr Lewis Macdonald MSP

Deputy to the Minister, with special responsibility for Transport.

## Minister for Finance and Public Services

## Andy Kerr MSP

Responsible for the Scottish Budget, European structural funds, local government and local government reform, modernising government.

*Deputy Minister for Finance and Public Services*

## Peter Peacock MSP

With special responsibility for budgetary monitoring and control.

## Minister for Health and Community Care

## Malcolm Chisholm MSP

Responsible for health policy, the NHS in Scotland, community care and food safety.

*Deputy Ministers for Health and Community Care*

## Hugh Henry MSP and Mary Mulligan MSP

Deputies to the Minister for Health and Community Care.

## Minister for Parliament

## Patricia Ferguson MSP

Responsible for parliamentary business, including Executive business in Parliament, liaison between the Executive and Parliament, public appointments, policy and quango governance, co-ordination of Executive policy and management of cross-cutting issues.

*Deputy Minister for Parliament*

## Euan Robson MSP

Deputy to the Minister for Parliament with special responsibility for the handling of the legislative programme in Parliament and the management of cross-cutting priorities.

## Minister for the Environment and Rural Development

## Ross Finnie MSP

Responsible for policy on the environment and on rural development, including agriculture, fisheries and forestry.

*Deputy Minister for the Environment and Rural Development*

## Allan Wilson MSP

Deputy to the Minister for the Environment and Rural Development.

## Minister for Social Justice

## Iain Gray MSP

Responsible for social inclusion, housing, equality issues and the voluntary sector.

*Deputy Minister for Social Justice*

## Margaret Curran MSP

Deputy to the Minister for Social Justice.

## Minister for Tourism, Culture and Sport

## Mike Watson MSP

Responsible for tourism, sport, culture and the Arts, the built heritage, architecture, Historic Scotland, lottery funding and Gaelic.

*Deputy Minister for Tourism, Culture and Sport*

## Dr Elaine Murray MSP

Deputy to the Minister with special responsibility for Arts and culture.

## Law Officers

*Lord Advocate:* **Colin Boyd QC**
*Solicitor General:* **Elish Anglolini**

## Scottish Executive

**Contact:** 0131-556-8400
e-mail scottish.ministers@scotland.gov.uk
website www.scotland.gov.uk

# The Scottish Parliament:
# Contact and Access

**To contact the Parliament**, write to the Scottish Parliament, Edinburgh EH99 1SP, telephone 0131-346-5000 or fax 0131-348-5601. You can also reach the Parliament Switchboard/Public Information on 0845 278 1999.

There are several e-mail options, depending on the nature of your business:

| | |
|---|---|
| Public Information: | sp.info@scottish.parliament.uk |
| Media Enquiries: | sp.media@scottish.parliament.uk |
| School and Colleges: | education.service@scottish.parliament.uk |
| Debates: | chamber.office@scottish.parliament.uk |
| Committees: | committee.office@scottish.parliament.uk |
| Recruitment: | personnel.office@scottish.parliament.uk |
| Public Petitions: | petitions@scottish.parliament.uk |

The parliamentary website is www.scottish.parliament.uk

**To visit the Parliament** in session, you can reserve up to five seats for each meeting, from seven days before the meeting, by contacting the Visitor Centre on 0131-348-5411. It may be possible, depending on seat availability, to attend a meeting by simply turning up and queuing at the public entrance. No tickets are required for the Visitor Centre, or to see the Chamber when Parliament is not in session.

**Groups** require a prior booking at all times and should contact the Public Information Service. Tickets are required to attend any **Committee** meetings and these are also available from the Visitor Centre on 0131-348-5411.

Admission to any of the public facilities at the Scottish Parliament is free. The **Visitor Centre** has an exhibition providing an introduction to all aspects of the Parliament. The **Parliament Shop** has a wide range of quality products, many exclusive to the Scottish Parliament. Both are located in the Committee Chambers building on George IV Bridge. The **New Parliament** building also has a Visitor Centre on Holyrood Road.

Visitors attending any meeting of the Scottish Parliament or one of its Committees are asked to observe a **Code of Behaviour** required by the

Presiding Officer. Members of the public must not applaud, shout or disrupt proceedings in any way. They should enter and leave quietly, switch off mobile phones, pagers and laptops, and obey instructions given by parliamentary officials. Also prohibited are the display of banners or slogans or the use of cameras or recording equipment. You can't paint, draw or sketch without prior authorisation. You mustn't eat, drink, smoke or read newspapers. Baggage should not be left unattended at any time.

# Scottish Parliament Committees

## Audit Committee

**Convener:** Andrew Welsh (SNP).
**Members:** Scott Barrie, David Davidson (Deputy Convener), Margaret Jamieson, Paul Martin, Lloyd Quinan, Keith Raffan.
**Remit:** To consider and report on any accounts laid before Parliament; any report laid before Parliament by the Auditor General and any documents laid before Parliament concerning financial control, accounting and auditing in relation to public expenditure.

## Education, Culture and Sport Committee

**Convener:** Karen Gillon (Labour).
**Members:** Jackie Baillie, Ian Jenkins, Frank McAveety (Deputy Convener), Irene McGugan, Brian Monteith, Michael Russell.
**Remit:** To consider and report on matters relating to school and pre-school education which fall within the responsibility of the Minister for Education; and matters relating to Arts, culture and sport which fall within the responsibility of the Minister for Culture and Sport.

## Enterprise and Lifelong Learning Committee

**Convener:** Alex Neil (SNP).
**Members:** Bill Butler, Annabel Goldie (Deputy Convener), Brian Fitzpatrick, Duncan Hamilton, Marilyn Livingstone, Kenny McAskill, Kenneth Macintosh, Des McNulty, David Mundell, Tavish Scott, Elaine Thomson.
**Remit:** To consider and report on matters relating to the Scottish economy, industry, tourism, training, further and higher education, and other matters within the responsibility of the Minister for Enterprise and Lifelong Learning.

## Equal Opportunities Committee

**Convener:** Kate Maclean (Labour).
**Members:** Lyndsay McIntosh, Michael McMahon, Gil Paterson, Cathy Peattie, Tommy Sheridan, Elaine Smith, Jamie Stone, Kay Ullrich (Deputy Convener).
**Remit:** To consider and report on matters relating to equal opportunities and on the observance of equal opportunities within the Parliament. 'Equal opportunities' specifically covers the prevention, elimination or regulation of discrimination between persons on grounds of sex or marital status, on racial

grounds, or on grounds of disability, age, sexual orientation, language or social origin, or of any other personal attributes, including beliefs or opinions, such as religious beliefs or political opinions.

## European Committee

**Convener:** Irene Oldfather (Labour).
**Members:** Sarah Boyack, Colin Campbell, Dennis Canavan, Helen Eadie, John Home Robertson (Deputy Convener), Lloyd Quinan, Nora Radcliffe, Ben Wallace.
**Remit:** To consider and report on proposals for European Communities legislation; the implementation of EC legislation; and any EC or European Union issue.

## Finance Committee

**Convener:** Des McNulty (Labour).
**Members:** Brian Adam, David Davidson, Donald Gorrie, Tom McCabe, Alasdair Morgan, Elaine Thomson (Deputy Convener).
**Remit:** To consider and report on any report or document laid before Parliament by members of the Scottish Executive containing proposal for, or budgets of, public expenditure or proposals for the making of a tax-varying resolution, taking into account any report or recommendation made to them by any other committee with power to consider such documents or any part of them. To consider and report on any report made by a committee setting out proposals concerning public expenditure; budget bills; and any other matter relating to or affecting the expenditure of the Scottish Administration or any other expenditure payable out of the Scottish Consolidated Fund, and any other expenditure met out of taxes, charges or other public revenue.

## Health and Community Care Committee

**Convener:** Margaret Smith (Liberal Democrat).
**Members:** Dorothy-Grace Elder, Janis Hughes, Margaret Jamieson (Deputy Convener), John McAllion, Shona Robison, Mary Scanlon, Nicola Sturgeon.
**Remit:** To consider and report on issues relating to the health policy, the NHS in Scotland, and such other matters as fall within the responsibility of the Minister for Health and Community Care.

## Justice 1 Committee

**Convener:** Christine Grahame (SNP).
**Members:** Lord James Douglas-Hamilton, Donald Gorrie, Gordon Jackson (Deputy Convener), Maureen Macmillan, Paul Martin, Michael Matheson.
**Remit:** To consider and report on matters relating to the administration of civil and criminal justice, the reform of the civil and criminal law, and such other matters as fall within the responsibility of the Minister for Justice.

## Justice 2 Committee

**Convener:** Pauline McNeill (Labour).
**Members:** Bill Aitken (Deputy Convener), Scott Barrie, Margaret Ewing, George Lyon, Alasdair Morrison, Stewart Stevenson.
**Remit:** The Committee has the same remit as Justice 1.

## Local Government Committee

**Convener:** Trish Godman (Labour).
**Members:** Keith Harding, Sylvia Jackson (Deputy Convener), Michael McMahon, Tricia Marwick, Iain Smith, Sandra White.
**Remit:** To consider and report on matters relating to local government and which fall within the responsibility of the Minister for Finance and Public Services.

## Private Bills Committee

**A Committee will be formed to consider each Bill, and will be named after the Bill.**
**Remit:** To consider and report on the Bill in question.

## Procedures Committee

**Convener:** Murray Tosh (Conservative).
**Members:** Susan Deacon, Donald Gorrie, Fiona Hyslop, Frank McAveety, Kenneth Macintosh (Deputy Convener), Gil Paterson.
**Remit:** To consider the practice and procedures of the Scottish Parliament in relation to its public business.

## Public Petitions Committee

**Convener:** John McAllion (Labour).
**Members:** Helen Eadie (Deputy Convener), Dorothy-Grace Elder, Winnie Ewing, Phil Gallie, Rhoda Grant, John Farquhar Munro.
**Remit:** To consider and report on whether a public petition is admissible; what action should be taken upon the petition.

## Rural Development Committee

**Convener:** Alex Fergusson (Conservative).
**Members:** Fergus Ewing (Deputy Convener), Rhoda Grant, Richard Lochhead, Jamie McGrigor, John Farquhar Munro, Irene Oldfather, Mike Rumbles, Elaine Smith, Stewart Stevenson.
**Remit:** To consider and report on matters relating to rural development, agriculture and fisheries, and other related matters as fall within the responsibility of the Minister for Rural Development.

## Social Justice Committee

**Convener:** Johann Lamont (Labour).
**Members:** Robert Brown, Cathie Craigie, Linda Fabiani, Kenneth Gibson (Deputy Convener), Lyndsay McIntosh, Karen Whitefield.
**Remit:** To consider and report on matters relating to housing and the voluntary sector and such other related matters as fall within the responsibility of the Minister for Social Justice.

## Standards Committee

**Convener:** Mike Rumbles (Liberal Democrat).
**Members:** Susan Deacon, Lord James Douglas-Hamilton, Frank McAveety, Kenneth Macintosh, Tricia Marwick (Deputy Convener), Kay Ullrich.
**Remit:** To consider and report on whether a member's conduct is in accordance with the Rules (in Standing Orders) and any code of conduct for members, matters relating to member's interests, and any other matter relating to the conduct of members in carrying out their parliamentary duties; and the adoption, amendment and application of any Code of Conduct for members.

## Subordinate Legislation Committee

**Convener:** Margo Macdonald (SNP).
**Members:** Bill Butler, Colin Campbell, Murdo Fraser, Gordon Jackson, Ian Jenkins (Deputy Convener), Bristow Muldoon.
**Remit:** To consider and report on any subordinate legislation laid before Parliament or any statutory instrument not laid before Parliament; proposed powers to make subordinate legislation in particular Bills or other proposed legislation; general questions relating to powers to make subordinate legislation.

## Transport and the Environment Committee

**Convener:** Bristow Muldoon (Labour).
**Members:** Robin Harper, Adam Ingram, Angus MacKay, Fiona McLeod, Maureen Macmillan, Des McNulty, Nora Radcliffe (Deputy Convener), John Scott.
**Remit:** To consider and report on matters which fall within the responsibility of the Minister for Transport and within the responsibility of the Minister for the Environment.

# Scottish Constituencies and their Representatives

| Constituency | MSP | MP |
|---|---|---|
| Aberdeen Central | Lewis Macdonald (Lab) | Frank Doran (Lab) |
| Aberdeen North | Elaine Thomson (Lab) | Malcolm Savidge (Lab) |
| Aberdeen South | Nicol Stephen (LD) | Anne Begg (Lab) |
| Aberd'shire W & Kincardine | Mike Rumbles (LD) | Robert Smith (LD) |
| Airdrie & Shotts | Karen Whitefield (Lab) | Helen Liddell (Lab) |
| Angus | Andrew Welsh (SNP) | Michael Weir (SNP) |
| Argyll & Bute | George Lyon (LD) | Alan Reid (LD) |
| Ayr | John Scott (Con) | Sandra Osborne (Lab) |
| Banff & Buchan | Stewart Stevenson | Alex Salmond (SNP) |
| Caithness, Suthlnd & Easter Ross | Jamie Stone (LD) | John Thurso (LD) |
| Carrick, Cumnock & Doon Valley | Cathy Jamieson (Lab) | George Foulkes (Lab) |
| Clydebank & Milngavie | Des McNulty (Lab) | Tony Worthington (Lab) |
| Clydesdale | Karen Turnbull (Lab) | Jimmy Hood (Lab) |
| Coatbridge & Chryston | Elaine Smith (Labour) | Tom Clarke (Lab) |
| Cumbernauld & Kilsyth | Cathie Craigie (Lab) | Rosemary McKenna (Lab) |
| Cunninghame North | Allan Wilson (Lab) | Brian Wilson (Lab) |
| Cunninghame South | Irene Oldfather (Lab) | Brian Donohoe (Lab) |
| Dumbarton | Jackie Baillie (Lab) | John McFall (Lab) |
| Dumfries | Elaine Murray (Lab) | Russell Brown (Lab) |
| Dundee East | John McAllion (Lab) | Iain Luke (Lab) |
| Dundee West | Kate Maclean (Lab) | Ernie Ross (Lab) |
| Dunfermline East | Helen Eadie (Lab) | Gordon Brown (Lab) |
| Dunfermline West | Scott Barrie (Lab) | Rachel Squire (Lab) |
| East Kilbride | Andy Kerr (Lab) | Adam Ingram (Lab) |
| East Lothian | John Home Robertson (Lab) | Anne Picking (Lab) |

| *Constituency* | *MSP* | *MP* |
|---|---|---|
| Eastwood | Ken Macintosh (Lab) | Jim Murphy (Lab) |
| Edinburgh Central | Sarah Boyack (Lab) | Alistair Darling (Lab) |
| Edinburgh E & Musselburgh | Susan Deacon (Lab) | Gavin Strang (Lab) |
| Edinburgh N & Leith | Malcolm Chisholm (Lab) | Mark Lazarowicz (Lab) |
| Edinburgh Pentlands | Iain Gray (Lab) | Lynda Clark (Lab) |
| Edinburgh South | Angus MacKay (Lab) | Nigel Griffiths (Lab) |
| Edinburgh West | Margaret Smith (LD) | John Barrett (LD) |
| | | |
| Falkirk East | Cathy Peattie (Lab) | Michael Connarty (Lab) |
| Falkirk West | Dennis Canavan (Ind) | Eric Joyce (Lab) |
| Fife Central | Henry McLeish (Lab) | John MacDougall (Lab) |
| Fife North-East | Iain Smith (LD) | Menzies Campbell (LD) |
| | | |
| Galloway & Upper Nithsdale | Alasdair Morgan (SNP) | Peter Duncan (Con) |
| Glasgow Anniesland | Bill Butler (Lab) | John Robertson (Lab) |
| Glasgow Baillieston | Margaret Curran (Lab) | Jimmy Wray (Lab) |
| Glasgow Cathcart | Michael Watson (Lab) | Tom Harris (Lab) |
| Glasgow Govan | Gordon Jackson (Lab) | Mohammad Sarwar (Lab) |
| Glasgow Kelvin | Pauline McNeill (Lab) | George Galloway (Lab) |
| Glasgow Maryhill | Patricia Ferguson (Lab) | Ann McKechin (Lab) |
| Glasgow Pollok | Johann Lamont (Lab) | Ian Davidson (Lab) |
| Glasgow Rutherglen | Janis Hughes (Lab) | Tommy McAvoy (Lab) |
| Glasgow Shettleston | Frank McAveety (Lab) | David Marshall (Lab) |
| Glasgow Springburn | Paul Martin (Lab) | Michael Martin (Speaker) |
| Gordon | Nora Radcliffe (LD) | Malcolm Bruce (LD) |
| Greenock & Inverclyde | Duncan McNeil (Lab) | David Cairns (Lab) |
| | | |
| Hamilton North & Bellshill | Michael McMahon (Lab) | John Reid (Lab) |
| Hamilton South | Tom McCabe (Lab) | Bill Tynan (Lab) |
| | | |
| Inverness E, Nairn & Lochaber | Fergus Ewing (SNP) | David Stewart (Lab) |
| | | |
| Kilmarnock & Loudoun | Margaret Jamieson (Lab) | Des Browne (Lab) |
| Kirkcaldy | Marilyn Livingstone (Lab) | Lewis Moonie (Lab) |
| | | |
| Linlithgow | Mary Mulligan (Lab) | Tam Dalyell (Lab) |
| Livingston | Bristow Muldoon (Lab) | Robin Cook (Lab) |
| | | |
| Midlothian | Rhona Brankin (Lab) | David Hamilton (Lab) |
| Moray | Margaret Ewing (SNP) | Angus Robertson (SNP) |

| Constituency | MSP | MP |
|---|---|---|
| Motherwell & Wishaw | Jack McConnell (Lab) | Frank Roy (Lab) |
| Ochil | Richard Simpson (Lab) | Martin O'Neill (Lab) |
| Orkney & Shetland | Jim Wallace (LD) Tavish Scott (LD) | Alistair Carmichael (LD) |
| Paisley North | Wendy Alexander (Lab) | Irene Adams (Lab) |
| Paisley South | Hugh Henry (Lab) | Douglas Alexander (Lab) |
| Perth | Roseanna Cunningham (SNP) | Annabelle Ewing (SNP) |
| Renfrewshire West | Tricia Godman (Lab) | James Sheridan (Lab) |
| Ross, Skye & Inverness W | John Farquhar Munro (LD) | Charles Kennedy (LD) |
| Roxburgh & Berwickshire | Euan Robson (LD) | Archy Kirkwood (LD) |
| Stirling | Sylvia Jackson (Lab) | Anne McGuire (Lab) |
| Strathkelvin & Bearsden | Brian Fitzpatrick (Lab) | John Lyons (Lab) |
| Tayside North | John Swinney (SNP) | Peter Wishart (SNP) |
| Tweeddale, Ettrick & Lauderdale | Ian Jenkins (LD) | Michael Moore (LD) |
| Western Isles | Alasdair Morrison (Lab) | Calum MacDonald (Lab) |

*Members of the Scottish Parliament elected from party lists by proportional representation are listed by region on pages 70–1.*

# Scottish Members of the European Parliament: Members elected from All-Scotland Lists (1999)

### Elspeth Attwooll (LIBERAL DEMOCRAT)

She graduated from St Andrews University but taught at Glasgow University. She stood for the Liberals/Liberal Democrats in Glasgow Maryhill five times in UK parliamentary elections, and for Glasgow constituency once in the European elections. She is a member of the Executive of the Scottish Liberal Democrats and President of the Scottish Women Liberal Democrats. In the Parliament, she is a member of the European Liberal, Democrat and Reformist Group.

**Committees:** Fisheries; Regional Policy, Transport and Tourism.

**Contact:**   0141-946-1370  Fax 0141-946-4056 (Constituency)
e-mail  eattwooll@cix.compulink.co.uk

### Ian Hudghton (SNP)

He was first elected to the European Parliament at a by-election (1998) following the sudden death of Allan Macartney. He had previously been a councillor in Angus District (becoming Leader of Council), then Tayside Region (Deputy SNP Group Leader). Professionally, he ran the family home-decorating business for twenty years. In the Parliament, he is a member of Green–European Free Alliance (EFA) grouping, an alliance of Greens and home rule parties.

**Committees:** Fisheries; Employment and Social Affairs.

**Contact:**   01382-623200  Fax 01382-604767 (Constituency)
e-mail  ihmep.ne@snp.org

## Sir Neil MacCormick (SNP)

He is son of the late 'King' John MacCormick, a co-founder of the SNP and organiser of the National Covenant Movement after the war. He is a graduate of the Universities of Glasgow and Oxford (Balliol) who returned to teach at Edinburgh as Professor of Public Law and sometime Dean of the Faculty. He is one of Scotland's most distinguished lawyers and academics – currently on leave of absence from Edinburgh – and was one of the very few SNP members who lent their weight to the Constitutional Convention. He is a member of the Green–EFA Group.

**Committees:** Legal Affairs and Internal Market.

**Contact:**    0131-225-3497 Fax 0131-225-3499
e-mail nmaccmep@snp.sol.co.uk

## David Martin (LABOUR)

He was first elected to the European Parliament (for Lothian) under the previous electoral system in 1984. He had served briefly on Lothian Region prior to that. He is a graduate of Heriot Watt University (Economics) and Leicester University (European and Employment Law). He worked for a stockbroker, then an animal rights agency before taking up full-time politics. He has been a Vice-President of the Parliament for twelve years, now Senior Vice-President dealing in relationships with national parliaments. He has published on European matters. He sits with the PES, the Party of European Socialists.

**Committees:** Budgets.

**Contact:**    0131-654-1606 Fax 0131-654-1607 (Constituency)
e-mail david.martin@ccis.org.uk

## Bill Miller (LABOUR)

He was first elected as the MEP for Glasgow in 1994 under the previous electoral system. He had been a Strathclyde Regional Councillor for eight years before that. He was educated at Paisley Technical College and Kingston Polytechnic. He supports Kilmarnock FC, who have also been making it to Europe in recent seasons, though not with the same success. Like all Labour MEPs, he is a member of the PES, and is Whip for the British group.

**Committees:** Legal Affairs and Internal Market

**Contact:**     0141-569-7494 Fax 0141-577-0214 (Constituency)
               e-mail bmillermep@aol.com

## John Purvis (CONSERVATIVE)

He first served as an MEP for Mid-Scotland and Fife from 1979 to 1984 before being re-elected in 1999. He was an international banker and has run his own finance business. He was educated at Glenalmond School and the University of St Andrews (his home town). As a Conservative MEP, he is a member of the Group of the European People's Party and European Democrats, sensibly shortened to EPP/ED.

**Committees:** Industry, External Trade, Research and Energy.

**Contact:**     01334-475830 Fax 01334-733588 (Constituency)
               e-mail purvisco@compuserve.com

## Struan Stevenson (CONSERVATIVE)

He has been in Conservative politics for thirty years, but without much reward till now. He was a member of Girvan Council, then Kyle and Carrick, but – despite three attempts – failed to get elected to Westminster. His last attempt was in the formerly safe Tory seat of Dumfries in Labour's first landslide of 1997. He also stood for Europe unsuccessfully at the 1998 by-election in North-East Scotland. He was educated at Strathallan and the West of Scotland Agricultural College, before joining the family farming business. Latterly, before being elected in 1999, he was a Director of a PR and lobbying organisation, PS Communications. He is a member of EPP/ED.

**Committees:** Agriculture and Rural Development

**Contact:** 01131-247-6890 Fax 0131-247-6891 (Constituency)
e-mail struanmep@aol.com

## Catherine Stihler (LABOUR)

She was elected as Catherine Taylor, at the remarkably young age of twenty-five. She was educated at Coltness High School, Wishaw, and St Andrews University and has an MLitt as well as her first degree. She has been a member of the Scottish Executive of the Labour Party and of the NEC. She worked as researcher for Anne Begg MP and was Organiser for visits to Scotland by Central and Eastern European politicians. She has quickly made her mark in the European Parliament, becoming President of the Public Health Working Group.

**Committees:** Environment, Public Health and Consumer Policy.

**Contact:** 01383-731890 Fax 01383-731835 (Constituency)

# Scottish Political Parties

## Scottish Labour Party

John Smith House,
145 West Regent Street,
Glasgow G2 4RE
0141-572-6900  Fax 0141-572-2566
e-mail: scotland@new.labour.org.uk
website: www.scottishlabour.org.uk

## Scottish Conservative and Unionist Party

83 Princes Street,
Edinburgh EH2 2ER
0131-247-6890  Fax 0131-247-6891
e-mail:
central.office@scottishtories.org.uk
website: www.ScottishTories.org.uk

## Scottish National Party

107 McDonald Road,
Edinburgh EH7 4NW
0131-525-8900  Fax 0131-525-8901
e-mail: snp.hq@snp.org.uk
website: www.snp.org.uk

## Scottish Liberal Democrats

4 Clifton Terrace,
Edinburgh EH12 5DR
0131-337-2314  Fax 0131-337-3566
e-mail: scotlibdem@cix.co.uk
website: www.scotlibdems.org.uk

## Scottish Green Party

14 Albany Street,
Edinburgh EH1 3QB
0131-478-7896  Fax 0131-478-7896
e-mail: info@scottishgreens.org.uk
website: www.scottishgreens.org.uk

## Scottish Socialist Party

73 Robertson Street,
Glasgow G2 8QD
0141-221-7714  Fax 0141-221-7715
e-mail: ssv@mail.ndirect.co.uk
website:
www.scottishsocialistparty.org

# Useful Addresses and Numbers

## Public Offices

**Commissioner for Local Administration in Scotland**
23 Walker Street, Edinburgh EH3 7HX
0131-225-5300 Fax 0131-225-9495

**Employment Tribunal**
The Eagle Building, 3rd Floor, 215 Bothwell Street, Glasgow G2 7TS
0141-204-0730  Fax 0141-204-0732

**Health Service Commissioner for Scotland**
28 Thistle Street, Edinburgh EH2 1EN
0131-225-7465  Fax 0131-226-4447

**Highlands and Islands Enterprise**
Bridge House, 20 Bridge Street, Inverness IV1 1QR
01463-234171  Fax 01463-244469

**Scottish Arts Council**
12 Manor Place, Edinburgh EH3 7DD
0131-226-6051  Fax 0131-225-9833
e-mail: administrator@scottisharts.org.uk

**Scottish Enterprise**
120 Bothwell Street, Glasgow G2 7JP
0141-248-2700  Fax 01141-221-3217

**Scottish Law Commission**
140 Causewayside, Edinburgh EH9 1PR
0131-668-2131  Fax 0131-662-9400
e-mail: info@scotlawcom.gov.uk

**Scottish Legal Services Ombudsman**
16 Picardy Place, Edinburgh EH1 3JT
0131-556-5574  Fax 0131-556-1519
e-mail: complaints@scot-legal-ombud.org.uk

**Scottish Parliamentary Commissioner for Administration**
28 Thistle Street, Edinburgh EH2 1EN
0845-601-0456  Fax 0131-226-4447

**Scottish Tourist Board**
23 Ravelston Terrace, Edinburgh EH4 3TP
0131-332-2433  Fax 0131-343-1513

## Independent Organisations

**Confederation of British Industry (CBI Scotland)**
Beresford House, 5 Claremont Terrace, Glasgow G3 7XT
0141-332-8661

**Convention of Scottish Local Authorities (CoSLA)**
Rosebery House, 9 Haymarket Terrace, Edinburgh EH12 5XZ
0131-474-9200  Fax 0131-474-9292

**Institute of Directors (Scotland)**
29 Abercrombie Place, Edinburgh EH3 6QE
0131-557-5488

**Scottish Trades Union Congress (STUC)**
333 Woodlands Road, Glasgow G3 6NG
0141-337-8100  Fax 0141-337-8101